DISABILITY

Disability

THE GENEALOGY OF A CONCEPT FROM PREHISTORY TO MID-20TH CENTURY

Patrick Standen

ONION
RIVER
PRESS

Burlington, Vermont

Onion River Press
191 Bank Street
Burlington, VT 05401

ISBN: 978-1-949066-96-8

Contents

1

What is Disability?

Prefatory Remarks: An Historical Overview

This work is an exploration of the history of a concept. Not a study of a word's etymology, but the idea that structures the word as it appears in many languages. It is a history of the concept of disability, the meaning of disability. Again, this work is not a formal etymological study of the word. Such a work would not work; instead, this is the history of the concept, which animates the term or ideas used across different cultures and in various human languages to express what is understood by disability or loss of function. As such, this is a true history of an idea. The idea: disability. The story is a tragic one. It is a uniquely human history replete with tragedy and horror but also full of courage and inspiration. Above all else, it is a history of our fellow humans. Specifically, it tells a story of those among us who lived with or are living with a disability; however, it is also about those non-disabled humans and, most notably, their reactions toward their fellow humans with disabilities and the language they constructed to understand the former. For as long as we have been humans, we have encountered disability, been disabled, cared for the disabled in their lives, and lived intimately with disability. While disability has been an ever-present phenomenon of the human condition, disability as a descriptive concept emerged as a category relatively late, both historically and culturally. It will arise in modernity.

Disability and disabled persons were so widespread in antiquity that little attention was spent describing and discussing them. It was too ordinary. Nevertheless, as we will come to learn, being disabled is anything but ordinary.

To briefly expand on this point, a biological species subject to evolutionary adaptation with unpredictable changes in an often-hostile environment means that disability has been ever-present in the human condition. Thus, in one genuine sense, it is our condition.

Our very physical selves and the laws of nature create this reality. Indeed, disability comes with being a physical body, a body given to aging, decay, debility, disease, and, in the end, death. We all fall apart, and yet we are not alone. We witness disability in the broader animal community, too. It is not uncommon to find an animal missing a limb, blinded, or born with a deformity, yet many still adapt and flourish. Such adaptations in the natural world are frequent when one looks for them. The problem has been that we rarely look for them. Modern discourse in science and especially evolutionary rhetoric has been highjacked and kept hostage by an unreal idealism, a fantasy of perfectibility (i.e., perfect-ability) that ignores the presence of or the salience of the deformed, different, mutated, and disabled. In any case, disability emerges naturally from evolutionary adaptation and genetic mutation and through human activity and artifice. Either through genetic variation leading to discrete somatic differences such as being born without sight, hearing, or missing a digit, or from a near-catastrophic event experienced in one's lived environment, disability and humanity are inseparable twins.

What is of particular interest is that disability has been framed and used as a binary concept. A discriminatory dividing line between the able-bodied and disabled based on arbitrary divisions from the broader physical differences and abilities continuum seems problematic. We then valorize this binary division and render the term on the right-hand side of the relationship as valuable while the left-hand is denigrated, despised, demeaned. It functions as more of a political division than a medical or scientific classification. It is the social construction

of disability. There seems to be no non-arbitrary reason for defining one person as disabled and another as not. Variations in strength, endurance, ability, mobility, sight, speech, and hearing exist as parts of a more extended, unbroken continuum in the human community and among individuals that defy these binary divisions. Yet, they persist. It is a political choice.

Disability is like the popular bumper sticker about the 4-letter word: shit happens. Disability happens. As with their animal cousins, people needed to learn to live with and thrive with their disabilities no matter how hostile their contemporaries or the world around them may have been toward them. The option was death. What is relatively new in human history is that since the advent of modernity, humans have sought to overcome disability, to deny it, to erase it. Modernity created the formal concept of disability only to attempt to eradicate it. To remove something, one must first identify it. As such, modernity and its ableist assumptions create the absolute nature of the concept of disability[1]. It has done this, however, only to attempt to eradicate it. But it has not always been that way.

2

Prehistory and the Archaeology of Care

History holds answers that we too often overlook. In a Berlin museum, a bust of an ancient Egyptian "Princess" exists with a noticeable, congenital cranial abnormality[2]. Very little has been written about her and her disability. What this bust provides is clear evidence that disability was present in the ancient Egyptian world. Further, it suggests that disability was neither shunned nor ostracized; it may even indicate that disability was considered a mark of beauty, something exceptional. The very presence of a statue depicting a person with a disability reveals, minimally, that disability was not perceived as a burden, deformation, or a flashpoint for discrimination. It suggests they ignored differences in body and ability in their canon of beauty and memorialization. The realism implicit in this work suggests that the artist had no concerted attempt to idealize the princess's physical attractiveness. She is beautiful as she is. Moreover, that her likeness was preserved indicates that she was a person of means, success, and respect.

History will not always be so generous. Later, we will see the ability to respect and perceive disabled bodies as worthy of art lose traction when encountering disability.

The statue reveals that the traditional Westernized standards of beauty and the conceptualization of a notion of a "normal" were absent for the early Egyptians. Moreover, this realism of dis/ability is some-

thing we will see evidenced throughout human pre-history. We will see these practices lose traction through subsequent civilizations.

In the Egyptian bust, we see deliberative efforts the sculptor made, the person or persons who commissioned the works sought, and the efforts of those who initially prized and preserved the statue for viewing as a work of art, of a memorial. Collectively, those efforts point to comfort with a disability; this comfort reveals a familiarity—a candor--an openness to disability that will vanish over the centuries. In the final analysis, many people thought the princess important and beautiful enough to portray her as she was and render her beauty in the permanence of stone for the coming millennia. We remember her still. Unfortunately, we will watch as that idea of acceptance of disability crumbles through subsequent history.

As we investigate our past with a renewed and critical awareness, we find compelling evidence of the ubiquity of disability. Its presence is persistent and undeniable. Archaeologists have identified remains as far back as 7,500 years of at least 30 cases of persons living with significant disabilities. Given the relative scarcity of the archaeological record, to have so many singular examples of individuals living with their disabilities demonstrates that disability was part of the everyday fabric of the ancient world.

Furthermore, there is significant evidence that early hunter-gatherer societies took the time to accommodate the needs of individuals with disabilities within their communities; these challenge most of our modern assumptions about such cultures. Not surprisingly, the presence of disability and the culture of care it presupposes ultimately and compellingly challenges our preconceptions about pre-historic peoples and how they would have treated persons with disabilities. We typically view pre-historic cultures as backward and sometimes cruel, eking out hardscrabble existences, but this material warrants a new examination of these assumptions.

To deepen our understanding of the ancient record, let us more closely look at the recent work of archaeologists Tilley and Oxenham of the Australian National University in Canberra. Their recent excavation of the remains of a young man who lived some 4,000 years ago in a region of northern Vietnam sheds considerable light on the pre-historic record. Tilley and Oxenham examined the site known as Man Bac and the remains of a young man, concluding that the young man was disabled at his death and burial. Furthermore, they determined that the manner and ceremony of his funeral suggest he lived with his disability. Like our Egyptian Princess, he was an important person worthy of an elaborate burial ceremony. This find provides evidence of an honor bestowed to an individual with a disability, not unlike our Egyptian princess. It opens the likelihood that others living with disabilities were in positions of respect.

Interestingly, the arrangement of this skeleton was not like the others; rather than being positioned lying straight, he was in a fetal position. Intrigued with the unique positioning, archaeologists used DNA testing to test the remains finding that his vertebrae were fused, possibly demonstrating that he was disabled from birth.[3] Discoveries of this sort led Tilley and Oxenham to advance a theory known as the "bioarchaeology of care." The bioarchaeology of care is a practice in archaeology where a researcher infers from the evidence the level of care rendered a person while living, based on their skeletal remains and burial method. Thus, it allows the researcher to extrapolate cultural practices based on the material remains of a past culture.

Another piece of archaeological evidence comes from Tilley's work re-examining the 1,300-year-old remains of a Nazca child who it is hypothesized had Potts's disease—a more virulent form of TB—and suggests that the child lived with his disability for several years before his death. Moreover, the child's remains are upon a stool—a practice breaking with the disposition of other Peruvian remains—suggesting to Tilley a culture of care and a community oriented to the child's specific needs. Writing in Ars Technica, Kiona Smith summarizes Tilley's theory:

"The fact that the Nazca Boy survived eight to ten years with such a serious illness is proof that he received the care he needed, and it seems he was cared for well; his skin, preserved by natural mummification for nearly 1,300 years, shows no sign of bedsores, which means he likely benefited from good hygiene and frequent position changes."[4]

In a similar vein, Hawkey's study of a disabled individual from the New Mexican Pueblo culture suggests an equally well-developed sense of community, compassion, and care. The care provided to disabled members of the Pueblo communities is striking and consistent with these other remains. The remains of these individuals with disabilities living in these widely disparate cultures point to a set of global practical realities: namely, the culture of respect toward the disabled and the concomitant need for others who would be in the position to care for them as well as the technology of care that relationship entails. Others may need to clothe, clean, and presumably, in some cases, feed the individual. These actions presuppose a continuity of care and concern for the disabled in these societies. We may extrapolate from such evidence that such care manifests a culture of care in these earlier cultures. Such a level of care suggests that ancient practices towards the disabled were far more compassionate and empathetic than we might typically assume about the pre-history of humans. The very presence of levels of care undermines traditional interpretations of how these cultures treated their disabled and challenges our assumptions about disability. Our traditional culturally enforced narratives would find confirming beliefs that the disabled would have been eliminated or euthanized in such societies. This evidence contradicts those assumptions. These ancient cultures start to look far more compassionate and caring than later, more modern societies.

Other discoveries point to similar findings from our past. One such case shows a man who lived up to 45,000 years ago, died about 50, and had one arm amputated. That he had lost an arm is remarkable, but that he did not die from the wound or subsequent infection but outlived the accident and flourished with one arm is even more memorable. Again, accommodations were likely necessary for him, assuming levels of care and concern we usually do not assign to ancient cultures. However, there is more evidence. Graves show evidence of traumas to the eye sockets and other deformities that would require a person to live with a disabling condition despite the relatively primitive circumstances and milieu of their lives.

Another example from the archaeological record attesting to this is the remains of the "Windover Boy," estimated to have lived some 7,500 years ago and with spina bifida. Based on this and other sources of evidence, Dickel and Doran published an article concluding, contrary to popular stereotypes of prehistory:

"Life 7,500 years ago included an ability and willingness to help and sustain the chronically ill and handicapped."[5]

Following Dickel, Dorn, and others, the increasing volume of archaeological evidence revealing the treatment of and presence of persons with disabilities indicates that disability has been a permanent condition of humanity. This evidence shows a culture of continual care and respect present; it suggests how things have not necessarily improved for the disabled through the subsequent advance of history. Later cultures and societies, as we shall see, often discriminated against and persecuted persons with disabilities at an increasingly alarming rate and incidence. Many examples from this and earlier periods show that persons with disabilities were a vital and appreciated part of their communities. That seems to change in modernity. As often as not, persons with disabilities are relegated to the side-lines of contemporary culture. We will see that these earlier practices of caring will, I maintain, become less widespread and often be replaced by less caring even if more technologically advanced forms of treatment from modernity onward. Perhaps these contemporary attitudes of discrimination are why previous archaeological researchers failed to account for the presence of a disability. If one is not willing to see disability as a value, then one may miss the evidence in front of one. At root seems to be the very modern practice of neglect. As Battles writes:

"Impairment and disability are fundamental human experiences across cultures, yet disability remains curiously under-studied and under-theorized within anthropology, particularly within physical anthropology and archaeology."[6]

The branch of archaeology that investigates the health of individuals via their skeletal remains is called paleopathology. Paleo-pathologists have long assumed that the presence of certain skeletal conditions (e.g., lesions) indicates that the person died from a disease. However, this approach overlooks the reality of many chronic diseases. Lesions, for example, take a significant time to accumulate on a person's bones. The upshot of this osteological paradox[7] is that a person from Palaeolithic times may have lived with a chronic disorder for many years before succumbing to the condition.

As a result of this evidence, the binary values of living/dead, healthy/unhealthy, disabled/able-bodied start to fall apart. This binary logic prejudices the sciences we rely on, and, in turn, scientists fail to see the presence of disability in ancient cultural remains. This prejudice is a prime example of the discriminatory logic of the Enlightenment where the object of investigation is pathologized—reduced to an ailment. This process treats the one pathologized as inferior and deviating from a purported norm. The upshot is that you are either living and free of lesions or dead having lesions. This dichotomy seems absurd. There is no possibility of living with lesions—read here, disability.

To be sure, extrapolating any generalization from human remains becomes highly problematic and contentious especially given the deep-set prejudices toward the disabled in modern academic, scientific, and medical communities. However, at a deeper level, the evidence of these and other remains and the likelihood that chronic disabling conditions were present in the lives of Palaeolithic humans leads us to the probable conclusion that individuals lived successful lives with these and other chronic diseases.

As much as an error in scientific reasoning, it seems equally a failure of imagination. When open to the possibility, disability seems to be ever-present and widely accepted in these cultures. This is something we will see in many historical periods and cultures, at least until the arrival of modernity.

It is also not that anthropologists or archaeologists entirely ignored the salient evidence of the disabled in earlier cultures. One of the first anthropologists to study disability was Ruth Benedict, the pioneer anthropologist who published a study of cross-cultural conceptions of epilepsy in 1934. But it would not in any sense become a widespread or generally accepted area of investigation.

Despite the archaeological evidence present and the appearance of a widespread acceptance of persons with disabilities, many early cultures would chart a different course and develop discriminatory practices toward the disabled. For example, as we shall see, the ancient Jewish cultural traditions of discrimination against persons with disabilities as expressed in the Pentateuch function as an example of the general attitudes we find. Here we find strict rules against allowing rabbis with disabilities to enter the inner shrine, the holy of holies. If anyone violated this prohibition, the offender was executed. Their disability was an insult to god. There is something very different here than in the treatment we witnessed in the earlier archaeological records.

In another example, early Greek practices of infanticide aimed at disabled infants reveal the inhumane practices aimed at the disabled, which we will find prevalent in subsequent Western society. Further, in many of the early myths arising from disparate cultures, stretching from India to Greece, we will read how these cultures ostracized and ridiculed the disabled. The question becomes why humans went from the earlier Palaeolithic and Neolithic protective accommodations of a culture of care to a pervasive form of ridicule, exclusion, and discrimination. Let us turn to the past and see if the history of disability will shed light on this development.

3

Bodies in Ancient Cultures

As odd as it may seem to the modern human, evidence suggests that the ancient Egyptians and others such as the Mesopotamians and ancient Indians seemed to tolerate persons with disabilities more readily than many modern cultures do. Why? We can only speculate, but it may have to do with the sheer preponderance of disability in the ancient world. Another factor may be that the religions and mythologies of binary exclusion -the bases of all modern creeds- have not yet taken hold of the human mind. All religions assume an exclusionary binary logic of us versus them, the chosen and the forsaken.

In the first instance, if the disability was as prevalent as it seems to have once been, as evidenced by the archaeological record, we may correctly infer that those with disabilities would simply not be the subject of widespread discrimination because being disabled was commonplace. In the second, it becomes clear that myths (e.g., Greek myths) and later religions (esp., Judaism, Hinduism, et al.) become the source for many discriminatory beliefs and exclusionary practices because of their very binary intellectual nature of us/them, good/bad, sacred/profane. The French historian of disability, Henri-Jacques Stiker, suggests that this phenomenon has to do with the inherent magical versus religious orientations of many of these cultures and their religions.[8] Stiker's approach partly explains why the treatment of the disabled seems qualitatively better in those earlier cultures. The disabled were treated better at this point in history than in subsequent cultures, including our own.

Following Stiker, in magical thinking--where everyone is mortal and forever outside the realm of the divine--no one has any particular advantage, and a degree of social leveling is at play. As such, there is nothing to set them apart from each other.

In this view, disability does not seem to matter--it is not a point of contention. In some of these ancient civilizations, we see, for example, dwarves being revered and held in high esteem and some preferential treatment for the blind. Ample evidence exists in pre-modern cultures, as in the indigenes of the Americas, that the disabled were accommodated as shamans; or given important social roles to occupy that fitted their specific capabilities. As Nielson writes in *A Disability History of the United States*, Native American conceptions of disability are unique in that they do not exist at all. Many native languages lack a word for disability. There is simply no equivalent or even translatable concept matching the concept of disability in many indigenous languages. Again, if disability remains constant in these traditional societies, we may surmise that those populations enjoyed and integrated persons with disabilities into all realms of their respective communities.

The key here is that they were not singled out because of their disability. The absence of a word to categorize does not point to a deficiency in the language nor to the lack of something to describe, but it may mean that there is simply no reason or desire to set that being apart from other beings. As long as the person was occupying a position, then there was no need to discriminate. Language begins by labeling and differentiating one thing from another for a specific purpose. The absence of a word suggests that there is no reason for a label, a difference. In this practice, one is a shaman, etc. but not a person with a disability. The primary locator of your identity was not your inability but your capability; it was not your disability but your ability. Such a designator rests on and highlights your function to society. The process becomes a matter of focus. One reading of the possible differences may come from specific metaphysical and mythological considerations that lay at the root of such belief systems and later structure complete worldviews.

In contrast to westernized language assumptions, indigenous American languages approached it from a different set of foci:

"The modern view of reality is based in straight lines and angles. When someone goes somewhere or gives directions, the method of orientation is based on 'straight ahead,' 'turn left,' and 'turn right.' But Nature doesn't work that way, and neither does the traditional person. Everything in Nature goes in curves and circles, and the same is true about our going about." –Distant Eagle[9]

When a culture chooses to see reality as flexible, circular, capable of iteration, multidimensional; or offers such a degree of variability rendering rigid standards meaningless, it treats persons with differing embodiments, abilities, and capabilities differently than one presupposing a binary logic. Here is the chief difference between the magical and religious mindsets. As the word's origins imply, religion binds one down; this binding is a rigid standard that excludes others. Accordingly, we see that those cultures practicing the magical treat persons -all persons and indeed all beings- with a greater degree of respect and accommodation. Because of this different conception of reality, indigenous people's view of the disabled was remarkably different from later, so-called advanced cultures. Those earlier Palaeolithic and Neolithic cultures likely practiced variations of the magic found in the indigenous American approaches. Those practices may account, in part, for the openness to disability we see in the archaeological record. It is undoubtedly at play in Egypt. In Egypt, a similar conception of the universe structured their response to disability, too. Egyptian mythological beliefs were closer to the magical than the religious: this explains the importance of our Princess. However, we see this manifest in other places too. Their magical view would percolate through different aspects of their culture. The political culture, as an example, may have played a central role in viewing disability differently than later cultures, too. That approach seems clear upon examining an Egyptian excerpt from the "Instruction of Amenemope," which calls for tolerance toward the disabled. It appears that Amenemope needs to interpret the magic for the rest of his Egyptians:

"Beware of robbing a wretch or attacking a cripple.
Do not laugh at a blind man, nor tease a dwarf, nor cause hardship for
the lame.
Don't tease a man who is in the hand of the god (i.e., ill or insane)."

There are several plausible interpretations of this passage: either the
law needed promulgation because of the social problems created by the
robbing or mistreatment of the disabled, or, what seems more plausible given what we know of ancient Egyptian culture, the disabled are
granted preferential treatment. This latter interpretation is strength-
ened when we recall that the disabled were viewed as occupying a place
that merited such treatment since their disability expressed a god's desire. We will see this turn to the divine become a problem for the disabled.

Again, recall our Princess. We are witnessing the beginning of a
transformation from the magical to the religious here. This movement
explains why a person was expected to act politely to those "in the hand
of God." In the religious view, we will see the emergence of the divine theory of attribution of disability. Theistic cultures, like the Egyptians, curry favor with the gods treating those closer to the divine with
a modicum of respect. However, this comes at a cost. We notice that
in the need for a proclamation about the disabled, we must first identify and describe a group as disabled. Here we witness a radical departure from the indigenous American and earlier cultural expressions.
The process of labeling the disabled as Other may find its roots here.
The religious view, like later scientific and medical epistemologies, sets
things apart, discriminates. As the poet William Wordsworth would
later write when distancing himself from the Enlightenment notions of
science and medicine:

"Sweet is the lore which Nature brings;
Our meddling intellect
Mis-shapes the beauteous form of things:--
We murder to dissect."

Centuries later, Wordsworth's Romantic critique of modernity attempted to break away from the obsolete and de-humanizing analyses

of the Enlightenment found in the binary epistemologies of the developing science and medical technologies. Read god, where Wordsworth wrote "nature," and his critique can be applied to the period where the religious emerges from the mystical.

In the ancient Vedic or Indian cultures, we find the earliest mentions of an assistive device for a person with a disability. The needs of the disabled will now become conspicuous. The first prosthetic is mentioned in one of the sacred texts of the Hindu tradition called *The Rig Veda*. Written around 3500 BCE, *The Rig Veda* is the first written record that mentions a prosthesis provided to a warrior queen who lost a leg in a battle. Highlighting an assistive device becomes a password for identifying the disabled. During the Khela battle, the Warrior-Queen, Vishpla, loses her leg in combat and is later fitted with an iron prosthetic allowing her to return to action and continue fighting. We notice a shift occurring here. The queen's disability becomes a foil for comment. From here on, the inclusion of disability within the sacred writings of Hinduism is generally conceived as unfavorable, and the disabled are typically denigrated in subsequent Hindu-influenced culture. This tale is pointing us to the thoroughly religious and non-magical aspects of Vedic thought.

This practice of discrimination stems from the Hindu belief in karma—a fundamental concept of the Hindu religion— that places the origins of a person's traits, characteristics, and circumstances to a divine order, a divine command. Again, the logic of karma is expressed in a binary fashion: good/bad, etc. Disability is viewed negatively, resulting from a divine act of retribution tied directly to one's agency. You are thought to be, in part, responsible for whatever physical ailment or disability you have been dealt. We are not directly in the hand of a god anymore but relegated to his priests and seers via the god's initial judgment of your guilt. Here the disabled become the object of punishment.

As so conceived, karma is primarily determined by the actions of one's previous incarnations or lives. In that case, there is an element of getting your just deserts or what you merit folded into this process as well: a degree of personal responsibility toward one's condition is implied. This element of duty, in some ways, makes it even more burdensome for persons with disabilities because subsequent Hindu-influenced cultures tend to denigrate physical difference and disability, seeing the disabled as meriting their condition. Thus, pity, compassion, or empathy become challenging when the person in question has brought their condition upon themselves.

The texts from Hinduism provide another example when in the Mahabharata, the blind king Dhritarashtra loses most of his sons in a war. His actions are viewed through his sense of revenge for his son's deaths: it is from his blindness. His loss of sight is used to explain the enormity of his rage. However, his is a complex characterization because he is not entirely evil if, for example, we compare him to Richard III.

Dhritarashtra achieves Moksha or enlightenment at the end of his life, yet it is suggested that this achievement is despite his blindness. We find a more robust and realistic portrayal in most Hindu characters: they are full of quirks and seem much more authentically human; nevertheless, the King's disability does not benefit him. In addition, of course, he is a vengeful murderer. His blindness becomes a fountain for his vengefulness--a character flaw that presumably derives from his blindness. This conceit will dog disabled people throughout later cultures and is like the modern stereotype of the embittered gimp that will manifest in later literary and cinematic aspects. This combination of inner psychological turmoil or fault will often be paired with an external flaw and become one of the most widespread stereotypes to affect the disabled.

The Hindu tradition presents us with the Gandhari King, Shakuni, a character of the Mahabharata and the principal belligerent of the epic war that unfolds in the story. He is in many ways the most excellent personification of scheming revenge and evil like Shakespeare's Iago and King Richard III. Both of whom coincidentally appear cruel and notably disabled. All three function as the scheming disabled villain-king. This conceit, incidentally, is found in all of world literature--Shakuni might be the first.

Shakuni was disabled by his father, Subala, who, we are told, twisted his leg permanently, disabling the child. He did this -we are further in-structed- to teach his child a lesson about revenge. It worked. Shakuni is the *cause de la guerre* of the Kurukshetra war fought between the Kaurava and the Pandava princes that serve as the central drama of the classic Indian epic. Inevitably, the vengefulness of the disabled will be the significant character trait we find in these tales. Expressly, Shakuni's bitterness implied throughout the legend stems from his early disablement by his father; the disability is the locus of his evil.

In later Hindu mythology, Lord Vishnu refused to allow a wedding for Lakshmi's sister, Alakshmi, because she is disabled. Alakshmi is of-ten described as disabled and always depicted as disfigurement or a long list of disabilities and ailments. Alakshmi is the goddess of misfor-tune and is present whenever bad events or emotions prevail or occur, such as ruin, destruction, horror, sloth, gluttony, envy, rage, hypocrisy, greed, and lust.[10] Vishnu arranges a marriage to a tree for her because no human or other god would accept a wife with a disability. In the Samudra Matahana, Alakshmi is portrayed as being "cow-repelling, an-telope-footed, and bull-toothed." She is seen as sowing discord, misery, poverty, and jealousy wherever she goes and is often associated with the destructive goddess, Kali.[11] As an indication of the extended reach and staying power of these tropes, in today's Indian cinema, Shakuni and Alakshmi are often depicted as disabled.[12]

The religious becomes the bedrock for the scientific and modern. However, the real power is how these images inform the political re-alities and affect everyday lives. As the blogger and Professor Michael Moore writes regarding the treatment of people with disabilities in In-dia:

"All of this received wisdom inevitably influences the behavior of believers toward the disabled. Before 1928, handicapped individuals in India could not inherit property. Yet, the abolishment of legal discrim-ination (Nagpal, 1983) has not changed social norms. A 2007 World Bank survey found that around half of the respondents in India believed "disability was always or almost always a curse of God." The survey tells us further that people with disabilities attended around half of the social and religious functions and often found themselves discouraged from attending marriages. The behavior of clergy provides another indication of intolerance of disabled individuals: According to Punbit (2013), extremist Hindu clergy at temples have started a drive to deny entry to disabled people.[13]

4

Buddhism: Compassion for All Living Things Except the Disabled

Following a recent UNESCO report on children with disabilities worldwide in June 1994, 92 governmental organizations joined 25 international organizations at the World Conference on Special Needs Education held in Salamanca, Spain. These representatives looked at the conditions of children with disabilities around the world and found some disturbing trends. In Thailand, for example, disability is viewed as a personal failure because of one's previous karma, and the report further highlighted that those children with disabilities were neglected and abused. In addition, researchers found that attending school is not a viable option for most children with disabilities.[14] In a nation founded on the compassionate principles of Buddhism, one might reasonably expect a different result. Still, persons with disabilities have traditionally fared little better under Buddhism than under any other of the world's religions. Indeed, and somewhat ironically, given Buddhism's acceptance of suffering, tolerance, and compassion, we find the condition of persons with disabilities to be much worse off than in secular societies in many cases. Thus, notwithstanding the principles of compassion, Buddhism scores little better than other religions in treating the disabled.

Buddhism as a world religion has offered much compassionate treatment toward persons with diseases and poverty. Still, it has never substantively challenged the general denigration of the disabled. The chief reason for this may be that despite the traditions of compassion, care, and pacifism central to Buddhist doctrine, it still relies heavily upon and is indebted to the basic tenets of Hinduism, especially in its appropriation and adoption of the concepts of karma, destiny, duty and natural law. These concepts, as we have seen, have a decidedly negative impact on those with disabilities. Thus, one of the significant differences we find in Buddhism is its pragmatic orientation.

Suffering is a central tenet of human existence for Buddhists—one of the Buddha's Four Noble Truths—so we might assume that disability would be treated differently from what we see. In practice, we find that persons with disabilities are often only understood as a being suffering and rarely as one who can transcend that suffering. Further, karma relieves practitioners from feeling compassion toward those who suffer and replaces it with, in many instances, scorn. Too often, that suffering is seen as merited or pre-ordained from karma, adding to the blameworthiness of the sufferer. Pity may become the only appropriate mode of acceptable moral or social interaction between the disabled and non-disabled. The narrowing of social interactions deprives the disabled and, by extension, the non-disabled of the fullness of their humanity. At best, the disabled, too often, become just an object lesson and a focus of opportunity allowing for others -the non-disabled-- to demonstrate and exercise their virtues of charity and an attenuated form of compassion even if it limits the disabled. The upshot is the effect of reducing the person with a disability to mere use-value. The reduction to utility is fundamentally dehumanizing. As a result, many persons with disabilities in Buddhist countries are treated as pariahs or outcasts. They lose all agency, humanity, and the respect those aspects might garner. Their unconditional worth is gone. Buddhist societies do not offer any natural way to assuage or alleviate this kind of treatment. Hence, the prevailing condition for persons with disabilities in Buddhist countries is equal to or exceeds the most appalling we find anywhere in the globe.

Moreover, and primarily because of the hegemony of the idea of karma, a disability in Buddhist and Hindu-influenced cultures is a variant of getting one's just deserts. Your past actions are the cause of your current condition. Therefore, your disability is, in some measure, your fault. There is no ready antidote available or remedy here. What is more, there is no escaping this cruel and viciously circular logic. For example, this is the logic of the Buddhist anecdote explaining how people came to be hunchbacked. It is based entirely on karma. Their disability is caused because they once scoffed at a Buddhist, "berated, and laughed at those bowing to Buddha."[15] Their condition, then, is due to their actions in a previous life and precisely their prior act of desecration. As a result, a two-fold effect emerges. First, it forgives the person who caused your disability in cases of accident, injury, negligence, or medical malpractice; second, it simultaneously locates the foci of the blame on the disabled themselves. The upshot is that it emancipates society from all responsibility and blames the victim.

It is unsurprising then that we find overt discrimination in Buddhist countries. Moore cites a 2013 study of Japanese Buddhists, finding that "68% of people with a disability say they have experienced discrimination."

For a contemporary example, the difficulties experienced by the disabled are echoed in the work of the 1994 Nobel Laureate Kenzaburō Ōe in his 1964 book, "A Personal Matter." It is a semi-autobiographical work where he delicately writes about a man's life and his disabled son. The book is based on Ōe's own experiences with his son, the composer, Hikari Ōe. Hikari was born with multiple disabilities, including autism. The book fictionalizes the obstacles the Ōe family faced when they went against the orders of the family doctor who wanted to abort the couple's son, as well as the challenges they faced as Hikari grew up in a prejudicial culture. The reality of the situation in Japan repeats itself in other Buddhist nations.

Moore shows that "the vast majority of people without disability feel that individuals who have a disability are treated like second-class citizens." Reducing one's status to a less than average level allows others to treat you as a scapegoat for their hate and frustrations. While we see this manifest in micro-aggressive behaviors directed against the disabled, we also see violent expressions of these beliefs sanctioned too. For example, we witnessed the violence play out in the 2016 mass murder of 19 residents with disabilities living in a home for the disabled in Sagimahara, Japan. The assailant wrote a letter to a politician claiming that he would "obliterate 470 disabled people." He based his reasons were on the notion that a disabled life was a life not worth living. If this was an isolated act, we could discount it as an aberration. But like other forms of institutionalized and structural violence against minorities, we see explicit prior cultural legitimation of violence against the disabled, which, in turn, abets and indeed encourages this kind of violent behavior.

5

The Beginnings of Western Prejudice against the Disabled

It is a well-established idea that Western culture is built on the binary logic of exclusion—us versus them dichotomy. Equally pervasive is the idea that we tend to fear and reject what we fail to grasp or understand. These two ideas meld into a widespread behavioral tendency. In many instances, fear is generated by the so-called "the other," "the outsider." What develops is an excluded class toward which violence and discrimination are directed and legitimated throughout human culture. We find this intensified in what we have come to identify as "Western" cultures. We see this as an operative, for example, in the scapegoat syndrome, ultimately having its origins in Jewish thought. The scapegoat is the practice of singling out a party or person for unmerited exclusion or derision. It is a subtle and powerful force in Western culture arising originally out of ancient Jewish religious practices. The origin of the scapegoats requires two goats: one is sacrificed to God and the other to Azazel. It is essential to notice that the priest who offers the scapegoat must look in the face of the goat he is sacrificing and be cleansed before returning to the sacred sites. Then, the scapegoat would either be released (shunned) into the wilderness or taken to a cliff and thrown off.

The scapegoat as a social phenomenon is where one unconsciously projects one's feelings of inadequacy and problems on the other. A form of psychological displacement or projection of fear and inadequacy where aggression and hostility directed at a sub-group or individual is legitimated. If that hostility is muted or sublimated, it manifests as acts of micro-aggression or subtler forms of socially accepted discriminatory practices. We find early examples of scapegoating in many cultures. Early Judaism would justify scapegoating in supporting texts, including Leviticus (16: 8-10). Here we see the origins of scapegoating, where the second goat is sent into the desert to atone for the community's sins. The word used initially for scapegoating was the etymologically obscure "Azazel" which would eventually find its way into various mythologies. Azazel, to whom a goat or goats was sacrificed, was a fallen angel or possibly a corrupted god who bedeviled humankind into fornication and lewd behavior. Azazel is the creator of cosmetics, swords, knives, and a whole host of accouterments that cause humans to sin by powerfully beguiling tools of wickedness. Later, he was viewed as the force that compelled women to use ornamentation, jewelry, and cosmetics. While there does not seem to be a direct connection to Greek mythology, the mention of his forging weapons connects Azazel to the Greek god Hephaestus, who is, incidentally, a jeweler—he made a necklace for the goddess Harmonia, and he was disabled.

Moreover, like Hephaestus, Azazel is the god that taught humankind the art of the forge and metallurgy. The ancient Greeks developed a scapegoating ritual where a disabled beggar -known as the pharmakos-was driven out of the city after some tragedy had struck. The pharmakos were ritualistically blamed for the disaster (e.g., plague, earthquake, or invasion). The pharmakos could be sacrificed and often stoned before being driven from the community. All this is cognate with Azazel and scapegoating. It echoes the myth of Hephaestus driven from Olympia by Ares and other gods because of his unsightliness. In modern Persian, when you want to point to someone being unjustly blamed, you use a proverb that roughly translates to "beheading the blacksmith of Balkh:"

"A Persian story about a ruler who heard a blacksmith had committed a crime in the city of Balkh, now in northern Afghanistan. In his desire to appear swift in meting out justice he ordered the arrest and beheading of the culprit. But, as Balkh was too far away, the ruler decreed that beheading any blacksmith would do. And yet his henchmen were unable to find such an artisan in nearby towns. All they found was a coppersmith in the city of Shushtar in western Iran. So, our zealous ruler called for the execution of the poor coppersmith of Shushtar lest the crime of the blacksmith of Balkh went unpunished."[16]

The similarity of these mythologies (Jewish, Greek, and Persian) focusing on blaming an individual for an event they had little or no role in suggests a shared, deeper origin. The suggestive notion that all four figures, Azazel, Hephaestus, Pharmakos, and the blacksmith from Balkh were craftsmen liable to bear scars and disabilities from their trades, must be considered. In addition to the fact that they were makers of things that could charm, interest, or capture one's imagination. We also see the link with cosmetics with these myths is preserved in, to some extent, with the development of modern plastic surgery, which is often used to "repair" or "reconstruct" body deformations. The origins of plastic surgery emerged essentially after WWI, where surgeons tried to reconstruct the faces of WWI veterans who suffered facial disfigurements.

We see the origins of this form of discrimination -of setting someone apart and opening them to censure, ridicule, or worse -in the deep cultural roots of Western culture: Jewish, Syrian, Persian, and Greek. Moreover, practices of exclusion abound in nearby cultures, including Mandæan, Sabean, and Arabian mythologies, and will later be adopted into Christian myth.[17] Consequently, it does not surprise us to find the origins of discrimination in the earliest foundational sources, such as the biblical and philosophical traditions of the Western project.

For example, in the Pentateuch, we see practices of excluding and segregating persons with disabilities from important ritual events and sacred sites. You will notice that it squarely places the origin of disability on the divine, in god's hands. Judaism will share the divine agency origin of disability with several other ancient cultures.

Early in Exodus (4:11), we find Yahweh telling Moses where disability originates: "Who gives man speech? Who makes him dumb or deaf, seeing or blind? Is it not I, the Lord?" One of the first textual pieces of evidence for the divine attribution theory of the origins of disability. The divine attribution theory of disability is a dominant and universal trope concerning disability in Western thought. After Yahweh articulates this claim, you may choose to define its meaning. You may value the gift ethically and existentially, but it is still conceived as a burden or an opportunity. The conflict arises because the society you were born into will not reciprocate that positive valorization of disability. Whether in Greek, Roman, Jewish, Christian, Islamic or later secular approaches, this origin story of disability is found throughout Western and Eastern approaches to disability.

The notion is simple. God made you what you are, disabled or not. If disabled, you are either an outcast to be scapegoated or, if the circumstances demand, you are only valued for what service you provide the group. In either case, some special treatment is expected. Inevitably disability sets you apart, for good or ill. Often, that treatment will be construed as unfavorable. For example, in Leviticus 21: 18-21, severe and extreme prohibitions are promulgated to keep the disabled from encountering the holy and engaging in the critical rituals central to the Jewish spiritual life:

"No man who has any flaws can come near. No man who is blind or disabled can come. No man whose body is scarred or twisted can come.[18] No man whose foot or hand is disabled can come.[19] No man whose back is bent can come. No man who is too short can come. No man who has anything wrong with his eyes can come. No man who has boils or running sores can come. No man whose sex glands are crushed can come."

There is little to no resistance to such a prohibition throughout history; indeed, there are no early discussions concerning the merits or exceptions. It has been taken to be an acceptable practice. As Stiker notes in his magisterial and groundbreaking work on the history of disability, "Corps Infirmes et Societes," the concept of "blemish" was used to segregate the disabled from the flock and limit one's access to the ritual sacrifices. As such, a blemish acts as a signifier representing a deeper set of unassailable symbols grounding practices. Because of its deep-set origins, there will be no significant resistance, and such methods will not be questioned until modern times.

In most cultures, blemishes carry an ontological significance deeply rooted in that culture's foundational stories and cannot be easily extirpated. Stiker shows how in the "Encyclopedia of Judaica," there is a laundry list of conditions that fall under the rubric of blemish used to discriminate against persons with disabilities. These include blindness and certain diseases of the eyes, injuries to the thigh, a deformed nose, lameness, the loss of a limb, skeletal deformations, muscle degeneration, a humped back, skin diseases, and the loss of a testicle and impotence. The prohibitions go beyond just the privileges of the priestly class; they extend to those who will be allowed to engage in combat "and no man, lame, blind, crippled or having an incurable defect of the flesh, or afflicted by an impurity...shall accompany them to battle."

Centuries later, the influential philosopher Rabbi Moses Ben Maimonides issued an apologia defending these prohibitory actions toward the disabled. We read this, for example, from his magnum opus, "The Guide for the Perplexed:"

A priest who had a blemish was not allowed to officiate; and not only those who had a blemish were excluded from the service, but also ... those that had an abnormal appearance; for the multitude does not estimate man by his true form but by the perfection of his bodily limbs and the beauty of his garments, and the temple was to be held in great reverence by all."[20]

Sadly, we see that after more than a dozen centuries, Jewish thinking still discriminated against the disabled. It will take until the late 20th century before we see attempts to redress these practices.

But this notion of blemish will echo down through the millennia and manifest in the early 20th century with the development of so-called "ugly laws" in the United States.

As a result of the blemish turned into disability, the disabled person under Talmudic law was restricted from worship in the congregation, thereby creating unbridgeable social isolation. This isolation becomes an abyss—this prohibition about congregating functions as severing any opportunity for connection with the community. If you cannot interact with a group of people, you will never benefit from knowing them, becoming comfortable in their presence, and cannot, therefore, learn from them; you will live comfortably in the prison-house of your prejudices. As a widespread normative hegemony, you will likely internalize these values making any positive re-interpretation all but impossible. Segregation enforces stereotypes. Stiker shows that the "disabled had the status of prostitutes or of women whom menstruation made unclean."[21] In this approach, the disabled are viewed as unclean and impure; therefore, it was the right course of action to be shunned and excluded. The disabled had no recourse; they could only live on the margins of Jewish society. Indeed, living is all they could do, for there is even an injunction about trying to overcome one's disability or better one's condition. Given the divine origin of disability, this makes sense. If God is the sole judge of justice in the created universe, how can I question the justness of my disability or resulting exclusion? It is addressed in a fable by Rabbi Ishmael when two disabled peasants work in unison to obtain the king's fruit and are duly punished. Here is the legend in full:

"A king, owning a beautiful orchard of luscious fruit, and not knowing whom to trust in it, appointed two invalids—one lame and the other blind. The lame one, however, tempted by the precious fruit, suggested to his blind companion that he ascend a tree and pluck some; but the latter pointed to his sightless eyes. At last, the blind man raised his lame companion on his shoulders and thus enabled him to pluck some of the fruit. When the king came, noticing that some fruit had disappeared, he inquired which one was the thief. Vehemently asserting his innocence, each pointed to the defect that made it impossible for him to have committed the theft. But the king guessed the truth and, placing the lame man on the shoulders of the other, punished them together as if the two formed one complete body. Thus, added Ishmael, will it be hereafter: soul and body will be reunited and punished together."

The moral of this tale suggests that one should merely accept one's given lot in life and not try to overcome one's limitations or form any associations with others in similar straits. The echo of this lesson would reverberate down the millennia.

There remains the strange and peculiar case of Jacob. The story of Jacob's disablement and what it presents to this practice of excluding the lame is little commented upon in subsequent literature, but his central position in Jewish thought requires a new look. Jacob is, of course, one of the significant figures in early Jewish thought and one of the crucial Patriarchs of the Israelites. Indeed, he is one with whom God makes a covenant. As such, Jacob's centrality to Judaism is a given, yet he is rendered lame, disabled. In Genesis 32: 22-32, an anonymous man with whom he fights waylays him on his way to Canaan. Fighting throughout the night, Jacob comes to realize that this was no ordinary human. It was an angel or possibly God himself. As dawn broke and the fight continued, the story goes that Jacob's antagonist suddenly struck him on the thigh, permanently injuring and disabling him because Jacob would not release him and let him go. Because of the angelic or divine blow, Jacob is left lame: Jacob is disabled from the fight. In Genesis:

"Then he said, "Let me go, for the day has broken." But Jacob said, "I will not let you go unless you bless me." And he said to him, "What is your name?" And he said, "Jacob." Then he said, "Your name shall no longer be called Jacob, but Israel, for you have striven with God and with men, and have prevailed."

Although he is disabled, Jacob is renamed. There is something important to this renaming. In a way, his renaming will allow Jacob to avoid being shunned and suffering the fate of others who were disabled. He is set aside by being elevated to a new and vital status with his disability. The account contains several plays on the meaning of Hebrew "Israel" — Jacob's new name--which sounds like the Hebrew for "heel" (recall Oedipus and Achilles) comes from the Hebrew words, meaning "wrestle," and, "god." However, the fact that one of the central figures of the Jewish religion would be simultaneously one of those excluded because of his disability cannot be the case. Jacob's disability marks him as different and therefore existentially and morally identifiable, but it also has the dual aspect of potentially making him an outcast with singular importance. In a sense, this might prefigure the struggles of the people of Israel still waiting for them. In a personal, existential sense, it could signal the battle that may linger for anyone who will encounter disability in their life. A struggle made challenging because of the mandates directed against the disabled. You will need to redefine—rename--yourself after a disability. In the re-appropriation of the new name, you must both let go of your past self with all that implies and simultaneously come face-to-face with a new reality. Society will be slow to accept you in your new instantiation.

Alternatively, the renaming may set Jacob apart and render him no longer disabled. Emerging here is the latter aspect of disablist creed where one is either defined by one's new classification as a disabled person; or viewed by the larger, able-bodied world as not disabled at all because one achieves accomplishments beyond anyone's expectation for the disabled. This latter attribution gives rise to the "super-gimp" designation that would emerge in the 20th century. Moreover, it will indirectly lead to the seemingly unending search for a "politically correct" term to label the disabled. Consequently, the 20th and 21st centuries will produce a litany of namings and re-namings—euphemisms-- from invalid to crippled to handicapped to disabled. More cumbersome phrases such as the "differently-abled," "handicapable," and the like would briefly appear only to fade away and be replaced by another term.

Traditionally, and in many instances, disability was conceived in many ancient traditions as an immutable condition caused by the caprice of supernatural or divine agency. We witnessed this conceit beginning in and with the stories of exclusion in Exodus and the Hindu and Greek foundational myths and continuing into the early medieval period with the syncretic belief that the influence of the planets caused the deformity of an infant's disability. Planetary influences functioned, it was believed, as vital factors in birth and often the cause of disability. It was building on the Hippocratic tradition that viewed planetary influences operating on the health of fetuses and stemming from an influential work—"De Humana Matura" attributed to Constantinus Africanus (the 11th century). In the "De Humana Natura," Africanus advanced the notion that planetary effects on fetal development were paramount in providing credence to the folk wisdom of the celestial origins of disability. Saturn was viewed as dominant in the first and eighth months of pregnancy, and children born prematurely were likely to be born with congenital conditions. The reason, Africanus argued, was that Saturn brought a "heaviness" to the fetus, cooling it too much and causing a lack of necessary nourishments for proper development. Thus, children born with deformations or disabilities[21] were called "Saturn's children." Indeed, Metzler lists the personality effects attributed to Saturn's children under this humoral model of health and all of which were negative:

"They were often sickly, pale, skinny, cold, rough, lethargic, slow, sad, or thieving and grasping."

Deemed as deficient by others and likely viewing themselves as being marked from birth as different, they would find themselves living under a cloud. Here, we witness the dual process of ostracizing and deferential treatment that many disabled still find themselves bound up with and involved in subsequent societies. You are simultaneously derided and special. Remarkable in this context is nothing to be desired.

6

Christianity and Disability

Although the disabled fared little better under the more extended history of Christian-dominated societies, Jesus' proclamation to assist the under trodden does indeed, at least in theory, carve out a space for potential acceptance of the disabled. The key here is in the actual practice; we will not witness any emerging autonomy of the disabled. Nonetheless, we hear this message of rejecting the idea of divine punishment strongly expressed in the Gospel according to John 9:2

"As he went along, he saw a man blind from birth. His disciples asked him, "Rabbi, who sinned, this man or his parents, that he was born blind?"

"Neither this man nor his parents sinned," said Jesus, "but this happened so that the works of God might be displayed in him."

During Jesus' life, the accepted practice would be to see disability and the disabled as culpable or blameworthy agents of their conditions: further, disability resulted from embodiment, corporeality, and therefore the loci of potential sin.

Let us return to the parable of the blind man. When someone asked the blind man what or who caused his blindness, we hear the long-standing assumptions viewing the disabled as having done something to merit god's punishment driving their condition. Thus, your misfortune was either your fault or one of your relatives. In either case, you would shoulder part or all of the blame for your disability. With this view, you were righteous when you discriminated against the disabled or excluded the disabled; they were, after all, justifiably the objects of ostracizing and, for some, ridicule. Jesus' simple rebuttal challenges this long-standing tradition. As such, his words and actions begin to desacralize the notion of disability and render it a naturally occurring phenomenon rather than something caused or brought on by divine agency or punishment.

As it would later develop, the Christian Principle of the Least embodied in the saying from Luke, "For he who is least among you all — he is the greatest" (Luke 9:46) would be used to offer a veneer of protection and respect to the disabled. We may take this to mean that the displaced will now be viewed as valued. The formerly dispossessed will, at least in theory, be granted a modicum of value. Under this re-evaluation, the disabled will be among those now given a better position alongside prostitutes and others formerly despised and deprived of respect, autonomy, and opportunity. Further evidence is found throughout the New Testament, where Jesus is described as showing kindness toward the disabled. There is, of course, the paralytic from Matthew (9:2-7). Also, Jesus offers respect to those who were lame, blind, and in other ways disabled. Building on this tradition and extending to those with mental disabilities, Paul would teach that Christians should offer "Comfort to the feeble-minded." In Paul's instructions, we see that Jesus' messages were coded to include the disabled into the fold of believers and change the very sense of disability's origin away from the divine attribution theory. However, this would not lead to a wholesale change in the lives of the disabled; there was not, nor would there be, complete acceptance for the disabled. To be clear, notice that Jesus seeks to cure the disabled, not accept them into the community. This effort will begin the long process of rehabilitating or healing the afflicted. Under the Christian prerogative, we cannot remain neutral and let a difference exist. An activist and interventionist mentality will view that it needs to be cured if an affliction is present. These two assumptions will remain unchecked and unexamined up to the present day.

What is more, the relief of disability seems to rely entirely on Jesus' whim --whether he wants to offer a miracle or not. Thus, disability is still conceived negatively and needs to be overcome -that is what a miracle is all about- transcending the natural. Moreover, this approach renders the disabled wholly dependent on the caprice of the caregiver or redeemer.

As the centuries unfold, the influence of Christian thought waned, and the old prejudices against the disabled prevailed. The disabled were viewed as the subject of god's punishment. In the Anglican tradition of the "Book of Common Prayer," we find the instructions for curates visiting the disabled and ill, and in "The Order for the Visitation of the Sick" we see a return to the old notion of divine agency when it asks:

"Are you persuaded that your sickness is sent unto you by Almighty God?"

In a more recent edition of "Book of Common Prayer," we read that the justification of disability lies with God: "whatsoever your sickness is, know you certainly, that it is God's visitation." In both texts, we hear that one's salvation rests on accepting that as a truism. If you are disabled, it is a result of god's displeasure with you, and your only remedy is to become an even more ardent practitioner of the religion. An irksome realization to bear for the person with a disability. You cause your disability, and your cure can only be achieved when you become a better Christian. It was not until 1958 that the Anglican Church would return to revise its attitude toward disability:

"It is cruel and false to brand every sufferer as a sinner: much suffering and sickness is due to the sin either of other persons or society in general."[22]

7

Islam and Disability

Compared to other religions, Islam is relatively tolerant of persons born with disabilities but looks less favorably on those who encounter disability later in life, stemming from the notion that Allah is compassionate and that wrong-doing or ill fortune stems from human agency. Instead, this view sees Allah's punishment as just because of that person's actions. Consequently, persons who develop a disability later in life tend to be viewed as those Allah did not favor and deserve less beneficence.

Nevertheless, in a religion with a single creator God who has created everything and everyone implies a positive value on all regardless of differences of ability. Therefore, liberal interpreters of the Qur'an may interpret Islam in this way, bridging as they often do from where the Qur'an addresses the issue in this way:

"O mankind, we created you from a single pair of a male and a female, and made you into nations and tribes, that you may know each other not that you may despise each other. Verily the most honored of you in the sight of Allah is he who is the most righteous of you. And God has full knowledge and is well acquainted [with all things]" (49:13)

The Islamic scholar Fethullah Gulen writes, "Islam promotes equality as the will of God Almighty and requires mutual respect of fellow human beings. Islam embraces every individual and every group with the same equality and warmth. It responds to the expectations and the needs of everyone in the same way.[23]" Yet such parity is lost in actual

practice in contemporary Islamic countries. The absence of consideration or respect has led to neglect in most contemporary Islamic countries.

However, what is peculiarly at odds with Gulen's interpretation is
the near-complete lack of voices of the disabled in present-day Islamic
states and the near absence from the historical record. This absence
may be attributed to how disability is largely ignored in the Qur'an. It
contains little reference to the disabled except within the context of the
requirements of Jihad and Haj. Where it mentions the disabled are ex-
empt:

"Not equal are those of the believers who sit at home, except those
who are disabled, and those who strive hard and fight in the Cause of
Allah with their wealth and their lives." (4:95)

In this regard, the Qur'an limits the access of the disabled to some
functions, including battle and pilgrimage, but as Stiker remarks, not
because they are unclean as in Jewish law, but merely because they are
deemed "incapable.[24]" The Prophet, although rebuked by Allah for his
treatment of the disabled, counsels others to treat the disabled respect-
fully, saying,

"No reproach to the blind, no reproach to the lame, no reproach to
the sick"

Doing so, he starts to erase the millennia-old practice of exclusion
aimed at the disabled in the ancient desert world. The absence of the
disabled could be due to the rigors of a harsh desert and or the semi-
arid environment and the social conditions that those deeper realities
gave rise to, or the longer traditions of infanticide of disabled children
inherited from the older Mediterranean cultures. Whatever the cause
or causes, the silence is complete.

In other Hadith -the collection of instructive sayings derived from
Mohamed- the Prophet recounts the story of Julaybib, one of his contemporaries and later a martyr for the faith. Julaybib, from whom many
later Muslims would refer to as an example of how to treat the disabled,
offers one insight into the lives of the disabled. Julaybib was poor and
deformed and, because of his disability, could not find a wife. However,

upon the Prophet's request, a wealthy noble family gave their beautiful daughter in marriage to Julaybib. It is telling that the etymology of Julaybib means "small" from the diminutive jalbab, suggesting that Julaybib was small and short, perhaps a dwarf. He was frequently described as being damim, meaning ugly, deformed, or repulsive. Is it his small stature or his ugliness that prevents his success at marrying, or do we see the beginning of a tradition where disability will be equated with ugliness? We notice in this story that the young bride-to-be does not elect to marry Julaybib, nor did her family offer the arranged marriage until the Prophet ordered it.

Later, the third prominent Islamic leader, Omar Ibn Al-Khattab, provided a blind boy's family housing near a mosque closest to the family after the child's father complained that his son could not reach a different mosque[25]. These examples prove that Islam was more comparable to Christianity than Judaism in evolving more liberal attitudes toward the disabled. However, the deeper cultural roots and prejudices would still prove dominant in shaping attitudes to this day. The prejudicial treatment of persons with disabilities under religious traditions is abundantly clear, and as Schumm and Stoltzfus conclude in their introduction to a survey of religious attitudes toward the disabled: [26]

"While religious attitudes and responses to disability are quite diverse, it is not uncommon for Jewish, Christian, and Islamic perspectives to mimic the medical model by connecting disabling bodily conditions with individual spiritual deficiency. There is a persistent tendency to associate disability with individual sin."

Finally, the range of cultural, economic, and political diversity of modern Islamic nations makes generalization risky. However, there is still an absence of disabled persons in Islamic cultures and a general practice of discrimination operating throughout the Islamic world.

8

Ancient Greece

Roughly contemporary with the ancient Hebrew culture that gave rise to the Pentateuch and the somewhat earlier Vedic civilization of the "Rig-Veda," the ancient Greeks developed their unique view of the disabled. They would similarly encode them in their critical cultural documents. Chief among these documents are the epic poems the Iliad and Odyssey but also in the later plays. They will serve, as will Jewish and to some degree, Islamic traditions as the fountainhead for much of the prevailing attitudes of the Western and later modernist worlds.

The great Homeric epics such as the Iliad and Odyssey would provide insights into the lives of disabled Greeks in antiquity. Still, the Greeks left an impressive pictorial record in sculpture and relief that neither the Jewish nor the Islamic traditions did. This graphic record of the history of the body is evident in the many sculptures directly from or derived from ancient Greek sculptors. It is no stretch of the imagination to assert that later aesthetic canons in the sculptural arts derive from these Greek origins. For example, the cult of the able male body we see in Michelangelo finds its roots in Praxiteles and other Greek sculptors.

The classical world's aesthetic preference for idealism found in the expression of the male nude, the celebration of male strength, the importance of male sexuality, and the traditions of male athleticism associated with the Olympiad, enshrines a conception of beauty that reveals much about their approach to disability. What the Greeks considered and found beautiful was the fully able-bodied male nude. Indeed, as Lennard Davis has argued, the very Western notion of beauty derives from a particular idea of an idealized male athletic body that precludes the disabled, the differently embodied.[27] This ideal found its grounding in the very notion of what qualifies as art. For example, the philosopher Aristotle (384–322 BCE) believed, as did many in Ancient Greece, that the flawless nude male was the highest archetype of beauty; indeed, Aristotle went further, claiming that women were but deformed men. He would hold this prejudice both in phenotype and rational ability. It reveals that he believed that women were inferior to men because they were "the first step along the road to deformity." In other words, women were not beautiful because they were lacking maleness and, therefore, closer to being disabled, which was understood as a lacking, an absence. A clear hierarchy is constructed, with the uppermost position being occupied by men. Women would come next, and the deformed and disabled would be placed on the lowest rung of Aristotle's ladder of prejudice.

Consequently, mere removal away from the male ideal was aestheticized as unattractive and eventually deformed. The philosopher argued that men were far better at reasoning and therefore free from constraint and more deserving of the accolades of beauty. The very notion of freedom is established with this hierarchy. These analytical skills would qualify as the prerogatives of citizenship open only to aristocratic males and rarely, if ever, to women, children, slaves, or, presumably, the disabled. Thus, Aristotle legitimized the patriarchal practices of ancient Greece and the negative attitudes toward the intellectually different and physically disabled.[28] Patriarchy, sexism, and ableism are intricately bound together in Aristotle's ideology of beauty. Much of the resulting political culture of Western thought is founded on these biases. Aristotle's predominance in the Western philosophical and intellectual legacy is without peer. As such, Aristotle's hierarchy of superiority would lay the later foundations for the evils of slavery, misogyny, and ableism legitimized and taken as customary in the Western world. Many within that tradition have been struggling against these biases for over 2,000 years.

Aristotle was, however, not alone nor a remote outlier in advocating practices of discrimination. Plato, his teacher, made eugenics part of his preconditions for his perfected city. Plato's ideal city is often known as the Kallipolis (Καλλίπολις) or the "beautiful" city and is a political embodiment of the aesthetics of able-bodied male privilege. We can see what is assumed with this terminology. The governing rulers—the Philosopher Kings—would start their climb to supremacy training as soldiers. What set them apart would be the fetishization of the rational detailed by Aristotle. However, to achieve this perfect state, all obstacles need to be eliminated. Enter euthanasia and eugenics, the twin legacies of hate that form the bedrock of Western culture's violence toward the disabled. Indeed, Aristotle would follow his teacher Plato in recommending euthanasia for all "deformed children." In Aristotle's "Politics," he called for legislation that would effectively outlaw disabled children:

"Let there be a law that no cripple child shall be reared."[29]

In this, he was slavishly following Plato, who, in his "Republic," argued for both vigorously enforced eugenics and a policy of ridding his ideal state—Kallipolis-- of any deformed or disabled progeny. To begin, he would say a state should carefully control mating and sexual intercourse, only allowing for children to come from "the best of our men and the best of our woman as often as possible." (Republic, 240-1). Then, building on this policy of selective breeding, he would counsel that any disabled child should be "quietly and secretly disposed of," giving rise to his advocacy of abortion for the creation of the ideal state. To be exact, Plato argued that a midwife could induce abortions in cases of older parentage and as a device for population control, too. Still, the original purpose of the practice is derived from cleansing the population of the disabled. The method of feticide was celebrated as central to the state and one he had found in practice in nearby Sparta. While we often blame Plato and Aristotle, they were mere mouthpieces for existing practices in many city-states such as Sparta.

In his "Republic," Plato held that those born with disabilities or deformities should be put away immediately in a "mysterious and unknown" place in the ideal society. In the Republic, he writes, "The offspring of the inferior, or the better when they chance to be deformed, shall be put away." In addition, he later advises future leaders, "This is the kind of medical provision you should legislate in your state. You should provide treatment for those of your citizens whose physical constitution is good. As for all the others, it will be best to leave the unhealthy to die and put to death those whose psychological condition is incurably corrupt. It is the best thing to do, both for the individual sufferer and society." Ever the fan of Sparta, the philosopher came as close as he dared to the Spartan practice of "exposing" a child to determine its mettle. Still, he will ground his position on the welfare of society. As we have seen, exposure amounted to leaving an infant unattended outside the city walls to see if the child was favored by the gods and of superior strength. Thus, Plato justified his theory of infanticide of the disabled on the grounds of the welfare of society. In his final work, "Laws," Plato wrote and defended a kind of an ability-related purdah or apartheid when he argued, "the insane should not appear in the city, but each of them shall be kept in the home by those close to him." Presumably, this accounts for emergent disabilities that do not manifest at birth. The practices of exclusion would take some time to achieve, but it would be nearly complete after two millennia.

Aristotle, ironically himself peculiarly short of stature and with a noticeable speech impediment, would follow his teacher's policy of advocating infanticide, as we have seen. Further, Aristotle claimed that the deaf and mute were incapable of reasoning since one needed to see to speak—vision central to Aristotle's epistemology. Spoken language was, for Aristotle, essential to Aristotle's conception of our true nature or function as humans, and it makes us the sole language-using animal. Speech-related disabilities, deafness, and blindness would likely have remained constant throughout human history, so Aristotle's advice would consign a significant number of Athenians to a literal, sub-human status. The scaffolding of oppression is built when Aristotle uses language as a key to rationality and humanity. We often celebrate Aristotle as the figure who privileged empiricism or sense experience, but one cannot imagine how he could have made these conclusions based on experience. It flies in the light of common sense and experience. He must have had minimal first-hand experience with either deaf or blind persons to draw such a staggeringly lousy stereotype. Nonetheless, his practice of demeaning and denigrating a fellow human to less-than-human status is the first step to the barbarity we witness in justifying killing those we have designated as less than us. The concept of the vilified other -the disabled- emerge here and will become one of the unassailable ideas of the western tradition.

Abortion, eugenics, and euthanasia are the triple foundations Plato attempts to create to develop a pure citizenry in his beautiful city, Kallipolis, and for which Aristotle will provide the arguments. For the disabled, this would begin the millennia-long process to rid the state and ultimately the world of the disabled. But, unfortunately, what would start in Greece--as a philosopher's theoretical, socially enforced infanticide--would later be developed into 19th and 20th-century policy of eugenics in the United States and later lay the foundation for the Nazi killing machine and globalized practices of genocide. While it would take 2,000 years before the Nazis would institute such widespread barbarism, we need to acknowledge that it is a central part of the Western tradition from the very beginning and such inhumane practices inform much of the intellectual heritage we inherit.

Although the extant collection of Greek art does include a few representations of so-called "grotesques," typically of dying and disabled war heroes, there are few actual representations of disability in the canon of Greek art. Still here, the ideal triumphs over the normal and the abnormal, the different, and ultimately, the disabled, but their presence is nevertheless of curious importance. The desires and visions of artists and patrons would be subsumed under the philosophies of the Greek ideal, making for a powerful synthesis of beauty. This conception of beauty frames the discourse on beauty and art for the next two millennia.

Take Polycleitus' "Doryphoros," a perfect example of the ideal male form and conception of the Greek ideal of beauty, and a piece that has wielded an enormous influence on subsequent notions of art and beauty. The athlete is well- and thickly-muscled and stands solidly and independently as the idealized able-bodied and perfected male--the perfected Greek citizen. Philosophy and art become embodied in this sculpture. Now, compare this with the later Hellenistic statue of the "Old Market Woman," whose body seems weighed down and heavy from the burdens of age and possibly arthritis. Her stooped and forlorn figure is in sharp contrast to the erect and solidly built Doryphoros. One is an idealized male form projecting a nearly impossible conception of beauty. At the same time, the other is a naturalistically rendered possibility of a body worn down by age, disability, and the difficulties of a hardscrabble life.

What lessons might we draw from this exercise? To begin, we can ascertain that art can project either an idealized type or a realistic one. Art and artists choose to depict certain aspects rather than others. This is a political choice; it represents their assumptions. As such, the artist's choice becomes an intentional -willful- and therefore a direct, political act. Whereas the philosophers would counsel eugenics and euthanasia in their theories, the artists would project that idealized world in their choices in art. Together these two poles become the two moments of a dialectic that will rise to a synthesis of discrimination against the disabled. That we will find so few depictions of disability in the canon of Greek art and later traditions signals the exclusion of the disabled body as a deliberate, wholescale political maneuver becoming an intentional ethico-political position. The philosophers and the artists win with their vision of the idealized. This vision triumphs over the everyday and the ordinary, the real lives and bodies of living humans. As such, the ideal is triumphant in the Western aesthetics of the body. A whole hierarchy follows, placing the male over the female, the ideal over the normal, and the abled body over the disabled. This victory sets up the peculiar and highly effective binary logic that still functions 21 long centuries later. For example, the art historian Kenneth Clark's insightful criticism of the restored Venus of Arles would represent a change. He criticized the sculptor Girardon for changing the statue according to the whims of the French King.

Girardon was ordered to smooth out the realistic details of the original sculpture by removing any depiction of ribs, muscles, or wrinkles because the King found those details distasteful. Beauty, by the rise of modernity, had unhinged itself from reality. The ideal is unreal. They are demonstrating aptly here how the aesthetics of the ideal decisively triumphs over the lived body in all its ramifications of seeing a physical thing subject to physical laws. The actual -the real- is surrendered for and replaced by an unrealistic ideal. If the actual body becomes jettisoned, what can we expect of the disabled? If the disabled are anything at all, are they not inextricably the embodiment of realism? The disabled body is what happens to a physical body. It is contra the aesthetics of idealism.

When we encounter depictions of disability in Greek art and literature, it is inevitably folded into mythological tales that warn us of the perils of disability. The moral is clear, and it is that disability and the disabled are dangerous and ought to be removed or avoided. In ancient Greek culture, the disabled, the ill, and the diseased would be seen as inferior and objects of ill will subject to the god's whims and capriciousness. If not extirpated, the disabled would be left alone to suffer their afflictions or visit malice upon others. The dispassionate gods would wreak havoc on the lives of the disabled and those who do not heed the warnings. The misfortunes of one's life rested solely with the gods and their whims, and one's physical condition was seen as the by-product of divine agency. Scholars suggest that the well-known and well-documented practice of "exposure" represents this pattern of belief.

As practiced in Sparta, a committee of elders called the Gerousia would review each disabled child and decide whether the child was fit enough to be a Spartan and should be raised[30]. A child born with any irregularity, disability, or deformity would be placed outside the city's walls and left there overnight alone or placed in a crater at nearby Mount Taygetos. If the child survived, it would invariably be inter-

preted as the gods looked favorably on that child; should the child die--
and exposure would have happened at any time of the year and in all
kinds of weather--then it was viewed as definitive evidence that the
gods looked unfavorably upon that child. One can imagine that children born with disabilities and any number of lesser conditions were
proportionally more likely to die because of this callous treatment, thus
confirming the assumptions of the culture of discrimination. Indeed,
given the inability of the human newborn to self-regulate its body tem-
perature, many non-disabled infants died unnecessary deaths too. Over
time, this would develop into and strengthen the culture of violence
aimed against disability and the disabled. The disabled were viewed
as weak and incapable of surviving: the gods had deemed so. Indeed,
scholars have postulated that in the mytho-religious nature of ancient
cultures, deliberately euthanizing a child through "exposure" acts as a
profound interaction with the divine. What gods deemed, humans ac-
knowledged and followed. The social and personal risk was too high
not to cower to the gods and the priestly caste that enforced dogma
on earth. The notion that to kill the disabled child was both an act of
mercy and a kind of propitiation to the gods becomes an accepted practice and belief throughout antiquity. All rationalizations aside, we moderns cannot get over the sheer barbarity of this custom, religious or not.
It reveals the worse elements of humanity. Attempts to justify and ra-
tionalize—usually, in hindsight—one's inhumanity through reference to
divine agency seems ingenuous.

Ironically and around the same time, Greeks did provide meager assistance to some disabled; inadequate provisions were made by both
Greek and later Roman communities to provide some modest living
stipends to disabled war veterans. Nevertheless, a willingness to accord
the person disabled later in life a small measure of respect as long as
that disability came about in service to the state. A level of respect interestingly not extended to those born with disabilities or disabled from
other misfortunate events such as labor or accident. Take the fragment
from the noted Attic orator Lysias titled, "For the Cripple" or "On the
Refusal of a Pension," where Lysias defends a disabled veteran of not

being eligible for a pension before the Boule—the city council responsible for doling out such annual stipends.[31] During the war with the Medes,[32] a few Greek city-states financed "physicians" to care for the war wounded and provide a modest compensation after the war, but this was not a widespread action.

Keep in mind that the case with Lysias must be litigated. This account alone tells us that such largesse was neither forthcoming nor commonplace. Despite the few overtures to some of the disabled, the lives of the disabled were, overall, miserable; as with earlier cultures, a superficial wound or injury could result in a debilitating condition, permanent disability, or death: such was the state of medical care in antiquity.

Neither the ancient Greeks nor the Romans possessed a word equivalent to our word "disabled." In contrast, however, to the indigenous American linguistic absence for the word "disabled," the Greeks did develop descriptors to categorizing disabled, and none of them were very flattering. The words they used reveal much that is consistent with a culture of discrimination. The Greek word commonly used was "teras" (τέρας), a root for the Greek words meaning monster; and, later in Latin, "monstrum" where many modern languages derive the word, "monster." The word's root would be used to name the division of medicine--teratology—the study of physiological abnormalities and disfigurements. The word is also used in the study of mythology concerned with fantastic beasts and monsters. Teratology was borrowed from the French "tératologie" coming from the Greek-τέρας-teras which meant a "sign sent by the gods, portent, marvel, or monster. "Ology," of course, is used to designate a discourse, science, theory, or study. These word parts functioned as the roots for later English words "terrible," "terror," "monster," and "monstrosity." For the Greeks and later Romans, the roots are the exact words they used to describe mythological monsters and beasts, preserving the divine agency conceit of disability. The Greek "teras" was akin to other Greek words that imply "wonder" or "awe." The word conveys the sense of "something so strange it should be watched." This sense would be preserved in the Latin "monstrum," meaning a hideous mythological entity viewed as an aberration from nature's order. In Old English, "monster" may derive from either "moneo," meaning to warn, or "mostro," meaning to show forth. In either case, the word invokes the double sense of a warning that simultaneously fascinates. The notion of something compelling that still intrigues us helps us understand why people with disabilities will later be used as freaks, sideshow wonders, and oddities well into modernity.

These words connote something physically, morally, or psychologically hideous, literally a "freak of nature." We see this used across world literature and through the history of fiction and storytelling. From folk tale ogres to Frankenstein, from stories of Golems to the Hunchback of Notre Dame, the conceit is preserved across many works of literature. First, however, it needs to be pointed out that the words are cognate with the Latin word "to instruct" as in the English word, "demonstrate," and in this sense, it could have an instructive or educational component built into it[33]. As such, we may learn from the monstrous as much as from the beautiful. Second, it can be awe-inspiring: a sense of the actual usage still lurking in today's word, "awe-ful." If we read it this way, something deemed awful can still be educational, edifying. There are many ways one may interpret this etymology. The first suggests we may learn from the awe-inspiring; second, it is aspirational. The latter will be how many of the able-bodied in the contemporary world react toward the disabled: a strange alchemy of inspiration and incredulity. Third, and finally, it may provoke fear. Fiedler, in his study titled, "Freaks: Myths and Images of the Secret Self," lists three subclasses of monsters: monstres par excess (monsters who are giants), monstres par default (monsters missing something), and monstres par doubles (monsters that have two of something: hermaphrodites). All three subclasses describe conditions that occur within the human condition but are rare enough to provoke awe. In short, they represent the possibilities of the disabled body.

Turning back to the Greek philosophical tradition and the intellectual foment of late antiquity, Saint Augustine (circa 4th century) would offer a gentler interpretation of this notion of the monstrous. Augustine would tease out the educational aspect of the awe-aspiring nature of the monstrous consistent with his Christian perspective. His interpretation suggests that the monstrous ought not to be shunned nor avoided. On the contrary, since it is god's work, it ought to be celebrated. His efforts would be consistent with Christian thinking of the time, especially when coupled with the Christian ethical "principle of the least" and Jesus' examples of rejecting the Greco-Roman and Hebraic concept of disability. Because of this movement away from Greek and Jewish proscriptions against disability, we see a potential transformative possibility emerging that will manifest in the development of hospitals and other institutions of caring in the Christian-influenced medieval world. Nevertheless, it is intriguing and highly informative to hear the different senses of the words used by the ancients to describe persons with disabilities as having qualities of both monsters and saints. Vestiges of these meanings will echo throughout subsequent millennia in their treatment and attitudes toward the disabled.

As we have seen, many Greek myths reinforce the negative stereotypes about disability, but there are a few notable exceptions. One such exception is the myth of the Amazons-the legendary Scythian warrior-women—who reputedly and doubtfully removed one breast to shoot bows and throw spears better but left the other breast intact to nurse. One of their queens, Antianira, who succeeded the legendary Penthesilea after the latter was killed in Troy by Achilles, was reputed to maim her many husbands. She preferred disabled lovers.

The all-woman cities of the Amazons would annually mate with a nearby town of all-males known as the Gargarians. If the offspring were female, the Amazons would keep her; and if male, surrender it to the Gargarians. Queen Antianira—whose name may etymologically mean "equal to men" or conversely, "opposing men" was, according to Greek myth, responsible for castrating or blinding all her servants and crippling her husbands. When asked why she disabled her many husbands, she reputedly replied:

"A lame man makes the best lover."

However, the bioarchaeology record casts a bit of doubt on this myth. Adrienne Mayor, professor of classical history and the philosophy of science at Stanford University, points to the lack of evidence for such claims; instead, citing a Hippocratic medical text, "On Joints," she offers a better explanation for such lameness from the Scythian habit of riding horses and their rigorous and dangerous lifestyle. These activities would produce conditions similar to lameness. This theory gains support from the recent discovery of the genetic evidence of hip problems found in Steppe area people's genomes suggests conditions identical to the lameness which ancient poets subscribe to the peculiar fetishes of their warrior queens[34]. Yet another mythological back-formation explaining the presence of disability in the region and justified by the Amazon's preference for disabled men were provided by the belief that the women warriors deliberately disabled their male children so they would not be able to go to war. While reputed to be fierce warriors, the Amazons opposed war and combat, more reluctant warriors than the war-crazed myths we usually hear. This opposition to war may explain why they would have disabled their husbands because disabling them would disqualify them for battle.

Again, the bioarchaeological evidence for this is slim to nil. Skeletal remains from the gravesites of this region show a remarkable parity among men and women with disabling conditions with wounds from either war or more pedestrian forms of violence or just the rigors of the hardscrabble life on the steppe. What seems clear--all myths aside--is that the presence of disability in the ancient Greek tradition looks more commonplace than usually believed; nevertheless, there is still much stigma attached to disability despite its ubiquity.

The idea that Amazons removed a breast[35] and castrated their sons results in a deliberate repositioning toward "abnormality" and, consequently, farther from the male-oriented notions of beauty and its corresponding ideals of harmony, balance, and proportionality promulgated by Plato and Aristotle. It also has the effect of moving the Amazon closer to maleness—removing a breast—while simultaneously making her an aberration (out of balance). These actions are a radical departure from the patriarchal Greek ideals. Castrating their sons and, for that matter, disabling their husbands move them away from the attributes and virtues of males celebrated in Greek thought. The Greek word for virtue, ἀρετή (arete), meant excellence or fulfilling a function. The function of a male would be tied up with his purpose: to reason, fight and reproduce. The Latins translated arete into "virtue," coming from the root "vir," meaning male sexual prowess. Incidentally, the word "virago" was later used to describe an aggressive woman. It was initially used to describe female warriors or women of masculine strength or spirit[36] and comes ultimately from the words, "ball buster.[37]"It is of note that it comes from Vulgate translation as a name used by Adam for Eve in the Old English.

The famous queen of the Amazons, Penthesilea, will appear in another context featuring disability in ancient Greek myth. Penthesilea was the daughter of Ares, and she reappears in tales about the Trojan War but not in Homer's Iliad. Instead, her story may come from the lost, post-Homeric epic, Aethiopis, where she battles Achilles, ultimately being slain by him. Achilles purportedly had fallen in love with her when he removed her helmet and gazed upon her legendary beauty. Heartbroken Achilles started to lament her death when Thersites, Achilles' disabled comrade, ridiculed and mutilated her corpse, enraging Achilles. Achilles retaliated and struck Thersites killing him. In turn, Thersites' kin, Diomedes, would avenge Thersites' death by dragging Penthesilea's corpse behind his chariot and throwing it into the Scamander River. It is told that Achilles would later retrieve her body from the river and give it a burial fitting a queen but not before committing necrophilia with the dead Queen; some legends go so far as to believe that she bore Achilles a son from the coupling.

The central Greek myth dealing with disability is the myth of Oedipus. It contributes to a culture and practice of discrimination against the disabled and frames the appropriate and expected behaviors sanctioned toward the disabled in Greek society. The story's centrality to Greek and later cultures is firmly established, but its straightforward and discriminatory attitudes and postures toward the disabled often go unnoticed. Most interpreters of the myth pay little attention to Oedipus' disability. The influence of the legend on thinkers from Hegel to Freud, Gide to Cocteau warrants a reconsideration.[38]

To begin, in ancient Greek, Oedipus means "club-footed," and Tiresias' prophecy to Oedipus' parents that their child, if not killed, is fated to cause problems is both a chilling defense of infanticide and a direct attack against a disabled infant. Indeed, the myth of Oedipus whose name, Οἰδίπους, literally means "swollen foot" is another example of the Greek's tendency to view disability as an act of divine retribution or divine punishment meted out by capricious gods. The child's disability results from the gods' caprice, and as unpredictable and inscrutable as the gods may be, they still only mete out punishment for just causes. The implication is that a character flaw must correspond with the person's disability and cause the initial punishment. The disability becomes the outward marker of that inner flaw endorsed by the divine authority. In this, Tiresias is just interpreting the gods' handiwork, reading the symbol. Despite being an advocate for infanticide, he comes off blameless. In most iterations, Tiresias is blind. This tension of the disabled condemning the disabled will be a significant development in subsequent cultures.

Tiresias's prophecy interprets the god's will, and he instructs Laius that the newborn child must die, or dire misfortune will be visited upon Thebes and his family lineage. Laius's compassion and refusal to kill his son and all that follows from that choice confirms the social stigmas of disability. He had been warned, and he refused. The gods' wrath will follow, and misfortune indeed comes to the family and Thebes. The lesson is taught. Disability is a scourge: it and the disabled must be removed.

The family's name bears witness to a lineage of disability. Oedipus'' grandfather's name, "Labdabos," means "lame." The prophecy of having a child born with a disability could not have been that earth-shattering, given that lameness ran in the family. So why kill the child? Tiresias' prophecy reveals a change in attitude toward the disabled. If Oedipus' ancestors lived and flourished with a disability, why, at this time, should we deny that opportunity to Oedipus and invoke technologies of extermination such as infanticide? In times of social crises, we often see persons with disabilities scapegoated, blamed, or bear the brunt of the impacts.[39] Thebes was at a crossroads, and the whole of the Attic peninsula was undergoing rapid changes and pressures, including periodic outbreaks of epidemics. When Oedipus tried to learn of the plague during his reign, the Oracle at Delphi informed him that the city's woes were due to him alone.

In a closely related incident from ancient Greek history imbued with a similar set of attitudes, the first tyrant of Corinth, Cypselus (c. 7th century BCE), had a disabled mother. His mother, Labda, was disabled in a similar way as Oedipus; her name, a variant of "labdabos," meant she inherited some form of disability possibility, a form of lameness at birth, and like Oedipus, she too was slated to be "exposed." However, her parents refused. Having given birth to a disabled son, she too balked at killing him as Laius would with Oedipus and her parents with her. In one iteration of the myth, she hid Cypselus in a chest. The etymology of his name comes from the Greek, κυψέλη, meaning "chest." Is it too far of a reach to see his chest as the first assistive device? However, the story that unfolds is radically different. His family is not riven with a tragedy like Oedipus'; instead, he goes on to be a successful and much-loved ruler. It was thought that he was so popular he could eschew having bodyguards.

Herodotus reports a different variation of the story where members of the opposing ruling family--the Bacchiadae--heard from the oracle at Delphi that the son of Eëtion--Cypselus' father--would overthrow their dynasty unless they killed his son. Thus, to salvage their power, they conspired to kill the baby once it was born. However, as Herodotus writes, the newborn smiled so endearingly at each of the assassins sent to kill him that none could go through with the murder. Whatever we make of these myths, it is clear that the child's disability sets them up for violent treatment.

What emerges here is that both Oedipus and Cypselus are viewed as threats to the social order because of their disabilities. Their respective disabilities identify them as a threat that threatens the social fabric and the political order. What differs between the two is that Cypselus would succeed as would his future generations, whereas Oedipus would not. Cypselus would find a way to flourish. Oedipus' fortunes would turn out differently. A few generations after Cypselus, Greek culture had shifted just enough to make a living with disability taboo. At least in the case of Oedipus, the moral is that it would have been better to have killed the newborn than suffer the social dislocation wrought by the difference, the disability. Of course, the moral one draws about the Oedipean tale is that refusal to do the gods' bidding brings trouble. The gods made it easy for humans. They marked the child with a disability. The rest was simple: kill the child, save the state. Allowing him to exist brought about the decline of the royal household and Thebes. It becomes a multigenerational stain.

A further tragedy visited Oedipus. He not only began his life with a disability but ends with another: blindness. The difference is one of implicit causation. He was born with his lameness; the blindness was self-inflicted. Living with the lameness causes his blindness. As Stiker eloquently puts it, "from head to foot Oedipus is transpierced with disability." It is as if the existential weight of his disability and the burden of the prophecy caused him to loathe himself so that he deprives himself of what little pleasure—his sight—that remained. He cannot bear to see how he has fouled things up. What a terrible message to send to a disabled child. Better that you should never have been born, but if born, get ready for a life of self-loathing.

There is this double-nature of blindness that is an interesting trope in this myth. Tiresias, the blind poet, is gifted with an uncanny sight into knowing the whims of the gods, while the tragic Oedipus blinds himself to avoid seeing the physical. In the former case, blindness is almost a gift enabling a special epistemic status to the seer; in the latter, blindness is punitive. Recall here the case of Stesichorus, a poet whom Zeus blinded for insulting his daughter, Helen. In both divination and poetry, the epistemic value lies in going beyond the ordinary, requiring attenuation of one faculty for the corresponding development of another. Tiresias is sensitive to what his blindness allows when he mocks Oedipus because his disability allows him, he claims, to "see" things Oedipus cannot:

"So, you mock my blindness? Let me tell you this. You [Oedipus] with your precious eyes, you're blind to the corruption of your life ..." (Robert Fagles 1984)

There is a bipolar phenomenology of disability present in the clash between the two disabled characters. Tiresias values the reality of blindness; his disability is an asset. Oedipus' disabilities, however, are liabilities. The two disparate phenomenologies of disability clash in the play. If there is a dialectical resolution, then it is in framing boundaries for the disabled. Accept the socially sanctioned role or perish.

In the first instance with Tiresias' loss of sight, now we understand the origins of the cliché about compensatory perceptions in individuals who have lost one perception become more acute in others. Tiresias's physical inability to see enables him to discern the divine. But only within a particular well-defined context. Oedipus' blindness functions as a limit. His loss of sight does not grant him any unique ability. Despite this, in the final play of Sophocles' Trilogy, "Oedipus at Colonus," Oedipus tries to understand his blindness as a kind of prophetic gift and responds to the stranger that although his sight is blind, his words are not. Nevertheless, little come to pass from this conjecture or interaction: he has not gained wisdom from his disability. His disability does not earn him insight but the loss of meaning.

Tiresias though blind, can see, whereas Oedipus blinded cannot. Tiresias claims to speak the truth, but Laius is blinded by love and arrogance. Oedipus can see but is blind to reality and, as a result, kills his father and marries his mother. These actions lead to the blinding of both Oedipus and Jocasta. The bad luck continues when Creon is blinded by ambition. The moral of all these stories is that whatever privileges disability may provide are not worth the gain in the final tally.

Another discriminatory practice emerges in the play "Oedipus at Colonus" that mirrors the Jewish prohibition of the disabled from entering sacred spaces. When Oedipus and Antigone first arrive at the outskirts of Athens, they enter a shrine sacred to the Eumenides, and the Athenians are aghast at an intrusion by such a person, a disabled person. Again, the violations stem from the dual nature of Oedipus being both a foreigner and disabled. We will often see this link between disability and foreignness made in subsequent cultures[40].

Apart from the other well-studied aspects of the myth, we see how the advice from Tiresias, blind though he be, to euthanize the infant parallels what may be viewed by today's well-intentioned counsel from doctors, nurse practitioners, and family planning advocates when a fetus with a disability is detected in the womb. The advice dispensed is that the "smart" or "practical" thing to do is to abort the child and if abortion is not your cup of tea, send the kid to an orphanage. How little we have progressed from the days of the ancients. The chief difference between the practices of the ancient world and today is that they would ground their practice in mythology and religion. Today, we justify our practices with a veneer of science and social planning masked in well-intentioned counseling. Nowhere did this mythology become more inhumane than in the social planning of the policy during the German Reich with its brutal T4 program. We will examine this dark period of history in a later chapter.

There is another version of the Oedipal myth that is worth reviewing. In this iteration, it is not the gods who disabled Oedipus but his father. Like the Amazons and the Vedic king Shakuni, Laius will cause his son's disability. After Tiresias prophecizes that Oedipus will eventually grow up to murder him, Laius pierces his foot and orders a servant to take him to the mountains to expose the child. The servant could not just leave the child, giving him to shepherds who provided a childless couple from Corinth with the boy. In this version-- and running parallel with the other myths-- a family member becomes the cause of the disability: the gods are blameless. In this version, Tiresias is freed from self-loathing, and the locus of disability is on the father, which, in turn, exonerates the gods.

This version suggests how the disability manifests of secondary importance to the kind of disability itself. His father's action lames Oedipus as the Amazonian women disabled their sons and husbands, and the Vedic king was rendered lame, each representing injuries or disabilities that would limit mobility. Arguably, the ubiquity of injuries that limit mobility (e.g., foot injuries) are viewed as far more problematic than other kinds of injuries. Nevertheless, mobility was essential to survival in the burgeoning world of settled living created by the advent of civilized (i.e., agricultural) cultures. Later we see a variation of this arise in the context of the disabled veteran, Philoctetes, too, but first, let us look at another veteran with a disability.

In Book II of Homer's Iliad, a seemingly minor character, Thersites, is introduced, by Homer, solely to function as the object of scorn and the brutal chastisement by Odysseus for criticizing the siege of Troy. We heard of Thersites earlier in conjunction with the Amazons, but here we look at the complete treatment of him in Homer's epic poem, "The Iliad." Significantly and quite out of context, Homer describes him as lame and therefore despicable, although interestingly still a warrior. Notably, he is given one of the few detailed physical descriptions of a character's body in all of Homer's corpus, and only one of two commoners provided a name[41] in the epic poem. Homer is typically reticent about such matters; here, however, Homer describes Thersites as a buffoon, who was "bandy-legged" and "lame of one foot," with "shoulders stooped and drawn together over his chest," and a head that "went up to a point."[42] If one reads the original Greek and avoids contemporary bowdlerizing it, one notices that Homer has Odysseus ridicule the diminutive size of Thersites' penis and draw attention to his impotence:

"I do not take hold of you and strip you —yes, even of the shirt that hides your scut!"

A scut is a short tail of a rabbit or other small animal, often a derogatory euphemism for a small penis. We will see that a common refrain throughout cultures used to ridicule males with disabilities is their perceived sexual inadequacy or impotence.

In any event, it appears to be because of his disabilities that Thersites becomes the focus of Odysseus' abuse. It is noteworthy that the belittlement occurs after Thersites dared to speak his mind and criticize

his leaders. After a ten-year-long and unsuccessful siege, similar senti-
ments must have percolated through the troops. Thersites alone dared
to voice these opinions; he will pay dearly for doing so. He becomes the
brunt of Odysseus's wrath, but one notices that Odysseus has chosen his
adversary with care. Recall Achilles' refusal to fight at the beginning of
the epic, which did not warrant a reprisal. Where was Odysseus' wrath
then? When, however, Thersites dares to criticize Agamemnon's failed
policies, Odysseus brutally assaults him. Why? Is it just to keep the soldiers in check, stem rebellion, and battle against poor morale? Perhaps.
But something else is going on here: then and now, power is too often and only directed against the vulnerable. The disabled become the
foil for the powerful. Why do Thersites' comrades join in and cheer
Odysseus' attack on so vociferously? Why do they not join him in his
rebellion? Why is there the implication that Thersites is meriting what
he deserves? It cannot be that suddenly all his comrades became zealous patriots or were convinced by Odysseus' flimsy arguments. No, it
is because Thersites' disability makes him a legitimate symbol of attack.
Precisely because of his disability, any attempt at confederacy is a step
too far. As any child with a disability can tell you, they were bullied,
teased, and ridiculed by their schoolmates and teachers because of their
disability. Children are taught and quickly learn to be mistrustful of difference and disability because it opens one to ridicule. This bullying, I
assert, leads to the intolerance we see manifest later in the adult world.
The subtle cues to conform to the assumptions about disability in society are real and powerful; in a way, they may be unassailable. They
are the unquestioned and unsupported assumptions of a culture. They
shape the world we see, and we allow them to become our normative
practices. We deeply resist identifying with the vulnerable, the weak,
the underdog. We may at times offer or side with the underdog, but
we strenuously avoid seeing the world through their eyes, their bodies.
That which is different or abnormal is socially unacceptable and therefore worthy of our disdain, our ridicule. Certainly, Thersites can attest
to that. The treatment of Thersites is the true legacy of the cultures of

antiquity that frame modern, contemporary society. It is a lack of empathy for the disabled.

Disability seems everywhere to cause able-bodied people an actual, visceral discomfort. Why? Is it a foreshadowing of their future lives, their impending physical decay, frailty, even death? Is it a fear of the inevitable dissolution of living in and with a physical body? We are all of us only temporarily able-bodied.[43] In this sense-both then and now-Thersites and his future brothers and sisters living with their disabilities act as a valve allowing the larger able-bodied community to attack disability and vent their deepest fears.

In addition to Thersites' disability becoming the object of Odysseus' scorn, Thersites is not given a genealogy or patronym by Homer, thereby suggesting he is a commoner and certainly not a deserving aristocrat. Homer's anti-democratic bent is evident. On the other hand, Achilles was shielded from reprisals precisely because of his aristocratic lineage. His privilege sets him above criticism. Not so Thersites. As Auburn Professor of philosophy, Roderick Long asks, "why does Thersites' call to return home end up being echoed in the poem by the handsome, heroic, and aristocratic Achilles, and yet nothing seditious is made of his remarks? There is no punishment. Remember that Achilles has his imperfection, flaw, dare we say, disability, too. His heel is a disability—yet another example of mobility impairment in the ancient world. Achilles' weakness—what else is it but a dis-ability—is never mentioned nor viewed with the same intent or social disapprobation even though he voices the same objections to continued fighting as Thersites. Class shields him to some extent, but his heel –disability—will be his downfall. Even the great Achilles is not immune from the deeper norm of culture. Money, power, or even having a goddess for a mother will not save you from disability and its social consequences.[44]

The difference in the treatment between Thersites and Achilles is the degree of disability inflected through the social class of Ancient Greece. Wealth and the opportunities it may provide will offer some relief and some relative advantages with certain aspects of disability, as witnessed between the different treatments of Thersites and Achilles. Still, the kinds of and nature of disabilities matter too, even if not in this case. There exists a dichotomy between the mildly disabled, who often reject the notion of disability and eschew any connection to the disabled, and the more severely disabled who cannot but be faced to accept their disability which will plague disabled communities over the centuries. There are, to be sure, other factors that contribute to these issues. Intersectionality plays a vital function on the identities of persons with disabilities from antiquity until today.

But let us return to the opposing camps along the Scamander River. Camps on both the Greek and Trojan sides must have had their share of combat wounded, and disabled fighters never mentioned. After a decade of war, where have all the disabled gone? The real-life toll of battle is not mentioned in the poem. All the heroes die heroic deaths; none suffers debilitating or lingering wounds or injuries leading to a lifetime of disability. We know from the archival record that Greek city-states did at times provide some pensions to their disabled warriors. We are not given any notion that fighting causes disability. The drum roll of martial enthusiasm hides the actual cost of combat. Recall how, with Lysias' case, those benefits were not forthcoming. One needed to continue fighting long after you left the battlefield. Why? The message here is that the disabled merit whatever treatment comes their way -privately and publicly- and are therefore suitable objects for scorn and abuse and denied any compensation. Better to die in some idealized version of battle than survive with scars, physical or mental[45]. Keep in mind that most persons with disabilities are found in society's lowest socio-economic classes and divisions. We know from historical research that those unmentioned disabled veterans were relegated to a life of poverty and that some city-states offered meager pensions for the soldiers' sacrifices. Still, again they would need to struggle for those pensions.

Later, prominent thinkers as disparate as Shakespeare, Hegel, Marx, Nietzsche, Kenneth Burke, and Edward Said would comment upon this particular episode in the Iliad regarding its potential social and economic function. Notably, none of them focus on the disability of Thersites only upon the social criticism of power embedded within Thersites' condemnation of Agamemnon. Such an absence of encountering disability misses the essential nature of the episode. For it is precisely Thersites' disability that makes him the center of the attack.

As such, Thersites' disability is a central conceit because Homer would need to make Thersites so offensively different, embodied as such "the other" that he created an unbridgeable abyss, a distancing, for the audience. One can discount his politically uncomfortable message of revolt because he is so outré, different. People will find it difficult to relate to such a characterization. In this sense, nothing works better than physical disability in creating distance. As the classical scholar Gerald Else puts it in his work on Aristotle's "Poetics":

"Greek thinking begins with and for a long time holds to the proposition that mankind is divided into 'good' and 'bad,' and these terms are quite as much social, political, and economic as they are moral. ... [I]t began as the aristocrats' view of society and reflects their idea of the gulf between themselves and the "others." ... [O]f course "we" are the good people, the proper, decent, good-looking, right-thinking ones, while "they" are the rascals, the poltroons, the good-for-nothings – in short, everyone else. ... The dichotomy is mostly taken for granted in Homer: there are not many occasions when the heaven-wide gulf between heroes and commoners even has to be mentioned."

And if Odysseus' brutalization of Thersites was not enough proof of the ancient world's discriminatory practice toward the disabled, Homer provides another example in the treatment of Philoctetes. A wounded warrior, Philoctetes, was abandoned by Odysseus on the way home from Troy for having sustained a foot wound. The wound, legend has it, came from a snakebite and not combat. Because of his injury, Philoctetes was unceremoniously abandoned by his comrades on an island, Lemnos. The justification or pretext for his abandonment is that his fellow Greeks cannot perform the necessary rites to the gods with a disabled crewmember. As such, his foot wound becomes more than a mere personal injury or a liability for fighting. It becomes an affront to the gods. As a form of religious pollution,[46] disability directly affronts the god's sensibilities, something we heard in Jewish prohibitions toward the disabled and folded into Oedipus' treatment at Colonus.

On Lemnos, Philoctetes spends nine years foraging and eking out a bare-bones existence while suffering from his wound that would not heal. The mythic parallel here is revealing because Lemnos was the island Hephaestus was exiled to after being thrown from Olympus by Zeus. Moreover, the Greeks believed that the volcano on Lemnos was the site of Hephaestus' forge. Historically, Lemnos was long associated with the Sintians, a Thracian people known by the Greeks as pirates and smugglers. Indeed, the word's root, Sintians, comes from the Greek "sinteis," meaning "destructive." Thus, it would come to mean "the raiders" or "the plunderers"--an outsider that can cause harm or one that needs to be removed or some damage will follow.

This reputation as a disreputable yet skilled person may come from the formation of the stereotypes we see developing toward the disabled when the person with a disability is marginalized. Because of this marginalization the person must develop compensatory skills and abilities to survive. It is also easier to augment those skills if the person is removed from everyday interaction.

The irony of situating two central Greek myths dealing with a disability on the same island merits scrutiny. Still, we need first to confront the apparent link between disability and isolation. Throughout history, the disabled have been subject to ostracizing, isolation, and forced removal. Hephaestus, Philoctetes, and Oedipus would become the harbingers of the routine practice of moving the disabled from mainstream society. The practice of creating places to warehouse the disabled is accepted uncritically well into modernity. It fits into the practice of using concentration camps, reservations, holding pens, prisons, detention centers, immigration, and refugee camps, rehabilitation clinics, hospitals, and schools for the disabled predominating through modernity.

But who exactly was Philoctetes? To begin, he was one of the famous Argonauts, one of the Achaean leaders, one of Helen's suitors, and the man who inherited the legendary bow of Heracles. But because of his suppurating foot wound, he would miss much of the fighting at Troy. Once the Achaeans learned from a prophecy that they would not win without him, they put aside their biases and fetched him posthaste. When he returned to Troy, he killed three men at Troy, including Paris, and was one of the fighters secreted inside the Trojan horse. One might speculate about the treatment of future disabled service veterans from this literary anecdote: a disability may be overlooked if there is some utility to be gained.

While some narratives suggest his wound was sustained in combat, several report Philoctetes' wound coming from a snakebite—this is Sophocles' favored interpretation. Philoctetes sustains the injury during a religious rite consequent to Heracles' funeral. At the funeral, only Philoctetes succeeded in lighting Heracles' pyre but at a cost. Compare this with Jacob's wrestling with an angel. In both myths, the protagonist who confronts the divine is dealt a disabling blow. In return for Jacob's wound, he becomes a central figure in the Jewish religion; for Philoctetes, he is gifted Heracles' bow. The bow, however, functions as his passport back to the larger world because it is his bow that will allow him success in combat and the reason the Greeks slink back to retrieve him.

Nine years after abandoning him to his fate on Lemnos, Odysseus returns to retrieve Philoctetes only because the prophecies tell them that the Greeks will never be triumphant in Troy without Philoctetes and Heracles' bow. We see here that there emerges a theme about disability shared in both Greek and Jewish myths. Disabled people may achieve their goals and be active members of society but at a high cost and only by simultaneously having some utility for that society. Friends, comrades, family, and sometimes even the gods may abandon the disabled without penalty or guilt; their use-value or worth is only a tool for others. Recall how in Sophocles' Oedipus at Colonus, both Creon and Polyneices sought to entice Oedipus back to Thebes when it proved advantageous to their political ambitions. One sees parallels in the 21st century how during his campaign, U.S. President Trump curried favor with gifts to organizations that assist disabled veterans when, in reality, he had actively discriminated against disabled service members in his many real estate holdings and was a known scofflaw when it came to implementing ADA requirements. The upshot is that the skills or aspirational stories the disabled may provide are the only things the able-bodied world values from the disabled. Their actual lived experiences and lives are of little to no interest. Their unconditional worth is absent.

Further comparison of the treatment of both Philoctetes and Oedipus reveals a stratagem toward the disabled in ancient Greek mythology.[47] Apart from the various myths, we again note how the advice to euthanize the infant (Oedipus) or abandon the comrade (both Thersites and Philoctetes) parallels what may be viewed by today's counsel from medical professionals when a fetus with a disability is detected, or the neglect we see toward disabled veterans face upon returning home. In both instances, the advice offered as compassionate is to euthanize the unfortunate.

9

The Disabled God: Hephaestus and the Forge

What can we make of a disabled god? Can there be such a thing as a disabled god? Typical theological definitions of god view god as a being that is perfect or without flaw. This reasoning rests on the notion that God is immaterial, wholly spiritual, and therefore not subject to the assaults of being a physical thing. Nevertheless, the Greeks preferred corporeal gods. Their gods became incarnate, embodied, and often perished. Zeus or any other god may become human and had the foibles err to the flesh. One assumes these gods were as close to flawless as humans could be, but a disabled god?

Apart from Hephaestus, there are a few other examples of Greek gods with disabilities. Scattered throughout Greek tales are examples of gods disabling gods. For instance, Erymanthos, the Akkadian river god, is blinded after seeing Aphrodite bathing naked; it reveals that human nudity is deemed so offensive and that the chosen punishment by the gods is permanent or temporary blindness. Could it be that what lies at the root of the fear of disability and, for that matter, nudity is located in the deeper, more primordial worries attached to the body and physicality itself? We seem to grasp our eventual disintegration intuitively as an embodied being and fear its dissolution.

In a sense, it is entirely predictable that any culture would extend all its beliefs through its political, economic, or religious practices. For a culture such as the ancient Greeks to discriminate against the disabled in its earthly practice, one would naturally expect the same in matters of the divine. Thus, we find Hephaestus facing discrimination from his fellow divines just as disabled people faced discrimination from their peers. There appears, however, to be more at play with the god Hephaestus than reveals itself at first glance.

Hephaestus is the artisan god of blacksmiths, craftspeople, artists, sculptors, and metallurgy in general. His Roman equivalent is named Vulcan. In Greek and Roman traditions, he is disabled and one of the older, more senior gods. Indeed, some textual evidence from the Linear B script suggests he is an early god. He joins the likes of Zeus and others, but there is a difference. He will carry the additional epithets such as Amphigúeis (Ἀμφιγύεις) or in translation, "the lame one" and Kullopodíōn (Κυλλοποδίων), meaning the "the halting one." He is disabled. His disability sets him apart from the other Olympians.

In both the Greek and Roman mythologies, Hephaestus was the son of Zeus and Hera. In another version, he was Hera's parthenogenetic child she bore in retaliation for a fling of Zeus that itself resulted in the parthenogenetic birth of Aphrodite. That both love and creativity are both born of illicit couplings are revelatory. There are other similarities. In both myths, Hera rejected Hephaestus at birth because of his "shriveled foot" and throws him off Mount Olympus to fall to the bowels of the earth (or Lemnos). This removal functions as a kind of divine instance of "exposure." The precedent is set. We can imagine that the ancients needed to justify their practices of infanticide and exposure. If the gods do it, we mere mortals ought to do it, too. The parallels with Oedipus seem too obvious to mention, but we again notice the ubiquity of mobility-related impairments to the lower limbs in these ancient myths.

Alternate traditions postulate that Hephaestus' disability resulted from being thrown from Olympia by Zeus after attempting to intervene on his mother's behalf when Zeus attacked her. This version alludes to the case of Oedipus, where Laius is the cause of Oedipus' disability. In both cases, a parent -a father- is the cause of the disability.

The contrast must be drawn with the Amazons, who as mothers, disabled their sons.

Looking at both interpretations side by side, one is a bit skeptical that an immortal would suffer a disabling injury from a fall, so there must be something more to the cause. It is perhaps understandable that the gods may punish humans, but how can one god punish another god, and why a life-changing disability for eternity? This scenario is possible only in a henotheistic religion where one god or a set of gods are more powerful than others. The confusing thing here is that the earlier gods, such as Zeus and Hephaestus, are usually the privileged gods over newer ones added to the pantheon. This changes with Hephaestus. Myths are rarely consistent, but in their inconsistencies, they often reveal an understanding of the ways of culture. Under all this detail, there is a "being" unjustly disabled by an influential figure.

Other interpretations viewed Hephaestus as not landing in Hades but, as we have seen, in Lemnos and in so doing becoming one of the chthonic gods of the island, where he was cared for by the people of Lemnos until he regained his strength. Along with the nymph Cabira,[48] he would sire a tribe called the Caberi, renowned through the Mediterranean as skilled artisans. Hesychius of Alexandria wrote that they were called the karkinoi—crabs—coming from the Greek "Καβούρια." The Caberi were believed to be amphibious beings who had pincers instead of hands that they put to good use as tongs in the arts of metallurgy. Could this be an early reference to a prosthetic? It also ties them to Hephaestus and further links creativity with disability. This latter conceit will be operative throughout subsequent literary and art history (e.g., Byron, Van Gogh, Toulouse-Lautrec, Degas, Chuck Close, et al.).

10

Contrasting Embodiments: Projecting Ancient Disability on the Big Screen

Lest the reader worry we are only addressing ancient history, let us consider how we moderns re-appropriate these images and their underlying concepts in contemporary culture and film media. The film plays a role in propagandizing discriminatory social attitudes and is never independent of ethical positions and political persuasions. Every choice the actor, editor, screenwriter, photographer, producer, or director makes reflects a normative projection of an idealized society. We see such a stratagem in the use of ancient myths in contemporary cinema. A modern artist takes an ancient myth or symbol because they see some relevant parallel in contemporary society or wish to propagandize consistent with what that myth typically stands for in various interpretations. Take, for example, Frank Miller's 1998 graphic novel, "300" and especially Zack Snyder's homoerotic film adaptation of the tragic battle of Thermopylae. Historically, the battle is when and where the outnumbered Greeks would lose to the larger Persian forces despite their heroic stand. But this David vs. Goliath conceit is secondary to our purposes. Let us look at the depiction of the warrior's bodies themselves.

In particular, the contrast between ability/disability and power/ powerlessness is evident in the Spartan "heroes" bodies compared to the Spartan-turned-villain, Ephialtes. Ephialtes is portrayed as a severely deformed and disabled Spartan in exile in the comic book and movie. In the book, we learn his parents fled Sparta to protect him from the Spartan practice of killing disabled and deformed children in their socially enforced policy of infanticide. Again, the parallels with Oedipus are striking. We witness a parent's love for their child transcending the social norm of killing their disabled child in both instances. But we also see in both cases that going against such practices brings ruin to both family and realm.

Ephialtes' narrative will follow similar lines to Oedipus' but converges because Ephialtes turns treasonous. To begin, Ephialtes wanted to help defend Sparta and volunteered to stand with Leonidas and his 300. Seeing his crippled body, the Spartans summarily rejected his offer, and because of this indignity, Ephialtes would go over to the Persians. His defection will enable the Persians to break the blockade. The realm is lost because of the treasonous act of a person with a disability. But make no mistake about it; it is his disability that functions as a determinant in his character.

In both modern interpretations, Ephialtes is disabled, whereas there is no mention of any such disability from the historic record. Similar to the case of Shakespeare and his rendering of Richard III as a hunchbacked villain, Ephialtes' disability has no historical warrant. In the original Greek source, Herodotus's "Histories" and his "Persian Wars," Ephialtes is never portrayed as disabled. Instead, the Greek word "Ephialtes" means "nightmare" and is analogous to a "Quisling" or "Benedict Arnold" operating as an eponym for a traitor. While he might be a traitor, disability just does not figure into it at all. In another historic example--a Greek kylix dated circa 410-400 BCE--we see Ephialtes without any sign of deformity or disability. He is battling the god Apollo in a gigantomachy!

He bears an inner flaw—hamartia—but no corresponding outer disfigurement is present. The imposition of physical disability is an instance of constructing an external flaw to match the character's hamartia or inner defect for dramatic purposes. We will see this trope being used throughout literature and film. If disabled people are to be feared or loathed, then it is easy to render your villains with markers to identify them unambiguously to the audience or the reader. However, the question remains why do the contemporary filmmakers choose to depict him in this way? What are the underlying assumptions and unchecked attitudes that they are expressing to the audience? Why do moderns decide to represent their villains as persons with disabilities?

The critical question to consider, I submit, is why a comic book author and a film production crew of the 21st century would choose to portray Ephialtes with a disability? What is the real intent of their message? We are looking at a deliberate revisionist and interjectory political and ethical position that sees disabled persons as scapegoats and deems those lives worthless. The result is the further social denigration and demonization of persons with disabilities. I do not know that there is a direct link. Still, it is not coincidental that a candidate for the Office of President of the United States would think it appropriate to ridicule a reporter with a disability a few years after "300" was released. The disabled become the foil for continued ridicule, discrimination, and violence.

It is curious that Ephialtes appeared as a giant in Dante's "Inferno" (Canto 31-34) and was seen again by Dante while visiting the ninth circle of hell. In this treatment, Dante accurately references the classical tradition that viewed Ephialtes not as a traitorous and disabled Spartan but as one of the demi-gods that would battle the Olympians. However, no sign of disability is projected here either. They are not present in the classical references until Zeus engages the Titans in the battle of the gods or Titanomachy. During this struggle, Apollo and Heracles blind the Titans. Zeus ends the Titanomachy -the Titan rebellion against the Olympians- by blinding all the Titans with a bolt of lightning. Taking advantage of their temporary disability, Apollo and Heracles shoot out Ephialtes' eyes, ensuring the Olympian victory. In passing, we note that it is another case where the gods are responsible for disabling. As we have seen with Tiresias, blindness was valued for its ability to provide deeper insight into the spiritual and metaphysical (literally, beyond the physical). It is also conceived as a form of punishment meted out by both gods (metaphysically powerful) and the political (physically powerful).

When the French engraver Gustave Dore illustrated Dante's "Inferno" in the mid-19th century, he did not render Ephialtes with any sign of physical disability at all. In the treatment of Ephialtes by Herodotus, Dante, and Dore, we see an honest appraisal of the character consistent with the mythology. However, in modern treatment, we see a deliberate denigration of disability.

Returning to "300," when we contrast Ephialtes' body with the bodies of other Spartan warriors—all chiseled and photo-shopped, projections of male ideals—we see the starkness of the hunchbacked, Ephialtes, and it is a clear contrast of embodied politics. Leonidas rejects Ephialtes not because of his inability to fight but because of his perceived limitations-- What they assumed they saw in his body. The privileged male ableist perspective brooks no challenge to its ungrounded assumptions.

We note that the condition of a disability is never sufficient for Hollywood; they feel the need to embellish disability using special effects, computer-generated imagery, and animation technologies to achieve over-the-top results. You see this in the CGI used to create Ephialtes' body. What is the purpose of all this re-visioning, this caricaturing of the disabled? All this effort to add to the drama of disability? One cannot but be reminded of the Nazi-era posters showing robust Germans carrying disabled citizens burdening the Aryan race and preventing it from achieving its historical domination. These posters blanketed Nazi Germany to sway public opinion toward the acceptability of exterminating the disabled. The portrayals of the disabled in these posters, while not as embellished as those in Hollywood, are still noticeably elaborated, caricatured, whereas the burdened German citizen looks as though he had stepped right off a pedestal from a Greek sculpture garden. To further their case, the Nazis used the embellished imagery in films, posters, and pamphlets as propaganda to prepare the German volk for their programs to exterminate disabled Germans and ultimately groom Germans for the Holocaust.

11

The Roman Period

The Roman epoch would not see disability treated any differently than in the earlier Greek period. Given the rise of medicine in the works of Hippocrates and Galen, one may assume that medicine would seek to offer some benefit to the disabled, but we will see that has not been its history. Despite the work and traditions of Hippocrates, Galen, and others, medicine would do little to either change attitudes toward the disabled or relieve the sufferings of the disabled. Instead, we shall see that the Western project of medicine is essentially an attempt to overcome disability and death. Having failed at overcoming either of these, medical practices and institutions will often jettison any care for or interest in the disabled.

In some aspects of Roman urban life, we find a modicum of improvement for the well-off Roman living with a disability, but these cases are rare. Although commoners with disabilities had a more challenging life, some dispensations were occasionally made for the upper and wealthier classes. For example, from the historical record, we know that emperor Claudius was born lame and lived with a speech impediment. Those disabilities did not prevent him from becoming the most powerful man in Rome. However, the average Roman citizen's life would have been much different from the Emperors'.

As with earlier Neolithic remains, the Roman archaeological record is replete with examples of Romans living with disabilities. Victoria Brignell reports, "5 out of 12 Roman skeletons uncovered in a group burial site near Cambridge, England were found to have a spinal deformity.[49]" She further points out, and this material has been corroborated[50] that many of the exhumed Roman skeletons bore the signs of severe gout, osteoarthritis, and other physical disabilities that would have made everyday life at the edge of the empire challenging. This research squares with the archaeological record that we were looking at earlier. It is prudent to suggest that many more people during the Roman epoch lived with similar disabilities even if we have not yet found their remains.

Actual descriptions of Romans with disabilities are difficult to come by because they accepted and adopted much of the aesthetic ideals of the Greek canon. The Romans may have conquered Greece and assumed the latter's gods, art, poetry, philosophy, but they also adopted their attitudes regarding the disabled. One exception we find to this is Pliny the Younger. Pliny the Younger, the chronicler of Roman life, colorfully described the life of a wealthy Roman citizen, Domitius Tullus, living with a disability:

"Crippled and deformed in every limb, he could only enjoy his vast wealth by contemplating it and could not even turn in bed without assistance. He also had to have his teeth cleaned and brushed for him—a squalid and pitiful detail—and when complaining about the humiliations of his infirmity was often heard to say that every day he licked the fingers of his slaves." (Letters 8, 18; trans. B. Radice)

In this passage, we learn of the difficulties of disability brought on by old age; however, we also realize that Domitius was a wealthy Roman citizen living with the relative comforts available to him and which were not available to your average Roman citizens. Domitius may have had someone to cleanse his teeth, but did his slaves have someone to clean their teeth if needed? Let us take the archaeological record reported by Brignell and others. We can take it for granted that not only was disability prevalent throughout Roman culture, but the lives of most Romans living with disabilities were not as easy as the life of a patrician such as Domitius, no matter his hardships. It reveals that Domitius does complain enough for Pliny to record the state and condition of his physical body. This suggests that there had emerged in Pliny and Domitius' time enough of a sense of luxury and social bias against disability for those who could afford luxury and live a life removed from the rigors of living with disability and were continuing to frame a negatively valued position toward disability. This movement occurs when disability manifests in their bodies or their lives, as in the case of Domitius. Naturally, they would ground those beliefs in the unassailable ideas of their times and cultures. The ideas ready at hand were the ones borrowed from Greece.

The concept and need to define disability emerge when persons with disabilities are no longer as widespread; as such was the case, we might speculate, before Greece and Rome. As Romans gathered the wealth and comforts of a complex, urban society complete with public health institutions (think aqueducts and sewers), medicine, and other comfort technologies, we are likely to see some disabilities appear and others are mitigated. Correspondingly, we are likely to see an effort to distance the body from its disabilities. Take the case of Domitius. The more removed from the ubiquity of disability, the more prejudices against disability emerge. Therefore, a new conceptualization of disability emerges with a whole new set of ideas on and about disability. To be sure, disability does not vanish, but one sets up presumptive normalcy if one can afford to lessen the effects through emergent technologies. In this view, one can complain, or one can bear disability as a silent witness; or, if you can afford it, one may find relief in a nascent technology of the body. Those persons living with spinal deformity buried in Britain that we looked at earlier seemed to be accomplished enough to undergo memorialization processes not available to all. Memorialization presupposes a level of social acceptability. Domitius' tooth-cleaning slaves, for example, were required to bear their afflictions silently and die only to be forgotten. This is also evident in the Roman Emperor and Stoic philosopher, Marcus Aurelius as he writes in his "Meditations:"

"Pain is nether unbearable not unending, so long as you remember its limitations and don't add to it with your imagination...What we cannot bear takes us away from life; what lasts can be borne...Pain in the hand or foot is not against nature, provided that the foot and hand are fulfilling their own tasks." (Aurelius, Meditations 7, 64, 33; 6, 33, trans Birley, 1966)

Marcus Aurelius would have known his share of suffering and in his years decamped away from Rome fighting, he would have witnessed many instances of disability, but he was a consistent Stoic and a member of the most prosperous and powerful class in Rome. He views disability as more minor a misfortune than Domitius did, but rather as a regular and necessary outcome of the universe, a natural law (logos). What is clear here is that we now see three ways disability occurs according to the ancient traditions. A disability may be from the capricious will of a god, sheer bad luck, or is woven into the fabric of the world. How you conceive of disability's origins seems to point to how you will conceptualize it and deal with it, personally, philosophically, or socially.

12

The Medieval Period: Christianity and the Disabled: Grace, Charity, and Innocence

With the emergence of Christianity in the late classical period, we witnessed a subtle change in attitudes toward the disabled. One can trace this to the inclusiveness of Jesus' ministry toward the lame, the disabled, and other social outcasts. The parable of the least and his outré behavior toward the disabled would slowly wield a powerful effect. Because of this inclusion, we see a more compassionate set of practices emerge in opposition to the older traditions practices in antiquity. Those traditional practices viewed disability as a blemish, an imperfection, or the result of a nefarious divine agency. The Greek, Roman, and Jewish traditions slowly gave way to a different approach, albeit one that does not entirely change the treatment or conditions of persons living with disabilities, but it is arguably an improvement.

Nevertheless, Jesus directly ministering to the lame, blind, and leprous challenged those traditional practices and set the wheel in motion for change. His actions, however, are promulgated as ideals to strive for and not norms to be necessarily realized and practiced, especially in the secular realm. For example, in Paul's letter to the Thessalonians, his advice to his followers is to "comfort the feebleminded, be patient with all men." The triune configuration of love, compassion, and charity are ideals to strive for in our lives modeled on Jesus. Still, the practical reality and pragmatic understanding is that we will all fall well short of realizing those ideals. These ideals work well for saints, but the rest of us fall well short of the mark. After all, Paul is reminding his fellow Christians of behaviors that they should be modeling and practicing. But why does he feel the need to issue such a directive? Why else would he write on the topic if there was not a problem in the first instance?

That Paul devoted time to remind his disciples of the need for compassion toward the disabled suggests a dearth of empathy in early Christian communities. Therefore, it is predictable that the earlier cultural practices of Greek, Jewish, and Roman society had become the normative practice even for Christians. Yet, the earlier cultural practices toward the disabled will permeate the newer Christian-oriented accretions.

Later, Augustine's theology centers Christianity upon the concept of grace, resulting in an equalizing of all persons in the eyes of God, disabled and able-bodied. In this sense, the Augustinian theology views each of us as stained with original sin but stained equally in the eyes of the Christian god. As Stainton suggests in his study of intellectual disability, persons with disabilities "achieve a status of equality unknown in classical thought."[51] This equality is framed in theory only. The actual lived conditions of persons with disabilities will not substantively improve in late antiquity. We cannot overlook the reality that many previous cultural practices will remain undiminished despite these ideas. Nevertheless, that there is a discourse of compassion now available bodes better for future cultural practices.

Despite the archival and archaeological evidence of the long-standing presence of persons with disabilities throughout history, there is little, as we have seen, recorded or remembered from their perspectives. To be sure, many would be isolated, segregated, or treated as outcasts, but they were present nonetheless. Common sense tells us that disability would be a steady constant throughout history, and yet their presence is one of absence. In this reality, the absence is an erasure of history.

Given the reality of physically demanding manual labor, the effects of a disease, war, and naturally occurring conditions, the incidence of disability would always be prevalent. Along with the absence of medical care and treatment and the natural lottery of congenital disabilities, injuries from hard labor and war, we might reasonably expect to find a steady population of persons with disabilities at any given historical epoch. Unfortunately, no studies can definitively address this issue, but it stands to reason and is common sense that the disabled were present in proportionately large numbers throughout history. What we lack other than academic disciplines are their stories of disabled people, their accounts. Surprisingly, what does emerge in the medieval period is the relative security and success that we find disabled people enjoying in Medieval Europe. The work of recent historians such as Baswell, Mezler, Wheatley, and others is uncovering hidden traditions and histories of the disabled in Medieval Europe, which, in turn, may cause us to change our perceptions of the disabled of this period. This recent scholarship suggests that while life would be difficult for the disabled and they would have had their share of problems, persons with specific disabilities might have fared relatively better during the medieval epoch than other periods in history. While this realization may enlarge our understanding of medieval history, we will still witness significant prejudices toward disability during this period and subsequent eras, too.

Throughout the long period from the collapse of Rome to the rise of modern society around the 1700s, many of the disabled will be kept -employed as a word does not work here-as court jesters, clowns, curiosities, and other oddities for the nobility as in the Holy Roman Empire courts.

During the Inquisition, the disabled may be charged with heresy, drowned, or burned merely because their disabilities linked them with the devil. As late as 1601, Queen Elizabeth's government would divide the poor into three groups labeling the disabled as the "helpless poor." From this evidence, we may conclude that the picture looked quite bleak for most persons with disabilities. Yet, we do on occasion find throughout medieval-era archives isolated examples of persons with disabilities succeeding. For instance, medievalist Christopher Baswell points out the accomplishments of Hermann of Reichenau or "Hermann, the Cripple." One of the most celebrated Latin, Greek, and Arabic scholars of the 11th century,"[52] he was born in Swabia to minor nobility and with a kind of paralytic condition that scholars believe was cerebral palsy, spina bifida, or spinal muscular atrophy.[53] He was also born with a cleft palate, had difficulty speaking, and used a specially designed chair to get around. Later in his life, he would lose his eyesight. Although primarily understood as a mathematician responsible for introducing the Arabic numeral system, his prodigious accomplishments include works on German history, musical theory, astronomy, and the composition of many hymns, including "Salve Regina." But, again, like the accomplishments of other persons with disabilities who were well off enough, most of the disabled of the medieval epoch were unremembered and forgotten.

In Medieval England, evidence of the lives of the disabled abounds, for example, in the research by Simon Jarrett, who focused on the presence of words such as leper, blynde, dumbe, natural fool, creple, and lunatick." The emergence of these words indicates that the disabled were a presence in everyday life."[54] The introduction of a host of words describing different conditions of disability is unique to this period and serves as ample evidence of the ubiquity of the disabled. Thus, we transfer from generic lump terms not distinguishing the salient differences occasioned by disabling conditions to a broader vocabulary rich in descriptions. One of the background assumptions that I am using here is that these words emerged as needed because the disabled constitute a significant proportion of the population. If this is correct, it suggests that the disabled were present in large numbers.

Since the disabled were ubiquitous, why are their accomplishments not mentioned apart from a passing or oblique reference to those like Hermann of Reichenau? One plausible answer would be that no one cared or noticed in pre-modern times since disability was widespread.

Suppose many were deformed or disabled by the rigors of pre-modern life by contagious disease (leprosy, smallpox), manual labor, accidents from daily activities, punishments for crime[55], or war. We might not draw attention to it because it is expected and commonplace. If we add the poor state of medical knowledge and the lack of the ability to successfully treat, intervene or cure the naturally-occurring presence of congenital disabilities, the numbers would predictably swell. As the historian of disability, Henri Jacques Stiker, suggests regarding the medieval society, the disabled would "simply melt into the crowd of the poor."[56] The question remains that we are confronted with both an absence and a silence.

Despite the more significant numbers, there were problems. During the middle ages, Europe had adopted the Roman tradition of the Justinian law codes concerned with the legal standing of people with disabilities that denied their right to make property transactions of various kinds. Persons who had been born with conditions such as deafness, blindness, or muteness, were, according to these legal codes, banned from specific transactions.[57] Similarly, the Theodosian Laws prohibited males with any physical impairments from earning their living as tutors for children[58]. There is no clear rationale for this type of ban.

We do find characters in medieval era literature having disabilities. Indeed, disabilities of all sorts, including deafness. For example, it is explored through a literary lens in the Wife of Bath's character in Chaucer's "Canterbury Tales.[59]" Chaucer's character is described as "somdeel deef" because of an abusive husband who beat her with a book. The contrast of literacy and deafness has intrigued Chaucerian scholars and others.[60] His Knight's tale centers on the physical embodiment and condition of many of the Knight's characters, too. The descriptions are revealing for their description of potential physical impairments and their ubiquity. For Chaucer and subsequent writers, these examples form a literary device that allows the writer to propel the narrative forward by focusing on the physical embodiment. This device functions as "a literary scaffolding," enabling the writer to explore various issues. Mitchell and Snyder name it, appropriately, a "narrative prosthesis." From Chaucer on, we will see many writers make use of this trope in their writing. We see instances of the disabled appearing in Medieval narratives but rarely in a realistic way but rather as foils for the author's projections.

Warfare, raids, and conquest likely contributed to the number of disabled, and both writers and poets would borrow from this surplus. One such process that doubtlessly added to the rollcalls of the disabled was the long period of Norse invasions. But the sword cuts both ways: not only would those beleaguered coastal citizens feel the impact of disability but so too their marauders.

During the Norse invasion of England starting in 865, one of the Viking leaders, Ivar the Boneless, lived with a disability. As the son of the semi-legendary, King Ragnar Lothbrok, Ivar was the commander of the great heathen army of the Norse that invaded and dominated Medieval England and Ireland in the 9th century. According to legend, Ivar was carried into battle on a shield or a palanquin by his warriors because he could not walk--a condition he had since birth or very early infancy. In 1949, Danish researcher Knud Seedorf wrote:

"Of historical personages, the author knows of only one of whom we have a vague suspicion that he suffered from osteogenesis imperfecta, namely Ivar Benløs, eldest son of the Danish legendary king Regnar Lodbrog. He is reported to have had legs as soft as cartilage ('he lacked bones') so that he was unable to walk and had to be carried about on a shield."[61]

From the Scandinavian Sagas, Ivar is described as 'lacking bones' and hence the sobriquet, "boneless." The mid-twelfth century poem Hattalykill tells us Ivar was 'without any bones at all, which, of course, is not possible but provides further textual support for his disabling condition. In Ragnar's Saga, Ivar's nickname is explained in detail. While aspects of the explanation have their roots in myth and folklore, the explanation was likely constructed to explain a disability that could not be otherwise explained. An alternative reading of "boneless" might refer to his inability to get and maintain an erection. Still, this reading seems far-fetched, although erectile dysfunction often results from a disability and would not be out of the question. Following this notion, it is interesting to note that in the 2016 BBC mini-series, "The Vikings," Ivar will be characterized as a vengeful sociopath bent on overcoming his sexual impotence. His cruelty is in sharp contrast to the sympathetic portrayal of his other non-disabled brothers. Again, in the cultural appropriation of contemporary artists, one needs to ask why the writers chose to portray Ivar in this manner, especially when there is no mention of similar actions in the Norse stories? As with the caricaturing of Ephialtes in the film "300," contemporary artists tell us more about their prejudicial attitudes toward the disabled than anything remotely historically accurate. The association of deviant sexuality and the disabled and the obsession with the sexual lives of the disabled are commonplace tropes throughout the history of the West. Whatever the true nature of Ivar's condition, his name is a "marker of difference," or a device used in the Icelandic sagas and other epics to signify identity and, specifically, in Ivar's case, to signify disability. This "literary scaffolding" or "narrative prosthesis" that Chaucer invokes to propel the narrative adds richness to his characters and functions as a foil to investigate or promulgate positions and ideas.

It is exceptionally revealing that in the annals of Viking history--especially in Ragnar's Saga—more attention is paid to Ivar's upper body size and strength than his disability itself. He had likely developed his upper body as compensation for the loss of his lower limbs. But this may function as the idea of compensatory faculty development due to the loss of some other faculty we witnessed with Tiresias. It is different in degree and not kind to the earlier notion linked with Tiresias and his blindness.

In Ragnar's Saga, Ivar's exploits are recounted that mention his strength. In a battle against King Eysteinn of Sweden, Ivar triumphantly wins the day by doing battle and slaying a mystical cow called Sibilja. His men carry him into battle on his shield, and he blinds the cow by shooting two arrows from his longbow. The Saga describes the longbow as large as a tree trunk, but Ivar was able to pull back and let the arrows loose as if "were only a weal elm twig."

From these and similar accounts, we may safely conclude that some medieval people with disabilities, such as Ivar and Hermann of Reichenau, flourished during their lives. To be sure, both Ivar and Hermann were members of the more powerful classes in their respective cultures, and, as such, accounts such as these tell us very little about the lives of ordinary people living with disabilities. Moreover, the untrustworthiness of fictionalized versions (e.g., Chaucer) does little to provide reliable detail.

Before the Norman invasion of the British Isles in the 11th century, we find traditional law codes enforcing rules against kings having any disability or impairment holding their titles and power and limitations on property rights and civil liberties for all the disabled. These laws--derived from their Roman legal inheritance--would legally frame obstacles for the disabled.

In other legal codes, as with the Irish law code known as Brehon laws, they do little to rectify the conditions of the disabled. The Brehon laws, for example, mention the practice of individuals being ineligible for kingship if they are blemished or disabled. In the legal tract Bechbretha, we learn of the account of Congal Cáech deposed because a bee blinded him; his blindness was thought to make his ruling impossible. No accommodation nor any provision could be made. Whereas Ivar's fellow warriors would accommodate him during battle, Congal's refused to make any changes. Nevertheless, the Brehon laws offer comparatively generous remedies for injuries and disabilities caused by intentional acts leading to disability, especially when compared to earlier Roman and Canon law.[62] The Brehon laws also made it illegal to ridicule the disabled and fined those who did ridicule the disabled: a sharp contrast to other legal traditions, then and now.

As we have previously seen, Christian doctrine developed during the early medieval period and would attempt to present disability as neither a disgrace nor a divine punishment for a specific sin; on the contrary, disability was viewed as a means of divine purification and a particular way of manifesting grace. In this approach, the presence of a disability placed one closer to the suffering of Jesus. This orientation toward suffering would create a space for care toward persons with disabilities. The caretaker would benefit by being close to the sufferer who, by extension, was near to Jesus. Indeed, the charitable ethics of Christian thought and the Christian ethic of "the least" would manifest the establishment of the institutions of care (hospitals, alms-houses, etc.) during the later-medieval epoch that start the technologies of care. These institutions would seek to redress the lack of care and concern for persons with disabilities, modeling their actions on the subversive ethics of Jesus.

The first medical institutions to care specifically for persons with medical conditions emerged in the Medieval period. These institutions provided care to many, including some disabilities and illnesses. Indebted to earlier institutions found in ancient Greece, usually located at or near temples dedicated to the god of healing, Asclepius, these institutions would provide minimal care. In Greece, these Asclepieia functioned as centers of medical advice, prophecy, and some treatments[63]. Later and around 100 BCE, the Romans established valetudinaria for the care of the sick, wounded gladiators, and injured soldiers, but they did not seem to be widespread. They were not places for severe or incurable diseases and disabilities, but they would function as the medieval-era hospital's predecessors. The original institutions we would most closely identify as a hospital would emerge in the medieval period established by the efforts of clerics. They are widely viewed as the first hospitals. "Hospes," the root of the words "hospice" and "hospital," derives from the Latin for "guest." Its origin may be traced back to the 10th-century movement of St. John the Hospitallier. This movement sought to comfort, treat, and provide palliative care for the ill, some of the disabled, and the dying. The order of the Knights of the Hospital of St. John of Jerusalem—the Hospitallers-- arose as a group of individuals associated with an Amalfitan hospital in Jerusalem where having dedicated themselves to John the Baptist, sought to provide care for injured pilgrims. Founded by Gerard Thom in 1023, their express purpose was to provide care for sick, poor, or injured pilgrims making their journey to the Holy Land. In the late medieval period, beginning around the 14th century, small hospitals attached to monasteries began to spring up to care for the ill and infirm. Known as "Maison Dieu" in France, the hospices became places of refuge and cared for many disabled except the blind, lepers, the incurable, and the paralyzed[64]. We see that even in the nascent institutions of care, discriminatory practices existed. Why the exclusion? These institutions would treat only cases that were promising or fatal. Death is becoming a practical cure-all. A person with an incurable disease or condition such as paralysis, deafness, or leprosy that did not lead to a quick death was excluded from seeking care at these institutions.

Many early hospitals would be allied with and adjuncts to more significant monasteries. By the advent of the modern period, hospitals start to branch out and become independent, public enterprises supported by the charity of wealthier citizens. As they developed, their mission changed from caring and hospitality to one exclusively concerned with healing. We need to keep this in mind. However, hospitals were often only open to a select number of individuals with certain kinds of disabilities. The dividing criteria seemed to be whether a person was either treatable or permanently disabled: if treatable, they were admitted and cared for; if the disability were permanent, they would not be admitted--the exception being those on death's door. This may come from the earlier practice evidenced in hospices. In addition, proscriptions limited lepers, paralytics, the blind, the deaf, and those missing limbs.[65] There were no specialized centers for care specifically for the disabled until the founding of the Hotel des Invalides in 1670 by Louis XIV, and even there, it was only for aged and disabled veterans. The consequence was that the blind, paralyzed, and those living with other disabilities were excluded and would need to endure the discriminatory practices at play.

So, where did they go? Where were the disabled in Europe during this time? It is hypothesized that they were likely kept at home or expelled to wander the woods or city streets. Recall Queen Elizabeth's draconian law removing the disabled -the "helpless poor"-from English institutions, effectively consigning them to life on the streets or margins of society. It appears that the disabled would find themselves cast outside any of the acceptable social institutions and therefore any benefits one could accrue from those same institutions. They would be on their way to becoming a permanent but invisible underclass. In such a state of neglect, no doubt their lives were, to borrow a phrase from Thomas Hobbes, "nasty, poor brutish and short." The French historian and preeminent scholar of childhood, Phillipe Aries, suggests that most disabled infants "accidentally" died early deaths by smothering or falling down wells[66]. Aries and others argue that this prompted edicts issued by bishops banning parents sleeping in the same bed with their children.[67] If you were born with a significant disability, your parents were likely to dispatch you. The ancient practice of exposure had taken a decidedly nefarious domestic turn. If your parents did not commit infanticide, then you were likely to become an outcast, a social pariah eking out an existence on the margins of society. The exception to this would be those disabled by war which may find a modicum of support in institutions such as the Hotel des Invalides. Until the establishment of the Hotel des Invalides, the historical record is eerily silent concerning the disabled.

In the 16th century, the Protestant Reformation witnessed Protestant Christians such as Martin Luther and John Calvin returning to earlier folk and pagan beliefs concerning the disabled that ran contrary to Christian belief. The earlier ideas- a residual of the classical and pagan past- believed that persons with disabilities were possessed by evil, demonic spirits. As a result, after the Protestant Reformation in 1517, persons with developmental disabilities were often denounced and treated as subhuman or second-class citizens worthy only of ridicule.

Evidence of the tenacity of the older ideas from antiquity can be found in the Malleus Maleficarum. Many historians believe its importance has been overstated. It is still a helpful index about the attitudes toward the disabled during this time. It is beneficial in assessing attitudes toward the treatment of disabled children.

When the Dominicans Henricus Kramer and Jacob Sprenger published their Malleus Maleficarum in 1487, they would pave the way for Luther, Calvin, and others to retreat to the older idea of the divine agency or supernatural origins of disability--setting back the conditions of the disabled in Europe. Kramer and Sprenger would argue that witches in league with demonic spirits were responsible for childhood disabilities. To this end, they developed their understanding of the so-called "changeling" (German, Wechselkinder). A changeling occurred, in this tradition, when a "healthy" child was stolen and replaced by a child with a deformity or disability. In book two, chapter VIII Kramer and Sprenger write,

"Another terrible thing which God permits to happen to men is when their own children are taken away from women, and strange children are put in their place by devils. For some are always ailing and crying, and yet the milk of four women is not enough to satisfy them." '

Beyond the literal reading of this, I believe, a more profound and more revealing truth about the times and their attitudes toward the disabled emerges. A disabled child may require more care, consequently requiring more scarce resources than a non-disabled child. The parent would find themselves strapped to provide that additional care for that child. Additionally, the disabled child may be viewed as an inadequate potential contributor to the household economy. I take it that is why there is the mention of the enormous breastfeeding demands of a changeling. No medieval peasant could afford three additional wet nurses for a single child, so it best to rid yourself of the child soon and not grow attachments to it.

It is interesting to note that the changeling's origin may arise from a system of ritualized rape—a host of devils cuckolds the father. A devil known as an incubus seduced the mother who becomes pregnant, but the devil uses sperm from the father. How? The incubus has stolen sperm from the father by a female devil--a succubus--who had earlier gathered it from a coupling with the father or obtained it from a wet dream that the father had:

"Some are generated by the operation of Incubus devils, of whom, however, they are not the sons, but of that man from whom the devil has received the semen as a Succubus, or whose semen he has collected from some nocturnal pollution in sleep. For these children are sometimes, by Divine permission, substituted for the real children."

In this strange taxonomy of developmental disability, the book identifies the third kind of changeling who appears in place of the original child:

"And there is the third kind when the devils at times appear in the form of young children and attach themselves to the nurses. But all three kinds have this in common, that though they are very heavy, they are always ailing and do not grow, and cannot receive enough milk to satisfy them...."

Mention is made of the changeling's body and its unquenchable needs for milk suggesting an economic motive for infanticide. Influenced by these and similar ideas, Martin Luther (1483–1546) views developmentally disabled and deformed children as "filled with Satan." In the infamous case of a boy from Dessau, there is textual evidence that he argued that the child should be drowned or suffocated.

"In Dessau, there was a twelve-year-old boy like this: he devoured as much as four farmers did, and he did nothing else than eat and excrete."[68]

When asked to justify his position, Luther is reportedly said, "because I think he's simply a mass of flesh without a soul."

Once again, we see at root that the reason for fearing the disabled child seems founded on its hunger and insatiable needs rather than its purported demonic origins. Its demands outweigh its purportedly evil nature. The demonic, however, was not entirely forgotten. To that end, Luther would exculpate the boy's killers from charges of the sin of murder or infanticide because the child lacked a human soul. It was "simply a mass of flesh without a soul." It was more demon than human. There is some debate over whether these were Luther's words, but they speak to the tenor of the times. These beliefs fit perfectly with John Calvin's (1509–64) theory of the elect and the corresponding notion of predestination. In this view, the lucky went to heaven, and the rest were slated for purgatory or worse, hell. The determination of the elite would be cast along the lines of physical embodiment. The result of re-establishing these beliefs and practices would provide authoritative corroboration for what many civil and church leaders would use to subject people with disabilities to discrimination. Over time, it would be the justification for using gruesome tortures to exorcise those demonic spirits. It must have assuaged the conscience of the judge and executioner to believe that the human they were torturing did not have a soul, was not even, technically, human. It was just a mass of flesh.

It has been suggested that many of the punishments meted out by Church officials were directed at individuals with disabilities who were scapegoated and wrongly blamed for more significant social problems or catastrophic events. As a result, we lose Jesus' message of compassion for the disabled by the end of the Medieval period.

Most Medieval-era Christians would continue believing in the divine agency of disability, but some would come to the idea that persons with disabilities were closer to God. They clung to a variation of the early Christian notion of suffering and held that the disabled were living their life of purgatory on earth. As such, they thereby accelerated their eventual passage to heaven. This belief allowed them to be understood as closer to the grace of God. Nevertheless, disability in this period will still be primarily viewed as something one merited. In Holland during the 16th-century, those with leprosy could have all their possessions confiscated and redistributed to others. There was also the sense that the leper had somehow merited their treatment and punishment.[69] Because you brought on your condition yourself, you ought not to receive any social advantage, dispensation, or entitlement that wealth could buy. The odd part is that the disabled now needed to rely on and receive charity from their fellows once dispossessed of their property.

People with disabilities may find themselves occupying another position in society: the butt of humor. In Desiderius Erasmus's The Praise of Folly, the main character, Folly, scornfully belittles Vulcan -the

Greek Hephaestus- as the limping blacksmith. Erasmus' example illustrates how even a god with a disability cannot escape the human tendency to pre-judge, belittle, and ridicule. The scorn is evident, but what
is of more interest here is that the gods themselves were neither immune from disability nor the ridicule associated with being disabled. If
one may ridicule a god, then there are no restrictions on the mere human or near-human. Making fun of the disabled is consistent with the
practice we find during this period and is present in the amusements of
the "fool" or "buffoon" or the court jester. Disability now becomes part
of the satirist or comic's panoply of insults. We see this expressed pic-
torially in some of Pieter Brueghel, the Elder's canvasses of the 1500s,
especially his work, "The Beggars" which was known as "The Cripples"
(1568). The canvas shows several men with disabilities begging outside
the city walls as a woman casually walks by, ignoring them. Each man
wears a cap identifying him as a member of a different social class. But
they also wear fox tails pinned to their clothing, and art historical scholarship suggests that these were worn as a symbol of ridicule donned by
the fool or buffoon.

Brueghel was not alone nor the first to mirror social attitudes toward the disabled. For example, an earlier Hieronymus Bosch painting, "The Ship of Fools" (1490 to 1500), depicts the practice of
displaying people with physical and mental disabilities aboard a ship
that would sail from port to port as an exhibition for the curious. A
common approach and later literary metaphor addressed in his preface
to Foucault's "Madness and Civilization," by Jose Barchilon:

"Renaissance men developed a delightful yet horrible way of dealing
with their mad denizens: they were put on a ship and entrusted to
mariners because folly, water, and sea, as everyone then 'knew,' had
an affinity for each other. Thus, 'Ship of Fools' crisscrossed the sea
and canals of Europe with their comic and pathetic cargo of souls.
Some found pleasure and even a cure in the changing surroundings, in
the isolation of being cast off, while others withdrew further, became
worse, or died alone and away from their families. The cities and villages which had thus rid themselves of their crazed and crazy could now

take pleasure in watching the exciting sideshow when a ship full of foreign lunatics would dock at their harbors."

The original metaphor of the "ship of fools" was introduced by Plato in book VI the "Republic" where he used the imagery of the "fools" to represent the ship of the state being taken over and governed by the unenlightened masses rather than an enlightened monarch, the philosopher-king. Identifying mental disability with the unruly mobs is a suggestive comparison that reveals much about the chief worries and concerns of the powerful classes in antiquity and later medieval and renaissance periods. The disabled, the anarchist, the critic, and the masses are all pitted against the powers-that-be because they threaten the sanctity of the status quo, the normal. The disabled are the outsiders and, as such, threaten the stability of the state. They remind us of Homer's Thersites, who critiques the Greek generals and will be viewed as a potential disruption of order. As Watson and Mann write in their highly informative text on the Disabled in Art History:[70]

"In 1494, German satirist Sebastian Brant adapted Plato's allegory of the ship of fools into a popular book that featured woodcut illustrations by Dürer and was the inspiration for Bosch's painting... The allegory features a vessel without a pilot that is populated by deranged, frivolous, and oblivious inhabitants who are seemingly ignorant of their course. A parody of the Church's "ark of salvation," Ship of Fools inverted societal norms and critiqued the church's mores and authority. The book became extremely popular, with six authorized and seven pirated editions published before 1521."

One may imagine how if a person had a disability in Renaissance society, they would then go to extremes to hide or disguise it. Of course, with diseases such as smallpox endemic throughout Europe, those who had contracted the disease and survived would live with identifiable scars that would remain all of their lives; many people would find no recourse but to bear their scars and disfigurements openly and with stoic resolve. Take the example from the Italian Renaissance of the Duke of Urbino. The Duke was a kind of a hired gun for the rich. He was a prosperous Condottiere who seemed to enjoy having his portrait painted. All the portraits of Federico depict his left side. It is widely held that he had suffered from smallpox, and his right side was deeply scarred and disfigured. It has been reported that he had lost his right eye in a jousting accident. He would then "hide" such conditions by only commissioning portraits from the left. A prominent feature he cannot hide is his nose. His nose bridge was apparently "whittled" down by surgeons to expand his eye's sight. The Duke's portraits underscore that those who could afford to disguise their conditions to avoid suffering the social indignities of being viewed as disabled or disfigured would do so. While the Duke's contemporaries would know of his condition, he would not let posterity in on his secret.

He would not have been alone. Many people would have been permanently scarred from disease, burns, and accidents; others would have been born with cleft palates, facial disfigurements, and more. Diseases such as leprosy and smallpox that were once endemic and widespread around the globe would have left millions disfigured and ostracized by their communities. Epidemiologists believe that the variola virus that causes smallpox has been with humans since antiquity. The earliest archaeological evidence of smallpox is found on the mummified body of Pharaoh Ramses of Egypt. With a nearly 30% fatality rate, smallpox is estimated to have killed 400,000 Europeans during the final years of the 18th century. It knew no class allegiance taking out five reigning European monarchs. In America, Presidents Washington, Jackson, and Lincoln, had all contracted smallpox but were lucky to have survived. That was not the luck of President Jackson's brother, Robert: he died from the disease. The great Sioux warrior and chief, Sitting Bull, had smallpox as a child. Disease and disability respect no class boundaries. Soviet leader, Stalin, had smallpox at aged seven leaving him scarred with pockmarks. As with Duke Urbino, Stalin had his handlers "touch" up his photos for posterity. Those who did not die would need to learn to live with scars that would have marred their faces and bodies and caused them social unease, embarrassment, and, sadly, social ostracizing. In about 2% of the cases, one of the complications would result in being permanently blind. In addition, painful lesions to the joints, mainly the elbows, often occur, causing severe and debilitating arthritic symptoms that may lead to many disabling conditions. The relative absence of dependable and effective medical treatment would have meant these diseases were incurable and largely untreatable. If one tore one's ACL while being pulled by his oxen ploughing a field, you could not get it treated by surgery.

The research above brings together much of what we have struggled to investigate and learn from the previous histories discussed in this book. We may provisionally conclude that the disabled are viewed as "the other" because their physical or mental condition is perceived as a threat to the natural, political, and divine order. For the good of society, such a threat must be kept isolated from the public purview or, failing that stratagem, removed entirely. In a world where adventitious disability could occur at any time, humor and ridicule will emerge as socially acceptable transferences in dealing with death, banishment, and exile in the Medieval period; still, occasional episodes of violence leveled against the disabled will erupt as in the inquisition. Eventually, with the rise of capitalism in the late Medieval and early modern periods and modern carceral institutions, we will see the profit motive becoming one of the direct relations of the disabled. As history unfolds, hospitals and a parasitical medical tradition advancing false cures and panaceas will emerge in these instances. The groundwork for the pre-conditions of modernity has been laid. Unfortunately, the arrival of modernity will not be much of an improvement for the disabled.

In summary, at the end of the religiously dominated period of the Medieval epoch and with the dawn of modernity, Western culture is developing a dual set of attitudes toward the disabled. On the one hand, disability is to be criticized and denounced as the devil's handiwork or an aberration from the natural order; on the other, the disabled may be viewed as closer to God because of their life of suffering. In the former instance, prejudice and violence toward the disabled are abetted and tolerated if not expected. At the same time, the result of the latter is the unenviable position of never being able to live up to culture's aspirational ideals and idealized projections. Your fallibility is, in this sense, entirely a foregone conclusion.

13

A Renaissance Interlude: An Outer Flaw: Shakespeare and Disability

Before we embark on our journey through modernity, let us take a tour of one of the most critical voices of the new world dawning, Shakespeare. Renaissance-era theatre teems with stereotypical images and portrayals of persons with disabilities. In Shakespeare, we find some of the most powerful renderings of these stereotypes; those that would, given his far-ranging influence, come to shape and alter the mental landscape permanently. Part of Shakespeare's gift is his uncanny ability to convey a character by a physical description. This ability to sketch a character builds on the stereotypes and assumptions of a culture. One thinks of the delightful rogue Falstaff and all of Shakespeare's many colorful physical depictions of his rotund form. His fundamental buffoonery is encapsulated in his countenance and comportment. But not all of Shakespeare's depictions are quite so kind-hearted. Whereas arguably, Shakespeare is lampooning Falstaff, others will be subjected to a more bitter draught. Take the example of Richard III. In real life, in the words of John Rous, Richard III was a "good lord," but the last prince of the House of York and the last of the Plantagenet lineage would be turned into the preeminent arch-villain by Shakespeare. Indeed, while Richard III was by contemporary's accounts perfectly hale, and the later King James I was described by a contemporary as having "weak legs" and was "unable" to stand, we see Richard becoming the object of ridicule. No tragic plays are dripping in self-loathing about James I. James I may have been secure because he was a theatre patron. Still, there is more at play, and Shakespeare and his contemporary playwrights never miss a chance to ridicule a patron. Why only Richard and not James?

Shakespeare in his second-longest folio, Richard III, describes Richard III-- the very model of the Machiavellian king--as someone who is an "ugly hunchback" and whom is "rudely stamp'd," "deformed, unfinish'd," and cannot "strut before a wanton ambling nymph." Shakespeare knew his audience, his political interests, and whom he should and could please. The times required an attack on Richard III, and Shakespeare dug into the prejudices against the disabled to transform Richard III into the unpopular regent. Note we learn from the classical playwrights and Shakespeare and his contemporaries that when you need to defame a person, you borrow from the store of available tropes such as those framed against the disabled and apply them to some facet that character's physiognomy. It is a recipe that all arts use to one degree or another. Shakespeare was just the preeminent master.

Let us look at the play itself. In the famous opening monologue, for example, the beleaguered King summarizes his existence with a monumental degree of self-loathing:

Into this breathing world, scarce half made up,
And that so lamely and unfashionable
That dogs bark at me as I halt by them--
Why I, in this weak piping time of peace,
Have no delight to pass away the time,
Unless to see my shadow in the sun
And descant on mine own deformity.
And therefore, since I cannot prove a lover

To entertain these fair well-spoken days,
I am determinèd to prove a villain

In this passage, Richard III is self-consciously attributing his immorality directly to his disability. In a sense, this sanctions his opponent's reprisals as morally justifiable. Here, we also witness the emergence of the culturally induced self-loathing that will be present in the lives of the disabled and strongly reinforced by cultural beliefs up to this day. Much later, this will be encoded in the notion of the "embittered gimp." Richard III is, of course, the first and perhaps most embittered gimp of all. In Shakespeare's deft hands, the character reaches heights of unimaginable and perhaps unsustainable self-contempt. But instead of letting him stew in his bitterness, Shakespeare has Richard III channel his self-hate into an act of conspiratorial revenge and anger that will become the very model for future villainy. Unfortunately, in lesser hands, the outward flaw is usually more pronounced than the inner struggle.

But keep in mind this is theater. As a note, in real life, Richard III was not disabled and, most importantly, there is no contemporary reference to his having any disability or physical malformation in the historical record at all. The first instances of such concerns emerged well after Richard's death and were part of a stridently anti-monarchical campaign bent on tarnishing the royals in general. In choosing to portray Richard III as physically disabled, Shakespeare's character's supposed inner flaws will be mirrored with the contrived outer disabilities. Shakespeare essentially invented the flawed physiognomy to go with his flawed inner hamartia so operative in all post-renaissance theatre. Aristotle had detailed the importance of the hamartia in his "Poetics," and theatre through the centuries will trade on stock characters manifesting corresponding inner and outer flaws; it is Shakespeare who turns this into an art form and not mere pantomime. But in Shakespeare's deft hands, he turns the character of Richard III into a disturbing social force with profound psychological undertones attendant with the trait of self-loathing. Due to his disability, Richard III describes himself in several instances with scorn as being "crippled." This self-hate renders any person with a disability susceptible to a lack of positive self-image or healthy self-love. And lacking any competing alternative model, the disabled internalize the dominant hegemony of disgust. All too often, the culturally reinforced stereotypes are internalized by the object of those stereotypes manifesting as self-hate.

As recently as 2012, the BBC television adaptation of Shakespeare's historical plays depicted Richard III's inner flaws arising from and stemming from his physical disabilities. Benedict Cumberbatch's acting lends a sinister dimension to his portrayal by hobbling around the set under the burden of a hunchback. Again, none of this is historically accurate. It seems that since Aristotle identified the hamartia as a central component to the essential elements of tragedy, writers find it necessary to embed the inner flaw into the body, always an outward, visible mark or disability. Shakespeare's place in the canon legitimized lesser authors' use of such blatant stereotypes.

Shakespeare would later revisit this conceit in "The Tragedy of Julius Caesar" when he provided Caesar with a convenient disability, "the falling disease" or epilepsy. In Act 1, Scene 2 of "Julius Caesar," Brutus questions Casca about the noises he and Cassius had been hearing. Casca tells Brutus that Caesar "swooned and fell down:"

"He fell down in the marketplace, and foamed at mouth, and was speechless."

This scene is essential because it publicizes Caesar's disability. Once his disability—a hidden disability without any external evidence—becomes public, it makes his eventual ostracization legitimate. The significance here is crucial. The disability cannot be hidden. No words can dissemble the reality of his flawed character. Brutus, gifted with Tiresias' insight, is not surprised about Caesar's disability commenting:

"'Tis very like: he hath the falling sickness."

Blaming his political indiscretions—his tendency towards tyranny on Caesar's disability—Brutus grounds his future act of treason as legitimate. It is as if Brutus and Cassius' conspiracy and future assassination of Caesar is justified because Caesar is disabled. It is again interesting that recent scholarship points out that there is simply no evidence to assign such a diagnosis of epilepsy to Caesar. Indeed, the original diagnosis was provided by Plutarch, who, of course, was not only unqualified to make such a medical diagnosis but was born long after Caesar's death. As Hobgood puts it in her insightful paper on Shakespeare,

"In casting its protagonist as an epileptic, Shakespeare's tragedy constructs the disabled body, and its diverse rhetorical significations, against a dominant, able body that represents power, productivity, and longevity. The drama appears, that is, to privilege Rome's "normal" bodies over its "extraordinary" ones. In his failure to thrive past the play's third act, an epileptic Caesar helps Shakespeare's tragedy perform, even in its most basic plot structure, and ableist politics."[71]

Having set up the moral justification of Caesar's assassination as a kind of blood-letting of the disabled commensurate with the ancient tradition of infanticide, Shakespeare has Brutus justify his action by "a medicalized rhetoric of disability that is entirely ableist at heart:"[72]

"This shall make
Our purpose is necessary and not envious,
Which so appearing to the common eyes,
We shall be called purgers, not murderers." (Act 2, Scene I)

The scene where Brutus argues that they will be viewed as "purgers" not "murderers" is entirely within the tradition we have mapped out in the ancient tradition of "exposing" the disabled. The action is reworded as not a killing but is viewed as returning the flawed vehicle—Caesar's disabled body-- to the gods in some macabre ritualized act of social cleansing. Therefore, the conspirators view their assassination as the removal of sickness for the good of society. As Hobgood concludes, "Caesar's assassination, for instance, is motivated by ableism, justified by his body's inability to conform to normative cultural expectations. His epileptic "lack" prevents his successful leadership while Brutus and Antony's able bodies are more suited to the task."[73] In addition, and finally, "Caesar's better parts," says a representative plebeian of the people, "Shall be crowned in Brutus." The better parts of Caesar are impaired by the flawed embodiments of the disabled ruler. In this sense, alone, we can see that Caesar's ambitions operate as the inner "hamartia" for Brutus and others, to which his "epilepsy" is the corresponding outer flaw. The two ideas run parallel, are commensurate with one other, and are believed to threaten the very order of the Republic. From Shakespeare on, discrimination against the disabled will take on a patriotic fervor.

14

The Enlightenment and Beyond

During the Enlightenment or the period from the end of the Renaissance until the beginning of the 20th century, it may come as a surprise that persons with disabilities fared little better than in earlier, un-enlightened times. Indeed, with the rise of science, medicine, and the attempt to "better" humanity through a host of therapies, we see modernity becoming a mixed blessing for the disabled. Just as different cultures and non-Europeans would suffer enormously under the heel of modernity's notion of progress, so too will the disabled suffer. While sciences and medicines will and did help improve the lives of the disabled, they will also bring unprecedented levels of violence and suffering to their lives. The older belief that disability was caused by divine wrath or demonic possession seemed to wane. Yet, the new "scientific" practices appropriated those older prejudices and grounded them in the new vocabulary of science and rationalism. The scientific disciplines emerging out of this period would treat the disabled as inhumanely in many regards as earlier periods. They would suffer the indignities of brutal and unfeeling classification, labeling, and then be subject to any manner of therapeutic or curative practices that would do more harm than good. Foucault, Cooper, Szasz, and others have covered modernity's treatment of mental disabilities, mapping out and analyzing its totalizing effects. Stiker suggests following Szasz's position looking at the period's mania for institutions, confinement, and the establishment of asylums might more appropriately be called "the age of madness." Many of the institutions developed during this period (e.g., asylums, hospitals) were purposely designed to remove persons with disabilities from the social milieu, to hide them from sight. The disabled were viewed as unsightly, an embarrassment, or what will prove to be as destructive, something to cure, treat or altogether remove or prevent from occurring in the first place. As Foucault has shown within the context of the treatment of madness and the insane, the Enlightenment was a significant turning point, a shift, in the Western project's conceptual understanding of madness, and we can extend this to its treatment of physical disabilities too. Where disability was linked to the divine and transformed into the foolish, by the 16th century, we see people fearing what will be reframed as "abnormal" or "unhealthy." In short, the ability to frame and classify the disabled comes from this period's mania for nomenclature and its obsession with normalcy. The medicalization and related pathologizing of the disability come directly from the Enlightenment. Much of it just to satisfy a bizarre curiosity of wealthy, European gentlemen scientists.

Western medicine has its roots in ancient Greece's search to end disease, incapacity and ultimately overcome death. In this sense, it has been a colossal failure. We tend to cherry-pick data to support our conclusions. If we could tally the numbers of dead, injured, maimed by medicine over the millennia and compare it to those fortunate few who did benefit, the numbers might shock us. Western medicine has always been concerned with ridding the old and disabled. In this sense, it has always sought to eliminate or remove, not expand nor enliven. It has developed a set of exclusionary normative practices that are less about well-being than about discriminating. The emergence of medical practices during the Enlightenment would create a zeal for naming, classifying, categorizing, and developing rigid frameworks to position those attributes and qualities that did not fit into the acceptable range of the normal. Such misfits would be viewed as pathological or untreatable-- dis-eased or dis-abled. The pathologizing of disability that would ensue led directly to attempts to remove the disabled from society. Recall, in the very dawn of modernity—the Renaissance-- Queen Elizabeth I in 1601 tried to save the crown some cash and issued orders that the "disabled poor—the lowest echelon of English society—were to be ejected from hospitals and monasteries forcing them to beg on the streets[74]." Because of these changes in mentalities, the fear of otherness at the root of these attitudes toward the disabled will be amplified, projected, and folded into the newly found institutions: leprosaria, asylums, hospitals, sanitaria. The origins of these institutions had less to do with any benefit that might be gained by the patient cum inmate but wholly to protect the larger society and its "normal" citizens situated outside the walls of the institution. Building walls of exclusion and identity becomes a common practice in modernity. The attempt to wall in the disabled is such that disability will be removed from sight. The age of reason built an architecture of fear and confinement. The spaces it delimited did not so much free humanity's physical problems as enclose and imprison them; this is in no place more evident than in the nascent institutions that would be used to imprison the disabled.

Despite its anti-religious orientation, the Enlightenment would continue and refine and, in its way, extend the practices of the shunning apostates -the heretical- found throughout earlier Judaeo-Christian and Islamic traditions. The apostates now, however, were not religious non-conformists but the disabled who would risk becoming even further isolated and marginalized in a society increasingly hostile to their very presence. Their very bodies become the heretics. There is double treachery to their bodies. It not only becomes the ground of their heresy from the normal, but it reveals their heresy in their incapacity. They cannot hide. The harelip, the stutter, limp, loss of function or limb gives them away as clearly as the mark of a criminal. The disabled become the modern apostate, the modern pariah. The betrayal of their very corporeality—their bodies-- has converted them to sinners against society. If they cannot be cured, they must be confined; extermination and eradication will be humanely proffered if confinement fails. The disabled will be herded together into permanent detention with all of the rest of Western society's outsiders and rejects-- the poor, the criminal, the mad, the sexually curious, the exotic, the foreign, the dark-skinned, et al.

Modernity's chief architectural embodiments are, after all, the reservation, the asylum, the clinic, the prison, the detention center, the workhouse, and, finally, the ultimate built space for confinement, processing, and removal: the concentration camp. The abattoirs of modernity are the purported institutions of care. The difference between these places is that the inmate's label determines where they are sent. One other difference stands out, in most populations isolated in prisons, workhouses, the confined are able-bodied. They can pose a real political threat because they can retaliate or escape. The criminal is always capable of striking back; the slave strives for manumission. The poor have nothing to lose but their chains and are always capable of revolt. The disabled, due to the limiting nature of their condition and their dependence on others, are simply and too often unable to defend themselves from attack. They may not be able to band together in solidarity or free themselves through revolutionary activity. Thus, making the disabled the ideal target for all the discriminatory hostility of modernity. Their forced institutionalization is nearly complete in modernity's quest for control over the other. Any escape is made almost impossible with widespread forced confinement emerging in the Enlightenment with its establishment of institutions and the corresponding mentalities and rhetorics of discrimination aimed at the disabled.

An unsavory and seemingly unassailable belief of modernity emerges here: we strike where we are most effective, which means at the weakest members: we go after those who cannot fight back. Foucault's notion of a praxis of unreason did not, however, go far enough. To be sure, the insane will suffer the "science of medicine," the so-called sacred cow of science, but the disabled will be the chief target of this new practice of exclusion and erasure. The curiosity and fascination practiced towards the disabled will transmogrify the medical practices of diagnosis, incarceration, cure, and removal. We are reminded here of Hippolyte from Foucault's Madame Bovary, who needs to be convinced that he is disabled because his club foot has never limited him before he is told it does.

In an acute and poignant sense, it is just the ancient practice of exposure made manifest and converted to a respectable medical institution. It is just going to happen either before birth or later in life.

It is no mere coincidence that this age witnesses an explosion in architecture. The physical space often mirrors the conceptual. We build according to our aesthetic and political values. Buildings are designed to let some people access power and others not. Our built space becomes our prisons, whether penal or not. Nowhere is this more clearly illustrated than in the well-studied, English institution, Saint Mary's of Bethlehem, which later became infamously known as "Bedlam." An impressive structure, St. Mary's would become an asylum for depositing the mentally disabled. As the Mayor of London, William Gregory, put it in 1450:

"A Church of Our Lady that is named Bedlam. And in that place be found many men that be fallen out of their wit. And full honestly they be kept in that place, and some be restored onto their wit and health again. And some be abiding therein for ever, for they be fallen so much out of themselves that it is incurable unto man."[75]

The key to his claim is that Bedlam was a place—a building—where those deemed insane (fallen out of their wit) would be kept "for ever." Receiving patronage from church and crown, St. Mary's would fit into the model of regulating normalcy emerging in the Enlightenment. At Saint Mary's, to supplement their income, doctors and administrators developed the practice of entertaining the populace with paid tours of the insane, revealing the kind of obsession the public had with those deemed outsiders and outcasts. As Leo Carey wrote in "Lingua Franca:"

"In contrast to the lock-'em-up-and-throw-away-the-key policies chronicled by Foucault, Bethlem remained open to the public through most of the eighteenth century and was a popular destination for middle-class London. "Unlike the silent mad in the Foucault model, the mad in Bethlem were talking politics and they were talking religion," says Roy Porter, a professor of the social history of medicine at London's Wellcome Institute. "You went along to Bethlem to hear the mad jabber." Stories abound of visitors to Bethlem being guided around by a "decent-looking chap," only to learn that he is in fact an inmate."[76]

The irony of the age of reason's obsession with putting away the mentally insane is that it found itself not knowing what to do with the physically disabled, especially those it could not cure. In the discourse of modern philosophy, the subject would be reduced to an object and, once reconceptualized as an object, lose any moral standing one previously might have had. All this results in the disabled being reduced to non-human status. This process of dehumanization we see here began, incidentally—and as we saw--in the attitudes toward the disabled in the late Middle Ages and Renaissance. Recall, here, the notion of a changeling where a disabled child had been exchanged for a non-human demon. The process of complete dehumanization was nearly complete as we approach the 20th century. It would need to develop a permanent and final solution, which would come with the twin totalizing cultures of America and Nazi Germany.

15

Colonial America and Disability: Of Witch-hunts and Outcasts

In 1637 the Massachusetts Bay Colony brought Anne Hutchinson to trial on charges of heresy. Hutchison was an outspoken member of a group of thinkers later tagged antinomians whose opinions often ran contrary to prevailing thought. One--in that grace was available to others, including women--was too controversial for many male church leaders. Hutchinson's stance on the convent of grace softened the rigid adherence of the Puritan's stand on Calvinistic predestination. Deemed heresy, his ideas placed her at risk of censure or worse. She refused to cavil to the authorities and opted to face trial. She would be found guilty and exiled, eventually settling in what would become the state of Rhode Island. But the long reach of the Puritans would harry her from exile, and she would need to seek refuge in the Dutch-controlled New Netherlands with her surviving children. New Netherlands was the territory claimed by the Dutch and extending from the Delmarva Peninsula to extreme southwestern Cape Cod, including settled areas that are now part of New York, New Jersey, Delaware, and Connecticut. Tragically her life would end in exile when a Siwanoy raiding party would kill her and all but one of her children during Kieft's war or Wappinger war (1634-5).

Here is where her story gets interesting. She was the mother of 15 children, and the forces allied against her would descend upon her misfortunes. Rumors circulated in the Colony that one of her infants had been born with a disability—local authorities deemed the infant "monstrous." The primary hypothesis of the Puritan divines was that she must have been consorting with the devil—an easy belief since she was already guilty of harboring opinions contrary to the elect. The accusation of disability at birth with supernatural evil is a legacy of the millennia-long belief that disability results from a divine agency. In this instance, the Puritans would link such a birth to the devil's handiwork, not god's. Covey, Winship, and others have shown that the Puritan belief toward disability was "unquestionably a manifestation of divine wrath."[77] The idea advanced first by Cotton Mather in his incitements railing against witches and other heretics united disability with self-agency, and his thought would gain much purchase in the minds of his fellow colonists. Hutchinson had been dogged by similar accusations before, during, and after her trial. These rumors and her subsequent ex-communication and exile reveal a side of the prejudice toward the disabled that would take root in the Americas. It was almost as if a heretic could be tolerated, but certainly not one giving birth to disabled children. Such superstitions went beyond human birth. In 1641 in New Haven, CT, a one-eyed servant was executed after being accused of "abominable filthynes" with a sow after she -the sow- gave birth to a piglet with one eye. Moreover, the piglet in question had a deformity shaped like a man's "instrum of generation."[78] Clear proof of the one-eyed servant's depravity.

These beliefs have a decidedly accusatory sense of self-responsibility, self-agency. The woman's actions brought about her infant's misfortune, and in the case of the accused servant, it was his base desire. In both cases, one's agency brought on the bad luck, the disability. Thus, the person or parent of the disabled child bears the total weight of responsibility. This fits squarely within the conservative protestant notion of self-agency. It harkens back to the idea that the parent's sin could result in the misfortune (i.e., disability) being visited upon the child.

In the case of the servant and Hutchinson, we witness one of the Western project's most scurrilous and most common forms of slander: sexual promiscuity united with the deep-rooted prejudices toward the disabled. The Puritans of the Massachusetts Bay Colony were not the first, nor have they been the last to stoop to such accusatory tactics. Accusations of sexually deviant behavior are often paired with other discriminatory beliefs to justify the prejudicial attitudes being forced on a group or person. If one stood out or made an argument against the status quo, or challenged one of its central tenets or practices, then one could expect slander accusing one of sexual promiscuity. Advocates for many causes would find themselves subject to these kinds of accusations: Suffragettes, abolitionists, and others were later to suffer these accusations.[79] As Snyder and Mitchell write in an endnote to "Cultural Locations of Disability":

"Patriarchal colonial authorities consistently linked the birth of disabled children with the blasphemies of women who sought to challenge male religious and civil authority."[80]

The Puritans of Colonial America imported prejudicial attitudes toward the disabled to North America from Europe. They combined them with a potent admixture of intolerance unique to the Calvinist notion of predestination they brought with them to the Americas. The upshot is that this combination of ideas would consign anyone either born with a disability or finding themselves disabled later in life to a life of neglect and social isolation. Theories of predestination were usually used to separate the "elect" or well-to-do from the misfortunes arguing along the way that such earthly benefits enjoyed by the elect were proof of god's initial favor. In contrast, the misfortunes of the poor and disabled were positive proof of god's displeasure. Keep in mind that isolation would be tantamount to a death sentence in the early days of colonization. The poor were forced to wear the punishment letter, "P," and we can assume that many colonists with slight or milder disabling conditions would find themselves in those numbers. No note was necessary when your disability identified your lot. The double-edged consequences of having a disability resulted in a loss of economic viability and the attendant social ostracizing.

To make matters worse, the scarcity of resources would cause communities to make choices that would be felt by the disabled far more keenly than the able-bodied. Indeed, only relatively healthy persons would likely have made the difficult, arduous journey. Still, many sicknesses, diseases, or accidents would have disabled many early arrivals to the new world. Moreover, the difficult sea passage itself may lead to disability conditions and diseases. And certainly, the first few lean winters would have caused several conditions and diseases. Finally, once settled, the early colonists either perish because of this lack of essential resources; or, because the rest of the community openly rejected and shunned them, find themselves exiled. The result, in either case, would be death.

Mental health issues in Colonial America were treated poorly as well. Given the state of mental health understanding at the time, it is entirely likely that the estimated 29 women who were hung or killed for accusations of witchcraft in the Colonies were individuals with mental health disabilities. The idea that women who were witches had willingly consorted with the devil was a vestige of the earlier European tradition we saw targeting the disabled and adding it to the widespread practices of misogyny, class bias, and other forms of prejudice, the utopian ideals of a new Jerusalem were looking less and less likely. As much as early Americans prided themselves on separating from their European ancestors, they imported most of their culture's forms and practices of discrimination in every shipload. While colonists brought invasive plants and animals and some diseases unknown to indigenous populations, they would also get a potent new stew of prejudices that still frame the mindset of 21st century Americans and their attitudes toward the disabled.

16

The Modern Promethean Fear of Disability: Frankenstein with an Attitude

In the mystical traditions of Jewish folklore, there are delightful and instructive tales of the golem. The golem tales are the tales found in Jewish folklore and mythology, and the golem is human-shaped magical being lacking a soul and made by a human. They are typically caused by Rabbis looking for a helpmate to assist with manual labor or during pogroms as a community defender. Unfortunately, the golem rarely provides the benefit he was initially made for, instead raining down destruction and misfortune on his maker. One of the key elements of a golem is its suggestibility. It will do as it is directed to do by its creator because, unlike humans, it lacks free will--an accusation often leveled against the disabled. Once initiated, the golem cannot veer from its predetermined path, and that path usually does not bode well for its creator, who is invariably killed by the creature. The lesson here is that one should not challenge god in his powers of creation; creation alone belongs to god. In some tales, especially in Prague and Poland, the golem wears the Hebrew word for truth emet on its forehead. The only way to stop the golem is by removing the letter aleph in the word changing it from "truth" to "death." In a 14th century commentary, Rabbi Jacob ben Shalom wrote that the law of destruction reverses the law of creation. In a sense, according to some biblical readings, the first human was a golem lacking the powers of speech and having a misshapen head. We can propose based on this reading that the entirety of the golem mythology is based on disability. The word golem in Hebrew occurring once in Psalm 139:16, may be viewed as meaning "raw" or "unfinished." clearly connoting a being not fully human or, in keeping with our interpretation, disabled. The word in Modern Hebrew means "dumb" or "helpless," again suggesting an aphasic disability. The expression then passes into Yiddish as a "goylem," further connoting clumsy or slow. Furthermore, these may be viewed as codes or euphemisms for disability. It is telling that in the 2016 Wikipedia entry for golem, a contributor writes that a golem is disabled because it cannot speak.

If this all sounds familiar, Mary Shelley will adopt and use much of the golem myth to weave a contemporary monster's most potent and famous horror story in her novel, "Frankenstein or the Modern Prometheus." In many ways, the novel is the emblematic novel of the enlightenment.

In 1816, while spending a cold and rainy summer visiting Lord Byron on Lake Geneva with her boyfriend, Percy Bysshe Shelley, Mary Shelley devised a tale about the modern golem that became Frankenstein's monster. Heeding Byron's prompt, they all agreed to create a ghost story and share it as they sat huddled around a large fireplace waiting for the inclement weather to turn. Building on tales of the golem from the Brothers Grimm and borrowing from the nascent fad of Galvanism, Shelley concocted a masterpiece of gothic horror. She was doubtlessly aware of the Galvanism of Luigi Galvani's studies of "animal magnetism" and other popular parallel movements such as Aldini's reanimation studies of 1803. Shelley would combine these with the golem into a captivating narrative of modern technology, basing her story on the cutting-edge science of her day.

In 1803, Aldini exhumed the corpse of a recently hung criminal—Thomas Forster—and tried to revivify him.[81] It is known that both

Mary and Percy attended similar demonstrations by Aldini in London. The spectacle stayed with the young writer because thirteen years later, it worked its way into her imagination to help create one of the most widely read and loved novels of all time, "Frankenstein or The Modern Prometheus." But it is also a cautionary tale of the rapacious aspect of modernity and the goals of science unleashed from human morality. Shelley's story would be the perfect admixture of 19th-century attitudes toward disability; in another vital sense, it is a parable for our times, too. Frankenstein, the golem that he is, is a helpless monster who depends on the welfare and good of others for his very existence. Man and not god creates him. Yet, society refuses him the very care he needs. They prejudge him, belittle him and scorn him. He brings to the forefront many latent fears of disability: fear of loss of bodily integrity, fear of science and medicine, fear of being a social outcast, fear of the other, fear of the grotesque. He is an insult to god, beauty, and the very scourge of a proper, well-working social order. He is the mad vision of science gone amok: A Promethean morality play. He is a metaphor for our helplessness in a cold and unfeeling universe, our fear of suffering, and our fear of death all rolled into one giant, clumsily ineffective, disabled body. His body is sewn together from the exhumed parts stolen from corpses and animals. As such, he gives rise to the many fears of contagious and infectious diseases of the 18th and 19th centuries, as well as the very subversion of humanity. He is less than human, although he is made mainly of humans. He is part animal and, as such, is outside the ken of the human. His very body dehumanizes him. His nature, condition, and disability will mean he will never be loved; he will die alone.

In terms of modern medicine and disability, many people disabled during life or born disabled find that their lives were saved or ameliorated by science but at a dear cost. Many would need to live lives changed and metamorphosed. As with Frankenstein's monster, so to the disabled are alive because of science, but it is an imperfect science: a science that can save their existence but not restore them to their former selves nor provide the level of care they desire; a science that will forever hold them in a position of awe but will wield an unrelenting power over them. Medical anomalies will be both salvaged and ravaged by medical technologies and permanently rendered oddities, curiosities. Their bodies may be healed by the parts of others (cadaverous transplantations) or animals (animal organs), or even technology (prosthetics) or innovative surgeries or technologies, but all this would come at a cost. What they will no longer be is wholly human. As such, they may find that their disabled selves will be limited, rejected by others, and at the end of it all, still cast as perpetual outsiders. The chief difference between being an outsider before the rise of modernity is that your status as an outsider is wholly dependent on systems and technologies of care.

Let us return to Mary Shelley and her story because we have one more character to flesh out: Igor. What do we make of Dr. Frankenstein's hunchbacked laboratory assistant? To begin with, he is not hunchbacked in the original story. There is no Igor in the novel. To be sure, Dr. Frankenstein has a hunchbacked assistant, but his name is Fritz, not Igor. Igor is a stock character in horror stories and folktales, but the Igor commonly associated with Frankenstein of popular imagination comes from modern cinema. He is a kind of cinematic golem, a celluloid golem first appearing in Frye's 1931 film and later in his sequels Son of Frankenstein (1939) and The Ghost of Frankenstein (1942). He appears as Ygor and is played by Bela Lugosi. However, Ygor is not hunchbacked in the original celluloid production starring Legosi but a blacksmith who had sustained a broken neck (an allusion to Hephaestus?). In the 1933 film the Mystery of the Wax Museum, the evil curator named Ivan Igor is the name of the mad curator of the wax museum but does not have a disability. In the 1953 remake called House of Wax, Igor is transformed into the curator's helpmate, deaf and mute. Film is borrowing the literary conceit of the evil character having a disability. Specifically, the hunchbacked assistant is usually fumbling and inept alluding to the long tradition of the buffoon or jester of the medieval courts and Renaissance theatre, often the only position a person with a disability could find in those times. Recall that many of the jesters were disabled or little people, and one had to "ham" it up with buffoonery. This acting would confirm the stereotypes of the disabled of the abled body viewers. As Arden Hegele ably summarizes in her paper for the International Gothic Association:

"Though the hunchbacked, devoted Igor is a relatively new addition to the Frankenstein cultural mythos, the origins of his character type are considerably older. To me, in his characteristics of physical deformity, unwavering allegiance to Frankenstein, and comic relief, Igor seems an unlikely blend of characters from early modern drama and nineteenth-century bel canto opera. As a hunchback, his most direct physical precedent is Shakespeare's villainous and scheming Richard III, though he may owe something to Verdi's ill-fated court jester, Rigoletto, who is a hunchbacked servant."[82]

Mention here must be made of the best-known disabled character in fiction, Quasimodo, or the hunchback of Notre Dame. Victor Hugo's 1831 work titled initially "Notre-Dame de Paris. 1482," introduced Quasimodo in a Medieval-era, unrequited love story. Its focus is as much on the cathedral and its environs as it was on the bell swinger's disfigurement until it was translated into English in 1833 by William Hazlitt[83]. Hazlitt was providing hungry English audiences with a book that appealed to their growing appetite for the grotesques, monsters, and oddities of the new genre of Gothic literature, as well as the nascent Victorian imagination for horror. Unfortunately, as we will see in the next section, such a hunger would be motivated by increasing pernicious stereotypes aimed at the disabled.

17

Ugly Clubs and the Cult of Beauty in the 19th Century

Throughout this history, we have seen how physical difference and disability had been used to stereotype, discriminate, and demean. At times, however, we have witnessed individuals with disabilities prevail against these obstacles and carve out a place and a living despite society's hostility towards them. One such feisty group of persons unwilling to accept the station handed them were a handful of British merchants, bankers, and ships captains who started the first "Ugly Club" in Liverpool, England, in 1753.[84] They called themselves the "Most Honourable and Facetious Society of Ugly Faces," and it consisted of bachelors whom each had facial deformity that, in their own words, made them look "odd," "remarkable," or "out of the way."

Members came from the prosperous classes of Liverpool, and any applicant had to have a facial disfigurement. However, simply having a physical disability was not enough. The rules stated that even if a prospective candidate were "humpback'd and leg'd and posses'd of all the perfections besides of the great and immortall worthy Aesop," he still would not qualify for membership. So, who was allowed to join? An entire range of various facial disfigurements and deformities were the basis for admittance ranging from "Blubber lips, little goggyling or squinting Eyes" to "a large Carbuncle Potatoe Nose."[85] Members satirized their looks and likely drew strength from their humor and camaraderie but were firm in their accepting only those with some kind of facial abnormality. In her research on ugly clubs, Susan Henderson tells us that only bachelors with facial disfigurements were admitted. The moment one of their members married, they were summarily kicked out of the club. The members were given a nickname that typically satirized their face and often came from an animal likeness that they were compared to:

"Their fellowship resembles a bestiary, with members described as 'shark,' 'pig,' 'eagle,' 'cat,' 'camel,' 'monkey,' 'cod,' 'hedgehog,' 'tortoise,' 'badger,' and other animals--with much ado about noses."[86]

Their use of animal nicknames reappropriates the strategy of reducing disabled people to an animalistic trait used in dehumanization, but here, the members are inverting that tradition. Henderson cites the cultural historian Peter Clark concerning the popularity and ubiquity of similar clubs throughout Europe. Clark estimates 25,000 such clubs might have been active in Europe in the 18th century, with over 130 in Britain alone. It is an open question to account for their popularity and why those already discriminated against because of their looks would form such organizations. We can, I believe, take a page from recent social movements, many of which choose to redefine a term of derision used against them and use it as a sign of empowerment. This lexical re-appropriation of a word or artifact is described within the fields of anthropology or cultural studies when a pejorative word used by a dominant class to insult or oppress a targeted group is adopted by that oppressed group as a tool of self-identity and is used by the targeted group as a source of community, or empowerment. Within the disability community, words such as "crip" and "gimp" are used by many contemporary persons with disabilities. The importance of such a term is precisely in who gets to use it. Only a member of that group is allowed to use the word. Anyone outsider using it is unacceptable. As such, the club's strict policies of club membership were a way of controlling their self-empowerment. In the 18th century, ugliness was seen as a significant flaw, and many influential intellectuals equated ugliness with immorality. In and throughout the 20th century, some American municipalities would go so far as to enact "Ugly laws." These clubs sought to reverse or undermine these tendencies. They would fail in thwarting that process. During the 18th century, we would witness the rise and growth of sciences that linked physiology with character and personality. The Swiss scientist, poet, and philosopher, Johann Caspar Lavater, in his "Essays on Physiognomy," claimed,

"Beauty and ugliness have a strict connection, with the moral constitution of the man. In proportion as he is morally good, he is handsome; and ugly, in proportion as he is morally bad.[87]"

Lavater's work would be widely read in France and Germany. Both nations form the epicenter of the enlightenment fuelling the nascent sciences of physiognomy and phrenology. Lavater's work influenced figures as disparate as Goethe and Blake and was central in developing the notion that beauty was directly related to one's spiritual and moral character. Closer to home, ugly laws were being passed and enacted. The great social critic Samuel Johnson, a subject of ridicule because of his odd looks due to scarring from smallpox and surgery from a lymphatic condition, would add to the link between disability and moral derision. Johnson knew firsthand as he was blind in one eye and partially deaf and would suffer from several conditions all his life.

Nonetheless, in his famous Dictionary in 1755, he would define deformity as something that provokes ridicule. This is precisely how the members of the ugly club found their greatest strength in re-appropriating the term and finding humor in their condition. Not all of the Ugly Club's contemporaries felt the same way. William Hay, a parliamentarian who had a hunched back, once wrote how he had never been a member of an ugly club. Hay went so far as to urge such clubs to disband because they provoke too much ridicule. [88] We know that Alexander Pope, who had a severe case of scoliosis and was the subject of a biographical study by Johnson, loathed the ridicule that his disability provoked in others. Thus, in this period, two clear and irreconcilable positions emerge in reaction to society's discriminatory attitudes towards the disabled: re-appropriation or pragmatic acceptance. Ugly clubs choose to attack the ugliness of social discrimination by re-appropriating and "owning" the very terms of their denigration as an act of empowerment. In contrast, others such as Johnson, Hay, and Pope chose to accept society's attitudes and still try to flourish under their hegemony, denying the social stereotypes.

Ugly clubs would continue to spread, eventually making it to America, landing first on college campuses. Some of the first to appear on American soil began at the Universities of North Carolina and Virginia, where they functioned as fraternities and social clubs. The clubs started to wane in the late 19th century with the advent of the tumult around the U.S. Civil war. Likely, the presence of returning soldiers with severe and life-changing disabilities from combat put an end to the nature of the ugly club. However, some sorts of injuries and disabilities just cannot be made fun of even by the disabled themselves. Ironically, we witness enacting "Ugly laws" passed and enforced in American cities during and after the Civil War. In 1861, San Francisco became the first American city to pass its law making it illegal to be in public if one was "diseased, maimed, mutilated, or in any way deformed to be an unsightly or disgusting object, or an improper person." Such laws would sound the death knell to ugly clubs. It was no longer funny to be ugly.

18

The Revolution Does Not Include You: The Politics of the Enlightenment and Disability

One of the chief intellectual characteristics of the Enlightenment and one that would influence the French Revolution was the misguided trust European intellectuals placed in the idea of progress. They would argue that this progress was readily achievable through the development of rational, scientific, and planned policies of social betterment. Reason and progress would solve all of our problems. Faith in the traditional order—the ancient regime-- was corrupt and inefficient. As cited earlier, Michel Foucault has skillfully charted the underbelly of this rhetoric of progress in Enlightenment mentalities. However, there is still no accurate, substantive recognition that many of the Enlightenment aims would occur on the backs of the disabled. The disabled became, in the discourse of the emergent technologies of the self and the sciences of the Enlightenment, the objects the social architects of modernity were attempting to eradicate in their projects. In the Enlightenment, whether in Baron Haussmann's demolition of unsightly Parisian slums or the forced removal of the insane to institutions, the modernist project of the Enlightenment sought to remove the abnormal, the inefficient, and the unsightly from view.

In France leading up to the 1789 revolution, a significant player in the revolution and a person with a disability, the wheelchair-using political figure Georges Auguste Couthon (1755-1794), is a fascinating illustration of these notions of progress gone amok. In many respects, Couthon symbolizes the set of contradictory attitudes and confusing actions of the revolution and one for whom the misguided policies aimed at removing the disabled were ironically embodied. Couthon played a pivotal role in the Assembly and was a significant legislator constructing substantive laws during his time as a legislator. But despite his accomplishments, it is his disability that would be the catalyst of his eventual disgrace and downfall.

Couthon lost the use of legs over time and relied on a newly designed gear-driven wheelchair for mobility. Couthon would use his wheelchair to get to and from his residence and attend the Assembly and other places he needed to go as a central figure of the revolution. In a way, Couthon may be viewed as the first of those tagged as a "super gimp." A "super gimp" in contemporary parlance is when the able-bodied world views a disabled person as inspirational and aspirational. In his case, Couthon's paralysis did not slow him down but catapulted him to more extraordinary and ambitious accomplishments. This outcome will serve as a template used to define later equally ambitious persons with disabilities. History has been less inspired by his example: less well-known as his fellow contemporaries Robespierre, St-Just, and Marat. Indeed, he has almost suffered a complete erasure from history.

To understand this erasure, let us look at an earlier portrayal of Couthon and then contrast it with more recent work. In the 1908 work, "Romances of the French Revolution," French historian Theodore Gosselin recounts a scene where Couthon encountered a large and unruly crowd. He describes it in a manner that lays the foundation for two things. First, it is an example of the nearly incredulous ability of some of the disabled; second, it simultaneously demeans Couthon by reducing him to his physical condition:

"This invalid in a bath-chair, who wished to contribute to the storm, appears amidst this outburst almost grandiose in his tenacity and energy."[89]

Gosselin has created the dichotomy of the disabled: super gimp yet still dependent. Gosselin, writing under his nom de plume, Georges Lenotre positions Couthon into a place where he is both pitied, described as an invalid, and, simultaneously, viewed as aspirational. The juxtaposition of the imagery of a disabled person being full of tenacity and energy creates the acceptable range discourse about disability in the post-modern era. This dichotomy sets the possible parameters of discourse around disability: ambitious but dependent. What seems odd is that nearly a century later, the Harvard-based, popular historian, Simon Schama, would describe Couthon dismissing the crowd as:

"It was broken by the cripple Georges Couthon, speaking from his wheelchair."[90]

Here Schama's word choice is more limiting. Schama is writing nearly a century after Lenotre and seems to have missed the disability rights movement. Moreover, Schama drops the aspirational option and prefers the limiting and derogatory descriptor "cripple" alone. By replacing the somewhat innocuous "invalid" with the accusatory "cripple," we see the failure of progress in modernity expressed in Schama's word choice. The choice of the word "cripple" in this context functions as a marker undermining any credibility of the person. Gone is the tenacity and energy, too. Schama's choice to describe a significant figure of such a historical epoch as "crippled" serves what function? Did it take a century to go from invalid to cripple? Perhaps we are witnessing the true nature of the Enlightenment mentalities as they regard disability.

Nevertheless, the underlying assumptions regarding disability reveal the power of discrimination at play in three disparate historical epochs: 1787-1909-1989. Moreover, it seems that the rhetoric and word choice become more evidently biased and directly violent in Schama's work than in Lenotre's. Thus, Schama's modernist rhetoric is decidedly influenced by two centuries of anti-disability prejudice. To be sure, the intervening period between the French Revolution and Schama's time would see the fruit of that discrimination bear its strange fruit.

However, a larger-than-life character and prominent legislator of such an important historic epoch ought to be better known. Equally, we may rightly expect our contemporary historians not to fall prey to the older prejudices but approach historical personages with a degree of honesty and accuracy.

Both Lenotre and Schama's writings are enthralled with the final days and manner of execution of Couthon. In Lenotre's work, he describes the final days of Couthon when Couthon would be seized from his home, beaten, thrown down a stairwell, and left for dead. Surviving, he crawled to safety outside his residence, where, as luck would have it, he would be stabbed, molested again, and for a second time left to die in an alley. Finally, Couthon's good luck would prevail. He would be found by loyalists and taken to the Hotel Dieu, where his wounds would be dressed, and he would be cared for by friends. However, his respite would be short-lived because not long after, agents of the opposing party found out that Couthon was still alive, arrived at the hospital, and dragged him to his execution. It is here where the story gets interesting, even if macabre.

Interesting because Couthon was responsible for the very law that would lead to his death: Couthon was the chief proponent and architect in the infamous Law of 22 Prairial--Loi de la Grande Terreur. This law would enable the Committee for Public Safety to condemn and summarily sentence suspects to death via guillotine without trial. Indeed, Couthon had been elected and served on the same Committee. From his appointment in May 1793, where he served closely with Robespierre and Saint-Just until his arrest in 1794, he would be responsible for the deaths of countless alleged anti-revolutionists. During that time, he authored some of the harsher laws promulgated--laws now leveled against him. Couthon suffered from his own hastily crafted and cruel laws. Under this law, executions would increase, and Couthon's allies, Robespierre and Saint-Just, would be summarily executed, too.

Ironically, both would be scheduled for execution on the same day as Couthon. Robespierre would be executed immediately before Couthon.

On that fateful day, Couthon and others would be carried in a tumbril—a slanted two-wheeled and open cart -to the Place de Revolution rolling past crowds that jeered, spit, and threw offal at the doomed men. He did not have his wheelchair and would likely have found the ride physically difficult. In addition, he had already survived several beatings and would be required to sit in a tilted cart unassisted. Once at the Place de Revolution, Couthon would be chosen first of the three disgraced revolutionaries to be executed. However, the crowds wanted Robespierre, and they got Robespierre. Thus, he would precede Couthon to satisfy the crowd's growing bloodlust. Having to witness the death of a close associate would have been difficult enough, but the scene described by Lenotre is even more horrible. Other historical accounts confirm Lenotre's tale as accurate, telling us that he could not be positioned correctly on the guillotine because of his paralysis. Unfazed by his pain, his executors would cruelly manipulate his body, forcing him into position for beheading.

Couthon's screams caused by the pain they put him in from forcing his body into position must have been shocking. But his screams seemed to whip up the frenzy of the crowd who called for more. They seemed to welcome the additional suffering Couthon was undergoing. In Couthon's case, his was not a quick nor an efficient death via the guillotine. His ordeal would go on for over a quarter of an hour. One wonders if the audience did not enjoy the extended torture of a person because of his disability. The executioners would need to hold Couthon since his body would not stay in the required position due to his disability. The effect of extending someone's execution while placing them in additional pain seems brutal, but according to accounts, precisely what the Parisians enjoyed. However, one needs to ask, was the barbarism a further excitement to the crowd because Couthon was disabled? Questions such as these are hard to answer, and we may never know.

19

The Early 19th Century in America: Disability as Social Burden

The early 19th century of America may be read as signaling a change in attitudes toward the disabled. This change, however, will do little to improve their social conditions despite efforts to lift the mass of Americans. As Americans began searching for a national identity in earnest, they quickly divorced themselves from many traditional religious obligations, class-based customs, and charitable institutions established by their European ancestors. Instead, they would try to erase any salient difference in a social experiment of democratic leveling or reduction of difference to the idea of the "common man," where, of course, the "common man" would be conceived in theory and practice as a white, non-disabled male. For better or worse, the disabled were going to be treated like everyone else. Starting, however, from the unequal footing, their ability to gain any social traction will be impossible. We will come to realize that any history of any subgroup in America is at best a checkered history. This history will be true for indigenous peoples, women, black and brown-skinned people, children, immigrants, the poor, and others, but it will be doubly so for the disabled in America.

The American Revolution period was advantageous for one group, the white male of moderate means in terms of political and economic progress. This group was formerly excluded from the corridors of power. In particular, this group would see their status rise during the populism of the Age of Jackson. Women, children, Native Americas, African Americans, indentured servants, immigrants, and members of many religious minorities would not fare well during this epoch. The disabled would suffer particularly poorly in early America. The disabled unmoored from care, albeit tenuous care of the institutions and supportive communities in Europe, would find themselves adrift in hostile waters in the new nation. At play here are the well-known concepts of manifest destiny and the Jacksonian emphasis on individualism and populism, which by mid-century Emerson would enlarge into his notion of "self-reliance."

Such a call for self-reliance would profoundly impact the disabled where the virtues of interdependence, community, and social support would be needed. Recall that in the 1700's care for the disabled fell upon the towns, so the decidedly antigovernmental twist to the conditions that would give rise to Emersonian self-reliance would hit the disabled harder than others. As the young nation expanded its physical borders, it sought to eradicate the boundaries between the disabled and abled bodied by viewing disability as a burden to the nation's potential successes. The practical aspect of viewing the disabled as no different than anyone else and therefore not deserving of any particular treatment, entitlement, or benefit would have disastrous consequences for the disabled in America. Salient differences would be erased, and the disabled would be melted into the melting pot of America.

The success of any given American citizen was attributed to that person's will to improve and better themselves alone by one's pluck and determination, rising in economic prosperity and gaining political power. But the practical obstacles of creating success were arrayed against you. The earlier Puritan practice of excommunicating or shunning those members it did not approve of would become the widespread practice of "warning out[91]" or "passing on" where the individual with a disability or their family was informed that they were not welcome in this community. It may even have meant loading the disabled person into a cart and depositing them in the next town. Colonial Massachusetts towns were allowed to deny residency to anyone they thought would rely on public support or dependency. Those persons deemed worthy of town citizenship could partake of the "freedoms" of town life, including property ownership, fishing, hunting, use of tidal waters, and pasturage. In short, to carve out a life. Denying a person access to these freedoms was equivalent to issuing a death sentence. In addition, of course, the incidence of any injury, disability, or physical difference could likely prevent or make it far more challenging to achieve any economic autonomy. The last state to abolish this practice of "warning out" was Vermont in 1817.

The emergent American ethic needed one to strike out on one's own and earn one's place in life. One did this by testing one's mettle by moving to the frontier, going west, pioneering, prospecting, homesteading, and ultimately, if lucky, prospering. Despite the difficulties of such living, failure in such a scheme was and is still viewed as self-caused. This naïve understanding of social forces, economies, culture, and class became one of the central identifying features of the new nation. If each individual succeeded, the belief maintained, so would the nation as a whole succeed. As the French philosopher and traveler Alexis de Tocqueville noted during his 1830's travels across America, Americans were so uniquely self-reliant that he found he had to coin a new word, "individualistic," to describe them. Unfortunately, the ethic of self-reliance transmogrified by mid-century into rugged individualism and social solipsism by the 21st century.

Because disability had been reconceived or pathologized during the enlightenment, any emphasis on individualism would pose dire problems for the disabled; the opposite of this new individualism is the social interdependency occasioned by disability. To borrow a phrase, it takes a village to raise a disabled child. Consequently, as Snyder and Mitchell write, any hint of disability and dependence would be viewed as contrary to the goals of the young and growing nation and its new creed of rugged individualism:

"The nineteenth-century approached dependency as a disservice to a nation that must invest it its manifest destiny.[92]"

Later in the early 20th century, this explains why FDR, his handlers, and the press corps would go to such lengths to "hide" his disability and use of a wheelchair. A disabled leader was un-American.

As a result of these exclusionary practices of the early-to-mid-19th century, persons with disabilities would be grouped alongside slaves, women, immigrants, and the indentured servants collectively occupying a zone of dependency, powerlessness, and endemic poverty. This mentality echoed in the scornful derision of Davy Crockett's disbelief when he lost the race for his seat in the U.S. House of Representatives in 1835 to a one-legged lawyer named Andrew Huntsman, saying,

"Since you have chosen to elect a man with a timber toe to succeed me, you may all go to hell and I will go to Texas."[93]

The invective evident in Crockett's words would be borne from the pervasive practices of the appropriateness of denying both political and civil rights for the disabled along with other members of the dispossessed occupying those zones of dependency. Deprived of economic, voting, and civil rights, the promise of the new nation's guarantee of rights and liberties would soon be seen as a hollow promise to the disabled as well as the other marginalized groups. People's lack of economic opportunities, freedoms, and liberties became a recipe for creating a permanent underclass. Moreover, the economic reality of the Jacksonian period would see the financial panic of 1819 and the depression of 1837 further threatening the new middle class and making it even more difficult for all, but especially for those with disabilities. Having no viable economic pathway, most Americans with disabilities sunk into lives of misery and poverty, eking out what living they could on the margins of society. They would turn to simple crafts, panhandling and begging, and, in some cases, crime to support themselves. Just as likely, they may find themselves uprooted, passed on, or placed into poorhouses or almshouses. These same pressures started to breed fear and distrust in many Americans toward the disabled, and they would start looking for scapegoats to blame. As Eric Foner writes,

"It was an axiom of eighteenth-century political thought that dependents lack a will of their own, and thus did not deserve a role in public affairs.[94]"

The disabled would, in turn, become scapegoats for others hurting from such rapacious economic times. Consequently, the disabled would be viewed as lacking a will to improve and would often find themselves blamed as a cause of the social and economic decay of the young nation. The view was that the disabled were a major burden holding back the nation's economic success. This unfounded rhetoric would find purchase throughout the 19th and later into the 20th and 21st centuries. Again, this would arise even though disability would have remained nearly the same in America as elsewhere through history and place. There seems no good reason for such a widespread prejudice. In fact, many Americans became disabled from the rigors of frontier life, disease, little to no access to medical care, and many of them would rise to prominence and flourish in the new nation. We know many prominent Americans were disabled even when the historical record glosses over their disabilities. In her research for her "Bold Women" series, Amanda Hughes reminds us how many important, and prominent Americans were disabled:

"Thomas Jefferson, Washington Irving and Cotton Mather had speech difficulties. The renowned artist John Brewster Jr. was deaf, Colonel William Prescott was visually impaired and Stephen Hopkins, who signed the Declaration of Independence, had Cerebral Palsy. He is quoted as saying when he signed the famous document, "My hand trembles, my heart does not."[95]

However, none of this could remedy the deeper cultural prejudices starting to sink roots in the new soil of America. Their successes, however aspirational, ran against the mainstream conditions and typical lives of most of their fellow Americans with disabilities. These conditions would prove to be as difficult as the ones they or their ancestors had left. It is important to note that each of the prominent Americans above had a measure of economic fortune and access to resources to make it in America. Not all were as lucky or so well situated. It is worth keeping in mind the tenuous nature of success for 19th century Americans; their hardscrabble lives were balancing on a thin line of the barest economic survival. There were many ways an early American could suffer an economic downturn leading to utter disaster. Persons living in or close to conditions of abject poverty could easily find themselves overwhelmed with a series of crop failures or due to being widowed, orphaned, or alcoholic. If one were already a member of a dispossessed group (e.g., woman, child, racial minority, indigene, religious nonconformist, etc.), then one's likelihood of success would be even more perilous and failure more certain. Adding the challenges of living with a physical or mental disability, and your fate was sealed. The promises of America were dashed.

20

The 19th Century Transatlantic Reality of Disability and Labor

By any estimate, life in 19th century America was challenging. The promises of an easy and bountiful life would prove an impossible dream for most immigrants. Living a brutal existence on the frontier, barely making a living, and carving out a sustainable farm from a vast and at times formidable natural world that Europeans were mainly unaccustomed to would prove challenging for the best. These realities would doubtless make life even more difficult for the disabled. Accidents leading to permanent disability such as the one that happened to Joseph Whiting Stock were common. Stock was disabled when a wagon he was repairing fell on him as a youth. His paralysis would not deter him from becoming one of the most popular "folk" artists of the 19th century. But the success of Stock would be uncommon. Accidents from farming, mining, lumbering, railroads, fishing, and hunting, as well as those related to the squalor and rampant diseases present in most of the cities and the challenges created by rapid urbanization and the pollution generated by the unrestrained growth of industry, would have kept a steady stream of the adventitiously disabled joining the ranks of those born with a disability. In this period, despite the demographic increase, we find that people with disabilities risked facing social ostracizing and outright rejection based on early American assumptions covered above. Still, the remnants of long-held prejudices from Europe and abroad would never be entirely jettisoned. One of the overlooked aspects of the metaphor of a "melting pot" is that you need to bring your previous culture's prejudices along with your other luggage. The old prejudices against people with disabilities would be brought to the new world, finding fertile ground to blossom and grow. The result is that the combination of the new discriminatory practices developed by the American experiment combined with the attitudes and beliefs from the immigrant's homes would conspire to check the potential successes of many Americans with disabilities. At best, the upper classes imbued with their Protestant ideals of an ethic of reform, progressivism and hard work would view the disabled as members of the 'worthy poor' so long as they could still be employed. Charity may be provided for them. Not so for "unworthy poor." The "unworthy poor" were more often those who, for whatever reason, could not usually work because of their disability. As a result, they would be relegated to the margins of society.

In some places, "Poor Relief" laws sought to provide some succor to this burgeoning and now chronic underclass. Workhouses might welcome the mildly disabled, but the more severally disabled would be routinely excluded--a practice imported from Europe.

As a result of the processes of institutionalization by the mid-19th century, most people with disabilities will discover themselves more and more dependent on innovations in the developing medical profession for cures and the largesse of the upper classes for their economic survival.[96] The sheer number of medical quackeries and nostrums would undoubtedly exacerbate the health conditions of many living with disabilities. The risks for factory workers were many, and the injuries often would leave one permanently disabled and no longer employable. The absence of any job-related insurance or support would further exacerbate the downward spiral of the disabled worker.

Ironically, many of those disabled were disabled because of working in the factories owned by the same class of fellow citizens that they would later need to turn to and rely on for charity. Thus, workplace injuries were high on the causes of disablement in the 19th century, and the dependence of the disabled became nested or embedded within the social fabric of the burgeoning industrial capitalists. As journalist Lisa Hix writes:

"Society didn't have a concept of "lacking ability" until industrialization, which, by the 19th century, had created an obsessive demand for "able-bodied workers" who could rapidly churn out mountains of goods."

Therefore, the very zeal for productivity, profit, and efficiency we see becoming part of the American mentality would create a new and subtle nuance to the concept of disability: it will be informed by those who cannot work. In short, disability in America will always imply disindustry, unemployability. In America, the crucial distinction became whether you could work or produce. One's self-worth took on a decidedly utilitarian flavor in the 19th century and remains essentially unchanged in contemporary America. Many of the concepts that constitute a notion of disability today promulgated by government agencies revolve entirely around one's employability.

As medicine lagged, the industrial capitalists were setting the terms of debate for the disabled. They alone were in charge. As a result, the young American republic was slow to adopt safety measures in workplaces and transportation compared to Europe. A cheap source of labor was essential to the developing industrial economies, and defining persons by their ability to work become the critical marker. As industrialization spread and the Protestant work ethic became engrained through all levels of society, the body became the battleground for citizenship: a good citizen was a productive member of society. A disabled body would be a problem. If a person was no longer physically or mentally able to be a productive worker, they were deemed defective, disabled. The able-bodied and financially secure upper classes of the 19th century could demonstrate their political and moral generosity by giving to charitable organizations that sought to return the mildly disabled individual to productive work. "Charities," says Jaipreet Virdi-Dhesi, "became popular avenues for the lay public to demonstrate their moral and social values as a way of contributing to national responsibility." [97] In addition, As Karen Bourrier explores in "The Measure of Manliness," one's physical appearance revealed one's moral character and chances at economic success. However, the values, appearances, and characters expressed were entirely cast along with a utilitarian and ableist narrative. The disabled themselves would be left entirely behind. Yet at the same time--the very centers of economic utility--the mills, factories, and manufacturing centers became the places of peril and disability. The very basis for American prosperity was the vehicle for disability and social estrangement. In the textile mills up and down the major rivers of New England, we would find a hazardous working condition where workers, including children, worked long hours on dangerous machinery. Because of the dangerous machinery, many would lose fingers, hands, arms, or worse. In a very palpable sense, America is built of the disabling of those who created it.

Exposure to toxic dyes, chemicals, and additives in wool and textile processing would lead to disabilities and disabling conditions. In addition, the deafening roar of the machinery would lead to hearing loss and impairment. Respiratory diseases became the norm from working in factories in the industrial regions of Europe, England, and America, including "shoddy fever' from inhaling the airborne particulates called by the workers "devil's dust" and first identified by the English doctor, Charles Thackrah in 1832.[98]

We can witness the result of these conditions on the workers' lives in accounts of the time. For example, in England, the testimony from a young mill worker, Benjamin Gomersal from Bradford, who worked in a worsted mill in Leeds at nine years old, records the dangerous and disastrous effects of working in a mill. He tells us:

"I was a healthy and strong boy, when I first went to the mill. When I was about eight years old, I could walk from Leeds to Bradford (ten miles) without any pain or difficulty, and with a little fatigue; now I cannot stand without crutches! I cannot walk at all! Perhaps I might creep up stairs. I go upstairs backwards every night! I found my limbs begin to fail, after I had been working about a year. It came on with great pain in my legs and knees. I am very much fatigued towards the end of the day. I cannot work in the mill now."[99]

In England, such testimonies would eventually reach the upper classes, who started to lobby for reform. In America, it was a slower and more protracted process; such accounts failed to be published or circulated. Not having a historic upper class desirous of providing charity, America's industrial magnates wanted only to engage in profit-making enterprises. Thus, they would forever be searching for cheaper pools of labor. If profit were their only aim, then business magnates would hardly offer capital to publishing houses that would be printing material exposing the dangers of their moneymaking enterprises.

Consequently, we do not see anything near the same response in America that occurred in England with the publication of William Dodd's "A Narrative of the Experience and Sufferings of William Dodd: a Factory Cripple," who recounts his life working in the mills from the age of five. The hazardous and treacherous nature of the work led to his disability. Dodd's first job placed so much strain on his "right knee" that the joint was permanently disabled. Remember that there would be no available medical treatment for such an injury. Within a few years, Dodd was, in his own words, a "cripple." He describes the difficulty his work caused on his joints:

"My joints were like so many rusty hinges that had laid for years. I had to get up an hour earlier, and, with the broom under one arm as a crutch, and a stick on my hand, walk over the house till I had got my joints in working order." [100]

Dodd's account would be widely circulated in England, but similar versions in America were rare despite overwhelming records of similar accidents and disabilities caused by industrial working environments. The photography of Lewis Hines for the National Child Labour Committee (NCLC), for example, would lead to reforms in child labor but not until well into the beginning of the 20th century. We are more likely to find sensational accounts of injuries such as the tragic injury sustained by Hannah E. Leary of Salem, Massachusetts, who operated a carding machine at the Naumkeag Steam Cotton Company. [101] In July of 1894, her hair was caught in the carding machine, and her scalp was partially torn off. The lurid accounts of her injury and hospitalization reveal macabre sensationalism we see in the "yellow journalism" of the time, but many injuries went unreported. We sense this because the original coverage by the "Boston Post" reported that a similar injury had recently happened to another worker in a nearby mill just a week before. What is telling is that the press and their readers would soon lose interest after hearing that she would recover from her injury. No books would be written, no legislation enacted to improve the unsafe working conditions. This is a sharp contrast to England. Dodd's England would be a more fruitful place for change than in America. The forces at play in America would be decidedly and firmly in the industrialists' camp who would resist all calls for improvement of working conditions of their laborers.

Back in England, Dodd's travails with industrial accidents and the authorities were not over either. He would later recount how members of his immediate family would be similarly disabled. His two sisters and brother-in-law were all disabled from their time in the factory. After one of his sister's hands was crushed and made functionally unusable, her employer gave her a total of 17 shillings for her injury--the equivalent of a week's worth of pay. As Dodd writes, "I need not say that she has been a cripple ever since, and can do very little towards getting a living." Dodd himself would later lose an arm while working as a mill clerk. Dodd would write the important and influential "The Factory System: Illustrated" published in 1842. His books would raise the hackles of the politicians and factory owners, and they would be attacked in the press as hyperbole. Dodd was even attacked on the floor of Parliament. He had hit a nerve; Dodd's books stirred controversy with the monied classes. Dodd was attacked in the House of Commons as a fraud and unreliable source by John Bright, an MP, and Quaker, who would argue while chairing a debating committee looking at the Factories Bill in 1844:

"I have in my hand two publications; one is The Adventures of William Dodd the Factory Cripple and the other is entitled The Factory System - both books have gone forth to the public under the sanction of the noble Lord Ashley. I do not wish to go into the particulars of the character of this man, for it is not necessary to my case, but I can demonstrate, that his books and statements are wholly unworthy of credit. Dodd states that from the hardships he endured in a factory, he was "done up" at the age of thirty-two, whereas I can prove that he was treated with uniform kindness, which he repaid by gross immorality of conduct, and for which he was discharged from his employment."

Despite saying he would not attack Dodd's character, Bright's charge of immorality and fraud would be a damning condemnation. Bright's accusations echo the kinds of rebuttals most disability activists face: the status quo always attacks them for being ungrateful. However, the cause of their troubles was due to their flawed character (gross immorality).

In Bright's case, he had a position he was protecting. Bright was a passionate advocate for "free trade," worrying that any bad press would hurt the British textile industry. Because of these pressures, Dodd would eventually be forced to immigrate to America. It is fascinating to note that while history loses track of Dodd, Bright would be honored by students at Cornell University as the first honorary member of their "Irving Literary Society" and even the socialist British historian, A. J. P. Taylor glowingly writes of Bright's legacy and achievements despite his blatant ableism:

"John Bright was the greatest of all parliamentary orators. He had many political successes. Along with Richard Cobden, he conducted the campaign which led to the repeal of the Corn Laws. He did more than any other man to prevent the intervention of this country (Britain) on the side of the South during the American Civil War, and he headed the reform agitation in 1867 which brought the industrial working class within the pale of the constitution. It was Bright who made possible the Liberal party of Gladstone, Asquith, and Lloyd George, and the alliance between middle-class idealism and trade unionism, which he promoted, still lives in the present-day Labour Party."[102]

Sadly, we would see these sorts of accolades piled on many other American politicians spouting prejudice toward the disabled.

With such a holy alliance allied against the disabled, it is little wonder that the lives of the 19th century disabled were so impoverished. The Victorian age almost single-handedly created the concept of the needy, disabled person. Social reformers of every stripe had indoctrinated the nascent middle classes into becoming obsessed with "normal" where normal alone meant able-bodied. And quite naturally, the able-bodied started perceiving the disabled as a social and political problem. A problem that needed to be dealt with and soon. Charitable institutions, workhouses, and similar institutions were set up as reformist causes, but the 19th-century notion of "kindness" would as likely kill you as save you. In England, mid-century reformist-minded doctors sought to improve the conditions of the institutionalized with a short-lived movement originating in the late 1700s called the "moral treatment." Advocates of this movement would take their lead from European hospitals to discourage physical restraints, such as shackles or straitjackets. But these reformist-minded individuals would be fighting an uphill and losing battle. By the mid-to-late-20th century, America completed its process of deinstitutionalization rather than supporting those needing institutional care and the institutions themselves. In short, it abandoned the maintenance of these institutions and those within them.

The entrenched powers of the 19th century medical and psychological communities, the educated and learned classes, financial power-brokers, industrialists, free-traders, and politicians on both sides of the political spectrum will join pro-slavery racists and populist demagogues into a singularly powerful "union" bent on oppressing persons with disabilities and erasing the contributions of persons with disabilities and driving them into hiding. More destructively, as in the well-known struggles of Helen Keller, Carrie Buck, and others, institutions and practices made it challenging for disabled people to make a life, any kind of life in America. However and tragically, as technologies and institutions became efficient, the emergent tendency to completely reduce or remove the disabled altogether became more destructive.

21

Slavery and the Disabled Narrative

To borrow and adapt a phrase from Karl Marx, heretofore all struggles have been the struggles of the disabled. Thus, it should come to little surprise to the critical historian that the attempted justification for slavery's frequent mention is made of ableist narratives. Indeed, in one manner, slavery is built on the very idea of the powerful binary of ideal versus disabled. A slave's worth was their physical strength, endurance, and ability, while worthlessness would be the opposing terms: weakness, lethargy, and inability. Given the predominance of the discriminatory beliefs and practices aimed at the disabled throughout Western history, it is almost necessary that we see advocates of slavery glom onto the pre-existing discriminatory rhetoric aimed at the disabled. We see precisely this attempt. The dominating slaveholders found it essential to use whatever ideological tools at hand to justify their inhumane practice. We see clear evidence of this in an article published in "The New Orleans Medical and Surgical Journal" that sought to "scientifically" demonstrate that any alleged difference between the races was due to physical deficits, "diseases and physical peculiarities of the negro race."[103] In short, slavery became necessary because non-white people were associated with and viewed as disabled and incapable of looking out for themselves. It was also believed essential to create a long-sought pool of cheap labor and a compliant workforce to fuel America's economic ascendancy.

In other quarters, arguments would be constructed to show that "under conditions of freedom and equality, African Americans were prone to disability."[104] North Carolina Senator and pro-slavery advocate, John C. Calhoun would argue slavery is needed precisely because of the excessive number of disabled former slaves (e.g., he cites the numbers of the deaf, dumb, and blind former slaves among others) that one finds in the North where the "ancient relations between the races" had been altered[105]. The mental gymnastics that the pro-slavery apologists contorted their rhetoric to to justify their inhumane practice of brutalizing their fellow humans could be found in the kind of theorizing of someone such as the American physician Samuel A. Cartwright who in 1851 delivered an address before the Medical Association of Louisiana where he first identified, drapetomania, a psychiatric condition that caused slaves to be possessed by an irrational desire for freedom and which would often lead them to do such foolish things as try to escape their bondage! His treatment for drapetomania? He prescribed removing both of the slave's big toes to prevent running away. Thus, the purportedly disabled are rendered more disabled and for their own good. Slaves could be further reduced to total dependence by disabling them. He defined a condition he called "dysaesthesia aethiopica" which he claimed causes slaves to be lazy. It is, I believe, essential to grasp that these theorists believed that these "conditions made themselves manifest in the bodies of the slaves." If left untreated, claimed Cartwright, the disease would lead to "lesions" and other physical disabilities. The entailment here is that slave owner--much like the superintendent of the asylum and the factory owner--meant only to help the object of his concern. Again we hear the echo here of the Victorian notion of "kindness" that was essentially going to maim and kill you. We heard a similar presentiment in the medical community and their desire to improve the disabled. Think of the character Hippolyte from Flaubert's Madame Bovary, where Doctor Charles Bovary tries to "help" him and his clubfoot only to make him worse off than he was before--this becomes a metaphor for the treatment of the disabled in modernity. Too often, for the disabled, the cure is as bad or worse than the condition.

Race narratives were not the only place where the dominant classes tried to extend their ableist hegemony over the dominated classes. We see it used in movements against women's suffrage, too. By attempting to legitimate their stranglehold of power by using "science" infused with ableist narratives, we start to see the unsavory side effects of the modernist project. Women were viewed as infantile, incapable of analytical acumen harkening back to Aristotle's idea that they were incomplete men or, to put it bluntly, disabled men. Quasi-scientific theories will abound, justifying these prejudices, and many rely on notions of incapacity, inability, or dis-ability.

Immigrants would find themselves on the losing side of the narrative as well. In 1855, Edward Jarvis was tasked with preparing a report for the Commonwealth of Massachusetts. He was asked to analyze the state of mental health of its poorer classes. The good doctor found that "Irish Labourers" were disproportionately found in the ranks of the insane in Massachusetts and concluded it was due to their inherent "lack of sensibility, "greater irritability," and "intemperance."[106] Again, these assumptions are based on lack of capacity or capability. These new citizens had recently emigrated from Ireland, escaping poverty and oppression looking for a more promising place of opportunity. Instead, they would find themselves being fit into a new medicalized subset of deviance and disability. It is important to stress that Jarvis set out to show that "idiocy" was due to several factors, including one's "physical condition." He argued that the recent influx of "aliens" has contributed to the rise of "idiocy" in the Massachusetts Commonwealth. This sort of stratagem becomes part of the long trail of anti-immigrant prejudices still operative in the 21st century. Jarvis will be building on the budding 19th-century tradition in the psychology of viewing mental disturbances as emanating from one's body. As such, the body can become a predictor of all kinds of instability, psychological and social. In the hands of the trained psychoanalyst who can "read" these predictors, it becomes a way to classify a person's future acts by just looking at their present physiognomy. These officials ally themselves with the wealthy and powerful, and you have a tool for oppression. In the hands of the wealthy arbiters of class, the body becomes the litmus test to segregate the dominant class from the outsiders: women, persons of color, the poor, the disabled, immigrants, and children. These stereotypes would parallel and legitimate the 19th-century sciences where phrenologists would claim that one's character is derived from the shape of one's skull. Phrenology or what was called "the only true science of mind," derived from the ideas of the Viennese physician Franz Joseph Gall (1758-1828) and his work, "The Anatomy and Physiology of the Nervous System in General, and of the Brain in Particular" and was later developed by Johann Kaspar Spurzheim (1776–1832) and George Combe (1788–1858).[107] Gall's original research was based on his observations of inmates in jails and asylums. From those observations, he claimed to detect traits associated with criminal and aberrant behaviors based on the prisoners' skull shapes and sizes. He would proceed, he believed, to name and correctly map the cranial bases for murder, theft, and so on. Gall's work gave rise to the idea of a "degenerate," meaning someone immoral or criminal. Reviewing the etymology of this word reveals its true meaning. Coming from the Latin of the late 15th-century word, "degeneratus" meaning 'no longer of its kind" and composed of the stems "de" meaning "away from" and genus meaning "race," or "kind," we see the ideological intents of this outlook. When later grounded in the burgeoning theory of evolution, the degenerate becomes the forces slowing the progress of evolution. In Italy, Cesare Lombroso had started using the new art of photography to photograph criminals to determine if criminals were degenerating physically. The founder of eugenics, Sir Francis Galton, used a similar technique to determine the "ideal" human body types by super-imposing overlapping photographs of "normal" bodies. Any excess or difference would be labeled as abnormal.

Spurzheim grounded phrenology in contemporary moral, scientific, and religious notions, building on Gall's theories and ideas; he would bring phrenology to the shores of America, where it would find a receptive and fruitful audience and thrive in the burgeoning middle classes. Spurzheim arrived in America in 1832 for a six-month lecture tour converting thousands of eager attendees, lectured at Harvard and Yale—and he spoke at Yale's commencement. His frenetic travels at the Ivy schools and other prestigious institutions may inadvertently have led to his premature death. Despite his short tenure in America, he would be hailed by Ralph Waldo Emerson as one of the world's greatest minds. The fast-paced tour would not only lead to his death but an even greater celebrity. No other than the esteemed dean of the Harvard Medical College, Dr. John Warren, would volunteer to perform Spurzheim's autopsy, John James Audubon sketched his funeral mask, and Harvard president Josiah Quincy arranged his funeral arrangements.[108] He would be bestowed with the honor of being buried in the Mount Auburn Cemetery, and his brain would be removed, preserved, and kept at the Boston Athenaeum for future study.[109] His influence was so widespread that the august medical journal the American Journal of Medical Sciences would eulogize him, writing: "The prophet is gone, but his mantle is upon us."

The mantle would soon fit another advocate. The British phrenologist George Combe would eagerly pick it up and don the mantle, further popularizing phrenology in America. His 1828 work, "The Constitution of Man," was one of the bestselling books of the nineteenth century where it sold over 200,000 copies in the U.S alone.[110] Phrenology influenced President James A. Garfield, who attended lectures on phrenology as a student at the Western Reserve Eclectic Institute (now Hiram College). Combe's work was made popularized by Fowler's New York-based "Phrenological Cabinet." The Fowlers became interested in phrenology while students at Amherst and opened a popular "clinic" to read people's skulls in New York City. Garfield visited the Fowler's establishment.

Orson Fowler, a ministry student and Amherst College graduate, became an enthusiast and started offering "readings" for 2 cents apiece. One of the readings was of his classmate and friend, the future Rev.

Henry Ward Beecher--the brother of Harriet Beecher Stowe. His skull, Fowler interpreted, showed evidence of a "strong social brain" with "very large Benevolence." Along with his younger brother Lorenzo, Orson crisscrossed the young nation expounding to audiences everywhere "the truth of phrenology," and many would buy into it. The brothers would "read" the young Clara Barton's skull and eventually settle down in New York City by the 1840's advertising phrenological profiles at their "Phrenological Cabinet." The "cabinet" would see many famous people walk through the doors to have their skulls assayed by the Fowlers. Phrenology became so fashionable in America that style-conscious women started adopting hairstyles to accentuate the more flattering aspects of their skulls.

19th-century notables such as Horace Greeley, Walt Whitman, Brigham Young, and P.T. Barnum joined President Garfield in having their skulls "read." Although decidedly in the minority, a few skeptics such as former President John Quincy Adams and Mark Twain would doubt phrenology's effectiveness. Upon the latter's skull, the Fowlers found a "cavity" where the ability to be humorous was located. Twain would prove the Fowlers wrong here, cavity or not.

All humor aside, phrenology was taken seriously by the mainstream medical and scientific communities. Indeed, after Garfield's assassination in 1881 by Charles Guiteau, phrenology was used as evidence during his trial.

"Several physicians who examined the accused were called by the defense to give their expert testimony. Dr. Edward Spitzka gave a lengthy analysis based on what he considered correlative neuroanatomy. Spitzka commented on Guiteau's cranial asymmetry, but conceded that the difference between the two sides of the brain did not "constitute a diseased difference."[111]

This American obsession with phrenology is a species of the millennia-long desire to establish an idealized body type. Constructing this hierarchy places an idealized type at the pinnacle. Unlike the earlier Greek attempts at building a hierarchical order of homocentric beauty or the Renaissance-era attempts represented by the Vitruvian illustration based on its idealized mathematical proportions, the modernist attempt starts to peer just beneath the surface to plumb the true depths of identity. The exact shape and stuff of your crania reveal your true and ineluctable nature. The next step will be to divine your genetic chemistry. In the context of the late 19th-century rise of science, these efforts will be used to justify a racial, sexist, and ableist hegemony over those placed on the margins of society.

22

Disability and Grotesquery in Flaubert's "Madame Bovary"

But before we turn to the twentieth century, let us look at how the mid-to-late-19th century frames the discussion around disability. Mention was made of a character -Hippolyte- from one of Flaubert's novels, "Madame Bovary." It is a central novel in the development of the modern novel and a useful barometer to the attitudes of middle-class culture on both sides of the Atlantic. In the final scenes of Flaubert's seminal 1857 novel, Emma Bovary -the novel's protagonist- is horrified by a blind and deformed beggar who accosts her while she is riding a carriage to Yonville. It is a pivotal moment in the novel. Yet, the character remains unnamed but returns later in the novel to pass beneath her window as Emma lies dying. Contrasting the depiction of Thersites where he is at least named, Flaubert's monster remains anonymous, stripped of all autonomy and identity. In his anonymity, he becomes everyman, or, to be more exact, every person's fears. The embodiment of Emma's fears is made manifest in the disabled body of a member of the "useless" and anonymous poor. Scholars variously interpret him as a symbolic personification of evil--the devil; or, somewhat rather more generously, as the concept of the normal which both Flaubert and his character, Emma, find so distasteful in Bourgeois France. His ugliness and the discordancy of his voice horrify Emma.

His presence signals the final collapse of Emma; and is, in a manner, a coup de grace signaling her incapacity and eventual death. This message is solidified by his re-appearance when he appears singing a funereal dirge under her window as she lay dying. As such, he acts as a sign of death; in this sense, he becomes Charon ferrying Emma over to the other side. As a psychopomp, the beggar Charon is typified as an old and unkempt man whose body is described as unclean, unsightly, and his eyes, as Dante renders them, unseeing eyes of fire. In short, characterizations of a person with multiple disabilities. He becomes every person's fears of bodily disintegration, death, and loss of autonomy at the root of most prejudices against the disabled. The beggar for Emma becomes her embodied Charon signaling her greatest fears. As we all do, she, too, has failed to live the lives we imagined burdened by the limitations of body and disability. Modern science and medicine and their promises to remove those limitations have failed.

It is, of course, well known that since antiquity, the blind are being given a significant role as soothsayers, prophets, and prognosticators capable precisely because of their loss of earthly sight. Seers from antiquity are often given this ability, as was Tiresias. Scholars of disability call this a "fantasy of compensation," and it is a common trope used when describing a person with a disability. Often, the belief holds that the loss of one human ability signals a greater sensitivity or keenness in an adjacent ability. Thus, we start the Western literary canon with the blind poet Homer, pass through Tiresias and Oedipus and arrive at Flaubert's Beggar.

We find it in George Eliot's club-footed Philip Wakem in her "The Mill on the Floss." Eliot grants Philip a greater sensitivity to art and people's feelings when compared to the other male characters in the novel. And while Flaubert's anonymous blind man functions as a prophet -though blind, he can see into the future and of Emma's impending death. However, he is only a minor, imperfect prophet -a prophet only capable of offering a bleak future.

But the blind beggar was not the first instance of Flaubert using disability in the novel. Earlier in the novel, Emma's husband, Doctor Charles Bovary, operates on the clubfoot of a village boy, Hippolyte. Clear parallels with Oedipus and Philip Wakem emerge here. We should emphasize that Hippolyte is perfectly happy with his disability and he in no way understands his club foot as a disability. Indeed, Flaubert presents an interesting situation here because Emma and the pompous, know-it-all, Monsieur Homais—the town's pharmacist—convince the unwilling Charles to perform the complicated surgery and convince Hippolyte he is disabled. They need to convince him that he needs mending in the first place. Hippolyte, as we mentioned, is unaware he is disabled.

Moreover, the surgery is less for any actual benefit Hippolyte might gain than in the name of progress and patriotism. Homais' patriotic zeal, ideals of perfection, faith in science, and Emma's distaste for the unusual are the catalysts for the surgery. As such, Hippolyte becomes a harbinger for how the disabled are and will be treated in the modern medical and scientific world. Those with physical differences are reconceived as disabled from around 1830, especially in France and Germany, when doctors start pioneering operations on so-called "orthopedic deformities." These "deformities" were viewed as aberrations in the body's symmetry, not necessarily a functional limitation. While Charles and Homais represent the new modern men of progress and science, Emma, the aesthetics of modernity, Hippolyte, harkens back to the medieval era where people seemed to accommodate living with a disability. He is unaware of any real problems caused by his clubfoot because there are none. His antagonists must allude to the future where such deviations from normalcy can and will be treated; to go untreated would be unfathomable, unmodern. Modernity convinces because it holds the promise of a future, a future, incidentally, that is empty of any meaning precisely because none of us owns a crystal ball or is gifted with prophetic vision. Medical science and mysticism unite in the promise of modernity.

To encourage the skeptical Hippolyte, Homais appeals to Hippolyte's sense of national pride and masculinity in an attempt to shame Hippolyte into the surgery. After all, with his ability "restored" he could ably serve in the army. Again, we see the identification of the social good—the society, the state—relying on the removal of disability. This is what finally convinces a skeptical Hippolyte to undergo the operation. An operation for which Charles knows as a doctor he is not qualified nor skilled enough to perform.

Immediately after the surgery, the local paper runs an article describing it with clear miraculous undertones: "Hasn't the time come to cry out that the blind shall see, the deaf hear, the lame walk?" The supernatural contrasts with the scientific by the scientific becoming mythic. In this sense, science uncovers what god designs. Modernity tries to redesign god's original flawed designs freeing his creations from imperfections.

The divine attribution theory of disability explained the origins of disability, and it would have structured Hippolyte's understanding of his clubfoot. Modernist science seeks to remove the flaws found in god's handiwork and replace them with the miracles of modern science. The surgeon becomes a wizard of sort straddling the liminal space between the divine and the natural. But lest we think we have traveled far from antiquity, recall that humans' overweening pride and ambition (hubris) was always punished by the gods (wrath): humans always get their comeuppance. The surgery is botched. Science fails to overcome what God wrought. As powerful as 19th-century science and medicine was, it was still beholden to the natural and supernatural realms. Man deposes but God or nature disposes.

The message cannot be more apparent to the young Hippolyte: He is standing in the way of progress, the future. Hippolyte himself is the source of his disability. This motif is common; disability is a character flaw willed by the very person with a disability. We see this motif in other works. For example, in Spyri's 1881 children's novel, "Heidi," Clara can walk only after Peter pushes her wheelchair off the mountain, leaving her no options. On the tail end of modernity, in James

Salter's "Open Faces," the protagonist threatens to shoot his paralyzed climbing partner, whom he believes can walk if he wills to do so.[112] The disability studies scholar and historian Paul Longmore calls this "the drama of adjustment." The blind, deaf, or otherwise disabled character is bitter, self-pitying, self-obsessed, and needs to be shocked back into normalcy. As in Salter's, these stories typically climax with an aggressive scene, in which a non-disabled character "grabs them by the shoulders and shakes them back to their senses." Charles, Emma, and Homias metaphorically grab Hippolyte and shake sense into him. Hippolyte is given little opportunity to voice his concerns about the surgery. He does not want the surgery and cannot understand or begin to fathom why the able-bodied world persists in viewing him and his clubfoot as they do. Like most people born with a disability, he does not conceive himself as disabled: his disability is his normative mode of being in the world, his whole comportment. One's phenomenological reality is what it is, disabled or not. Following this, it should be patently offensive to tell a person that they are disabled when, in the entirety of their prior phenomenological experience, they have never known another embodiment, much less a loss of functionality or ability. Another cannot rewrite someone's phenomenology. Hippolyte's perceived "disability" serves as a positive ability for him. His clubfoot is the strongest of his two feet, and he puts his foot to good service. In every way, his disability serves him as an advantage. When he puts his good foot forward, it is his "disabled" foot. This pride is what bothers Emma and Homais so much. Yet, he acquiesces and permits the surgery; his consent is his downfall. Hippolyte's consent has the function of alleviating any potential wrongdoing and culpability from Charles and, by extension, Emma and Homais. The disability and the failure to recover lay squarely upon Hippolyte. That Hippolyte ultimately sanctioned his damaging operation results in he alone bearing sole responsibility for it. The wizardry of Bovary's surgery is revealed for what it is: false magic. The central point here is that the person with a disability is always implicated and viewed as responsible for their disability.

Predictably, the operation is a terrible and catastrophic failure. The leg becomes infected, develops gangrene, and has to be amputated by the famous surgeon, Canivet, who is called in to save the day, if not the leg. Again, Charles' incompetence is demonstrated; Homais' rhetoric empty and Emma's aesthetics shallow. Hippolyte loses his good leg.

This episode is a cautionary tale about the claims of science and medicine for Flaubert. In a world without proven and reliable antiseptics, the operation seemed foolhardy, and its gruesome conclusion foreordained, but modernity builds its promise on risk. The loser is Hippolyte; he risked it and lost it all. Science and medicine walk away. All the promises and dreams abetted by Homais' hyped-rhetoric prove to be false and empty. The state does not care whether Hippolyte lives or dies. He will never serve in any army.

As such, modernity's promises will prove a hollow one for the disabled, too. Hippolyte becomes the emblematic human with a disability. The only worth you have is that your body becomes the battleground for experimentation in the struggle of science and religion. Hippolyte becomes imprisoned in his guilt because he succumbed to the very dream of the able-bodied world. Their vision becomes his nightmare. He had internalized the rhetoric of modernity's promise. He was born different and modern science would redefine him as abnormal and promised to improve him. It convinced him he must change for the future. He consents, and in consenting, he loses. Science and medicine are blameless and free to stroll into the 20th century.

As we have seen, this dyadic symbolism of the necessity of corresponding an inner with an outer flaw abounds in all the literary arts of the Western project. We saw the proliferation of this practice in antiquity. In and through the selected works of the literature of modernity, we witness the same phenomenon: from Melville's Captain Ahab in Moby Dick to Walt Disney's Captain Hook; from Hugo's Quasimodo—whom Hugo described as "an almost" and as "pope of fools" -- to Shelley's Frankenstein, inner evil or tragedy is always partnered with an outward manifestation of a physical flaw or disability. The implication is that, in some sense, the disabled person's character is to blame.

Classical and contemporary literature depends on this symbol. We find examples of characters with physical disabilities from Dickens' Tiny Tim to Quilp and Nell from the "Old Curiosity Shop" to his wheelchair-using pair Paul Dombey and Mrs. Skewton sitting in her three-wheeled wheelchair in "Dombey and Sons." It is found all through modernity, as with Jake Barnes in Hemingway's "The Sun Also Rises." It is in other arts too. It appears in the musical arts in Verdi's Rigoletto, and it is ubiquitous in film (e.g., Freaks, Doctor Strangelove, etc.). It is everywhere.

No genre in art is immune. From the visual arts to the pictorial to modern cinema, artists depend on the stock tropes of presenting disability within a highly derogatory caricature. There is always an outer, physical flaw corresponding with the tragic or comic character's inner flaw (hamartia). What started as a literary device of spectacle is now a powerful and unassailable cultural assumption of today; it has passed from art to everyday living. Oscar Wilde's dictum about nature rings true here. Nature is now reconceptualized through our art. Art imitates life. Art has appropriated the practice of demonizing the disabled, and now we see it in life.

In modernity and its bastard child, post-modernity, we find something more subtle emerging too. It is not always the villains who are the only ones with the two matching flaws, the inner and the outer. At times, the protagonist of the narrative -the hero or heroine- may have a compensatory flaw that compels the narrative. Providing the flawed or disabled character with superhuman skill is a variation of compensatory fantasy. We often find it in aspirational stories and mystery, fantasy, and Sci-Fi genres. As Jennifer Laing writes looking at mystery,

"Let's look at Sherlock Holmes, for example. In the two modern portrayals of him, both the big-screen treatment with Robert Downey, Jr. as Holmes and the BBC re-imagining of a modern-day Holmes with Benedict Cumberbatch, give us a Holmes with all the signs of Asperger's syndrome. His inner genius is mirrored by his outward social awkwardness characteristic of the syndrome. This disorder is characterized by poor social skills, keen attention to detail and trivia that seem inconsequential to most, and high intelligence and devotion to rationality. Or, in a word, Sherlock Holmes! Holmes's obsession with crime-solving matches the obsessions of many of my students with Asperger's, which have ranged from memorizing personal information of the people they meet, to drawing detailed sketches of Roman soldiers, to creating technical manuals to spaceships that don't exist."

In this interpretation, the inner flaw is coupled with an additional affect flaw of greater range or sensitivity. Typically, this conceit holds that the development of another augments the loss of one ability. Thus, the dyadic symbolism of inner/outer is now joined by a third dialectical stage as witnessed in Conan Doyle's Sherlock Holmes: the outer and inner flaws will be joined by an intellectual or cognitive abnormality of extraordinary ability. Thus, we have three stages of the dialectic: outer flaw (disability), inner flaw (obsessive-compulsive disorder or Aspergers), and compensatory ability. In this new triadic formulation, we get the genius or the mad scientist of modernity and post-modernity. Thus, we get Sherlock Holmes, Dr. No, and Professor X, but it began with the forerunner, Doctor Viktor Frankenstein. Let us now turn to a monster of a different kind: war.

23

The Missing Limb: War in the 19th Century - Take Two

From the stump of the arm, the amputated hand,

I undo the clotted lint, remove the slough, wash off the matter and blood,

Back on his pillow the soldier bends with curv'd neck and side falling head,

His eyes are closed, his face is pale, he dares not look on the bloody stump,

And has not yet look'd on it.

-Walt Whitman, *The Wound-Dresser*

During the U.S. Civil War, more than an estimated half a million Americans lost their lives and suffered combat wounds that would leave many of them permanently disabled. So many servicemen were wounded that the United States General Hospital, based in Alexandria, Virginia, published two weekly newspapers titled "The Cripple" and "The Crutch." Many of the Civil War-era wounds resulted from the technological advances in weaponry, artillery, and ordnance. Alongside the relatively primitive state of medicine, including scarcity of clean hospital environments and a lack of antisepsis, the wounds often proved fatal. In terms of weaponry, the breech-loading rifle, innovations in rifling,[113] and explosive shells were responsible for increasing deaths and the overall severity of wounds. One of the more lethal innovations was the invention and availability of the minié ball, a conical-shaped bullet of soft lead with three greased grooves along the outer base designed to mushroom upon impact. The impact caused more extensive damage to flesh and bone as it changed shape on impact. On average, it would enter two to three inches into the soldier's body, dragging skin and dirty clothing into the wound, increasing life-threatening infections. The injuries caused by the minié ball were unprecedented and of such a different class of injuries than those caused by smoothbore musket balls used in earlier conflicts.

Consequently, battlefield physicians were entirely unprepared for the kinds of wounds that they and the field hospitals would encounter. Accounts of damages from the minié ball that struck bone were often so destructive that they necessitated amputation.[114] The resulting infections from wounds and amputations alone would cause secondary infections leading to gangrene and sepsis that in the 1860s would often be fatal. It is difficult to estimate the total number of surgeries, but conservative estimates place the number of battle-related surgeries at approximately 60,000. About three-quarters of those operations performed in battlefield hospitals or nearby clinics during the war were amputations.[115] Some amputations occurred under such duress and haste that they would have required follow-up operations to save the wounded soldier. The effect of this consigns the soldier to a lifetime of permanent and nagging disability. Confronted with little training, poor hygiene, and the sheer volume of the wounded, physicians were under enormous pressures to perform rapidly and under dismal and dirty situations. They were operating in unsanitary conditions with little adequate anesthesia and no way to sterilize equipment or hands. Further, their understanding of germs and the need for sterile conditions was limited by the then-current state knowledge of germs and contagion. While their heroic efforts doubtlessly saved many, they would be given the macabre sobriquet, "butcher" by the wounded and non-wounded soldiers on both sides of the battle lines.

Alfred Bellard's memoir, "Gone for a Soldier," would provide an eyewitness account to such horrible conditions and experiences. Bellard was a private enlisted with the 5th New Jersey Volunteers serving in many battles, including Williamsburg, Second Bull Run, Fredericksburg, and Chancellorsville. Unfortunately, his luck would run out at Chancellorsville, where he would be seriously injured, requiring multiple surgeries to recover.

In his diary--not published for over a century later in 1975--Bellard wrote candidly about the field hospitals: "The doctors were busy in probing for balls, binding up wounds and in cutting off arms and legs, a pile of which lay under the table." His experiences would be memorialized in his drawings accompanying his words.

After his leg wound healed, Bellard would re-join the army fighting with the newly formed Invalid Corps (later renamed the Veteran Reserve Corps). The Invalid Corps was established by the federal government and organized under General Order No. 105, U.S. War Department, dated April 28, 1863.

The idea of an invalid corps was not new. An invalid corps existed during the U.S. Revolutionary War, started by General Washington after his crushing defeat at the Battle of Long Island. While Washington ultimately ordered it established, Major General Henry Knox conceived the idea, who submitted a request to the Continental Congress on January 3, 1784. The first corps included only disabled officers. They would be assigned to the garrison at West Point. Congress established it on June 20, 1776, placing Colonel Lewis Nicola in charge. Eventually, the order established eight battalions. They would see "light service" mostly in mid-Atlantic and northern states deployed in places such as Philadelphia, Vermont, and West Point. Such corps can be traced back to similar units in France in the 1670s.[116] In fact, by 1702, there were 61 similar companies of soldiers with disabilities serving in the French military alone. Established, in part, to help employ disabled veterans in war-related work and free up fresh, non-disabled soldiers for front-line combat duty. In the original American corps, the returning disabled service members were given only half-pay for their service. The Corps was mainly used for security detail and other non-combat functions.

The Civil War-era Corps was composed of three battalions. Your assignment depended on the nature of your disability. The first battalion was composed of men -officers and enlisted- with relatively lesser disabilities and who could still carry a weapon and march in formation. These men were sent back to combat to perform limited roles. The second battalion consisted of soldiers with more severe disabilities and pressed into service as prison and federal building guards. Finally, members of the Third battalion would be used in hospitals as cooks, nurses, ward masters, clerks, and orderlies.[117] Members of the Invalid Corps came to be known as the "Cripple Brigade" and were not offered the financial incentives granted to re-enlisting soldiers or new Union recruits. However, by statute, they should be paid on par with all other servicemen.

Further indignities were piled on the corps when their fellow servicemen would greet the battalions with a derogatory song mocking the disabled soldiers. Its singing became popular during the war. Here is a single stanza from the chorus:

"Some had the ticerdolerreou,
Some what they call "brown critters,"
And some were "lank and lazy" too,
Some were too "fond of bitters."
Some had "cork legs" and some "one eye,"
With backs deformed and crooked,
I'll bet you'd laugh'd till you had cried,
To see how "cute" they looked."[118]

During and after the war, many disabled veterans would find that the meager pensions offered by the Federal Government for their service were simply not enough to support themselves and their families after the war. The post-war economic slump and dismal reconstruction further exacerbated the situation of many veterans. Neither state nor federal agencies provided relief for such circumstances. These circumstances would fuel many ordinary citizens to develop and spread stereo-types about the missing work ethic of returning soldiers with disabilities. As a result, many would see the disabled as feeling entitled or living off charity. We see this in the song's words alluding to the stereotype that the unemployed, disabled veteran is "lank and lazy" and "too fond of bitters."

Practically speaking, one can well imagine that with the many botched surgeries, untreatable pain, alcohol was their only option for pain management. As a result, many turned to self-medicating with alcohol leading to chronic rates of alcoholism. While 19th-century American alcohol consumption was moderate, many veterans would abuse alcohol leading to severe impacts for communities. By the 1880s, for example, many public schools in New York and Pennsylvania were required to teach students about the dangers of alcohol. After the war and a failing economy in the challenging post-war reconstruction pe-riod, many disabled veterans were reduced to begging for alms. In 1864, the Invalid Corps was renamed the Veteran Reserve Corps to end the mockery of these soldiers. By 1916, the federal government's expen-ditures on Civil War pensions exceeded $5 billion and had cost more than the entire cost of the four-year-long conflict.[119] The rising costs and decidedly negative opinions of soldiers with disabilities would lead American politicians to look for cheaper ways to recruit and maintain armed services and ultimately culminating after WWI to develop phys-ical therapies as low-cost rehabilitative strategies to return veterans with disabilities back to the workforce. Linker covers this area in her book, "War's Waste: Rehabilitation in World War I America," where she details how rehabilitation would become the government's official policy to "rebuild war cripples" in subsequent conflicts; indeed, the very discipline of physical therapy would arise as a result of these two con-flicts, the Civil War, and WWI.

As self-defining as the Civil War was for both the participants and the broader nation, the bloodletting would seemingly prove too painful for the young nation's memory, and the sacrifices of the soldiers would be too quickly and deliberately forgotten. Genuine concern for the disabled veterans faded into the more palatable, politically convenient, and sanitized memorialization of the heroic with public statues, parks, and patriotic events. As Americans on both sides of the bloody conflict sought to put the tragic memory behind them, the fractured nation would increasingly ignore the plight of the living disabled, who were now aging and increasingly impoverished. We see evidence of this marked change in the many editorials railing against the disabled veterans as "money-grabbing dependents." Such derision would be found in cartoons like the 1882 editorial cartoon titled "the Insatiable Glutton."

The veteran volunteered and paid the cost and was ridiculed by his former comrades in song and the larger society with scorn and neglect. He was repaid for his sacrifice with contempt, satire, or indifference solely because he was disabled.

Less obvious but equally profound in their impacts in changing attitudes toward the disabled were the technological innovations in rail, communication (i.e., telegraph), photography, and the press, which would wield subtle but permanent and profound effects on the subsequent practice of war and its victims especially on those who witnessed or survived it. However, the significant innovations directly affecting the lives of the disabled would occur in the advances made in emergency and field medicine. These innovations would allow many of the wounded who certainly would have died in previous conflicts to survive, albeit often with disabling new realities. All told, the cumulative effects of these developments and innovations would produce a boom in the number of disabled Americans and bring the idea of the disabled veteran to the nation's consciousness.

A good indicator to measure the explosion of the disabled is to look at the rapid increase in the production of artificial limbs: about 150 patents were issued for artificial limb designs between 1861 and 1873. In 1862, the Federal Government provided disabled veterans up to $75 to buy an artificial leg, $50 for an arm, and by 1864, the Confederacy was doing the same.[120] Compensation for losing an arm or a leg was a practice stemming from earlier sea-faring and piratical traditions. In his "Icepick Surgeon," contemporary science writer, Sam Kean, writes:

"Pirates got 600 pieces of eight for losing a right arm, 500 for losing a left arm or right leg, 400 for losing the left leg, and 100 for losing an eye or finger.[121]

The ubiquity of prosthetics bespeaks the need. But the amount paid out was little compensation for the lifelong loss of wages that the men faced due to their war injuries. Nonetheless, these men were eager to erase their injury and return to some level of social function. They desired to fit in and erase their disabilities, revealing much about Civil War-era attitudes toward the disabled. In some cases, they would succeed, and in many more, the burdens, costs, and derision would become insurmountable obstacles. Of course, the nature of disability would forever be changed after this conflict, but there were momentous changes about to occur still, and for these, we will return to Europe.

24

WWI and Disability: The
Real Cost of War

"For Disabled men the war did not end in 1918. It was a
long and tragic serial lasting, for many, for a lifetime."
-Mr. Baxter, Limbless Ex-Servicemen's Association

If the American Civil War fundamentally changed how combat and war were to be waged and the disabled it created, then the First World War would witness injuries on a grander scale and with graver severity than in any previous military conflict. This tectonic shift in scale was due, in part, to the sheer volume of combatants. The global reach of combat and the very nature of trench warfare would also contribute to the sea change. It has been estimated that nearly 8 million European service members would return home permanently disabled after the Great War. While not the bloodiest human conflict, 30 years before 20-30 million died in the 14-year Taiping rebellion, and the Crimean War was more deadly for British soldiers, the war changed the scale of death and disability in the modern world. In France, the wounded were called mutiles de geurre or those "war maimed."

Their wounds were serious: amputations, paralysis, disfigurement, chemical burns, and a new hidden malady "shell shock" that wreaked the toll on the mental health of the combatants. Today shell shock is understood as a species of post-traumatic shock. It is recognized as a severe and limiting psychological disability, but at the time, it was oft viewed as an excuse to avoid war or blatant cowardice. By the end of the war, the British medical corps had dealt with 80,000 cases of shell shock, but millions more went unreported or ignored due to the controversy surrounding the diagnosis. Some did seek to change this scenario. Shell shock was the subject of insightful and important literary interest due, in considerable measure, to the great WWI veteran writers Henri Barbusse, Wilfred Owen, Isaac Rosenberg, Siegfried Sassoon, and Edward Thomas. These writers experienced the horrors of the trauma first-hand from their respective combat experiences in WWI. Some of them—Owen, Rosenberg, and Thomas—would die on the front. The poets would, through their poems, bring much-needed attention to the condition, although it would still not have much impact on most people's understanding of the diagnosis. However, for the mainstream, the disorder was dismissed by many as "quack psychiatry" despite the thoughtful and timely attention that Ernest Jones, President of the British Psycho-Analytic Association, colleague and translator of Sigmund Freud, paid to the disorder and those suffering from it. Jones would situate the soldier's reactions as a fitting response to the "abrogation of civilized standards" one experiences while in combat. He would write:

"'...to indulge in the behaviour of a kind that is throughout abhorrent to the civilised mind.... All sorts of previously forbidden and hidden impulses, cruel, sadistic, murderous and so on, are stirred to greater activity, and the old intrapsychical conflicts which, according to Freud, are the essential cause of all neurotic disorders, and which had been dealt with before by means of 'repression' of one side of the conflict are now reinforced, and the person is compelled to deal with them afresh under totally different circumstances."[122]

Jones, the writer-veterans, and others sympathetic to the men's experiences were decidedly in the minority; most people, including many within the upper ranks of the military and government echelons, were skeptical or openly dismissive of the existence of such a condition at all and still preferred to label those with shell shock cowards or shirkers: they were blaming the victim for their disability. For example, if shell shock occurred without a nearby artillery blast, the soldier was not given a "war stripe" for a wound; the denial of the medal was a slap in the soldier's face. Some men were even placed on trial for cowardice or desertion, and a few executed for cowardice. While even military officials recognized that soldiers might crack under duress, a long-lasting case of shell shock was almost inevitably viewed as an example of a shortcoming in one's character. This assumption squares with the emergent notion that one was in some sense responsible for one's disability. This belief would continue well after the war and in many quarters in other 20th and 21st century wars. For example, in a post-war testimony, WWI, British Field Marshall John Gort infamously said that shell shock was not found in the "good" units.[123]

Many of the injuries and reactions were brought on by the continued development and refinement of arms and weaponry first developed during the Crimean and U.S. Civil Wars, including heavy, short- and long-range artillery fire, rapid-fire machine guns, hand grenades, tanks, and the use of poisonous gases such as chlorine and mustard gases. These innovations and refinements, as well as the strategies of continual artillery barrages and the gruesome reality of long-term, trench warfare would lead to a range of injuries, diseases, and impairments often resulting in long-term disability, including limb mutilations and amputations, facial disfigurement, burns, blindness and the devastating psychological effects of shell shock. Artillery would count for most injuries and deaths. In Britain alone, over 1,640,000 British soldiers were wounded. That would amount to nearly 30% of all British troops who served during the war.[124] Many factors affected the rehabilitation of these soldiers, including inadequate state provisions allocated for disabled soldiers, the pervasive negative attitudes toward disability, and the soldiers' treatment, preparation, and training. Back at home, Britain would not readily absorb the volume of returning soldiers with disabilities and found itself increasingly relying on private charities to provide relief for the soldiers' needs. However, well-intentioned charity lacked the necessary resources or expertise to provide adequate levels of care for the volume of returning disabled veterans.

Because of the conditions away from the front, several national programs would be established. As Du Feu of the University of Aberdeen reports:

"Charities were especially prominent in the management of the severely disabled who needed longer term care, for example, paraplegic and limbless ex-servicemen. The Queen Mary's Star and Garter home for paraplegics was established to care for and rehabilitate paraplegic ex-servicemen by light work such as knitting. Curative workshops were established alongside orthopaedic hospitals and encouraged rehabilitation of soldiers by use of massage, gym equipment, and manual work to aid psychological and physical restoration."

Du Feu continues describing some of the institutions deliberately founded or developed to address the needs and medical care of the disabled serviceman:

"The first curative workshop was set up at Shepherd's Bush Hospital in 1916 and was largely the work of King Manuel, who raised funds privately. By 1918 there were 16 throughout Britain which enabled rehabilitation of many men. The Soldier's and Sailor's Help Society trained disabled men in their workshops as they had been doing since the Boer War. Roehampton and Brighton hospitals for limbless soldiers instructed men in various occupations such as carpentry, shoemaking and electrical work. Chailey and Agnes Hunt's Orthopaedic Hospital, which was formerly for crippled children, began to take in wounded soldiers. Each solider was paired with a child to boost their morale and inspire them. The men also undertook manual tasks and training at curative workshops to allow them to work, which was how "the dismembered could become full citizens again."[125]

One group of disabled soldiers returning to Britain who would often receive 100% of their disability pensions and relatively greater support were those who endured the horrors of facial disfigurement. WWI would witness an increase in facial injuries due to trench warfare and the use of poisonous gases. While the benefits were greater for those with these injuries, those benefits came at a high cost. In Britain, reports historian Suzanne Biernoff, "very severe facial disfigurement" was one of the few injuries for which a soldier received the full pension—the thinking being that it compromised one's "sense of self and social existence"[126] She further explains that those wounded "are almost condemned to isolation unless surgery can repair the damage." Since reconstructive surgery was still in its infancy, the early attempts at surgically restoring the soldier's face were likely limited. Indeed, the modern medical specialty of reconstructive surgery owes much of its existence to these sorts of injuries sustained in combat during WWI.[127] The French called such wounded soldiers les gueules cassées (men with smashed faces). Recovery from such a wound would take a lifetime, if at all. In addition, multiple surgeries and social unease would add to the long-term costs of these wounded soldiers.

A member of the British Army's medical corps, Harold Gillies, from New Zealand and a physician trained at Cambridge University would be tasked to take on these horrible wounds.[128] Gillies, an otolaryngologist, is today widely considered the father of modern plastic surgery due to his innovations working on and with soldiers with facial and other forms of disfigurements. Working as a surgeon in London when the war broke out, he would volunteer and serve in Belgium and France, bringing his skills to war and learning techniques on reconstructing soldiers' facial injuries. Upon returning to England, he convinced the Army's chief surgeon, Sir William Arbuthnot Lane, to begin the first facial injury ward at the Cambridge Military hospital in Aldershot. With the volume of injuries increasing, they would eventually establish a hospital devoted to facial reconstruction at Sidcup with over 1,000 beds. There Gillies and others would perform more than 11,000 surgery on some 5,000 veterans.

The cause of many of the facial injuries came from shrapnel and machine gunnery when soldiers in trenches would pop their heads over for a look and come back down, missing a nose, an ear, a cheek, or an entire face. Having witnessed these gruesome injuries, Gillies would call for plastic surgery units in the field hospitals. Back home, he and other surgeons would experiment and devise ways to reconstruct facial wounds building on essential skin grafting techniques established in Germany and the Soviet Union that offered the wounded veteran a chance to re-integrate back into civilian life. In addition, Gillies worked closely with artists and sculptors to capture the injured soldiers' faces and reconstruct them. One of the sculptors he worked with was Kathleen Scott, the widow of Capt. Robert Falcon Scott of the unfortunate 1912 Antarctica voyage. She once remarked, "men without noses are very beautiful, like antique marbles."[129] Other artists made prosthetic masks for the disfigured veterans, such as Anna Coleman Ladd and Francis Derwent Wood. However, Scott would be alone in seeing the beauty of such heroes; most people's reactions were of a different sort.

As mentioned, Sidcup, England, a quaint town southeast of London, was to become one of the homes for a hospital dedicated to WWI soldiers with facial disfigurements. Another hospital, Queen Mary's Hospital, started as a facial reconstruction unit in 1917 but converted to a general hospital. By 1925, funds disappeared for any ongoing veteran care.[130] The presence of the disfigured veterans was too much for many of the locals in Sidcup. They petitioned the town leaders to address the issue, and the town council created a series of unique blue benches for the soldiers. The benches served as "a code that warned townspeople that any man sitting on one would be distressful to view." Accordingly, the good citizens of Sidcup knew which benches to avoid, so they were not upset by seeing the men who had sacrificed so much.

Many artists would join Kathleen Scott in her appreciation of the soldiers and be ahead of the general population in this regard. For example, Otto Dix and George Grosz would include images of the facially mutilated men in several of their post-war paintings.

Despite the efforts of WWI disabled service members trying to integrate back into their communities and pick up lives they had left before the conflict, many would find crucial resources lacking, and they were altogether ill-prepared for the kinds of discrimination they would face. It was not only people's sensitivity to their appearances but the difficult adjustment of joining the ranks of the disabled and needing to face the millennia-old prejudices arrayed against the disabled, which left many hopeless. Additionally, a general lack of central planning and the absence of any national coordinating effort would ultimately leave many crucial areas under-served, and veterans were left to their own devices. Existing therapeutic programs for the disabled were often irrelevant to young soldiers' lives, experiences, and realities. Knitting, for example, was one such therapy. A very unreasonable expectation that a young man recently returned from the rigors of front line combat in trench warfare would take to knitting as a future occupation. Such therapies would be as impractical as they were misguided. The foolishness of such projects is staggeringly monumental. They would return to built environments that were inaccessible to those with mobility impairments. Universities would not accommodate them, and the kinds of work opportunities would be few.

Unlike their peers in Europe and the U.S., British veterans with disabilities failed to become a potent political force in the inter-war period.[131] They placed their trust in a public that they believed to be more sympathetic to their plight than government agencies or private charities proved to be or warranted. Sadly, both the public and the governments soon failed to offer any salient support. Any trust the veterans placed in these institutions would be short-lived. As the post-war economy began to stagnate, disabled veterans found that their needs were relegated to a second-class status. Indeed, as an example, after the war and to mark the Allied victory over the Axis powers, London celebrated with the largest parade it had ever witnessed. But it was an incomplete celebration; disabled veterans were excluded from participation. The "Times" effused about the inclusive nature of the parade as marchers representing Greek, Romanian, Serbian, and other allies "passed before our eye" but conspicuously absent were the very British servicemen who had fought and suffered in the war. The men who had made the most significant sacrifices were forced to sit on the sidelines as non-participants. It was as if the public cringed at any reminder of the actual costs of warfare. J. B. Brunel-Cohen, a newly elected member of parliament and a disabled veteran himself, spoke in defense of the excluded servicemen saying:

"The dead are brought to memory by the Noble cenotaph, the lucky living are in the procession, but where are the wounded? Surely it would not have been too much to have had even one lorry load just have given the crowd an opportunity of showing their appearance."[132]

But the larger public had grown weary of the war and all things associated with it. A younger generation wanted to move on and did not care about the soldiers.

The disabled veterans wanted more than merely pensions and parades; they were searching for respect; and, like all humans, their dignity. They did want a place in the parade, a place to be remembered. But they also wanted recognition and respect. Instead, disabled soldiers too often found themselves forgotten. Upon returning to a rapidly changing culture that was desperate, trying to ignore the horrors of the war, the disabled veterans would be relegated to the ash pile of history. In a similar cultural reaction to that which ensued after the American Civil War, Britons, too, grew tired of the soldier's plight and stories of war. The Roaring 20's, with its booze, flappers, jazz culture, and cynicism, the "lost generation" did everything it could to distance itself from the war and ignore those potent reminders of recent history.

The post-war reconstruction would, as Cohen describes it: "condemn the British disabled to a life on the periphery."[133] Ezra Pound's famous dictum about the need to modernize modernity to "make it new" would settle in the oddest places. The recently disabled found themselves old, attenuated, and in the way overnight: they would either be made new again through nascent technologies or find themselves in peril by being cast as outsiders. They would be all of 20 or 30 years old by the war's end.

The accounts of their struggles and the dismal and inaccessible living arrangements are hard to read, but they speak to these veterans' resiliency. Several archival reports recount how wheelchair-using veteran's homes were located on top floors lacking bathrooms in places where the doorframes were too narrow to allow passage for wheelchairs between rooms. Somehow, many of these men were able to eke out their existence in such circumstances. It must, nevertheless, had to have occurred to them just how modernity could devise clever new ways to maim and injure but not, unfortunately, heal or accommodate. Sadly, the WWI veteran might go from the confines of the trench to the confines of a single room. It must have seemed that their sacrifice was in vain.

The day-to-day difficulties were not of interest to any charitable organization, and people seemed to have had their fill of human suffering. They craved youth, abandonment, and the comforts of forgetting. The carefully cultivated apathy of the modernist ethic of the 1920s would cruelly turn a cold eye toward the disabled service members. For example, many insurance companies refused to insure disabled veterans; and when they came to die, their widows had no way to bury them. One would find that one could not survive alone sewing and selling poppies in a highly competitive capitalist economy. The challenges faced by many WWI veterans would partly fuel much of the post-war literary despair you find in some English and Modernist writers who had survived the war. They would attempt to deal with disability and injury in their writing, but they also needed to tone it down to sell their books. You see this in the tangential manner in which writers from Ford Madox Ford to Ernest Hemingway dealt with disability in their novels and stories.

In Germany, disabled WWI veterans fared better than their former opponents, but the unmet promises of the Weimer Republic would start to disappoint and leave disabled veterans in need. To this point, Cohen reports, "the bitter discontent of German veterans has puzzled historians."[134] Comparatively, the German veteran had the most "progressive" pension of the period: the pensions embodied in the 1920 National Pension Law carried significantly more political and civil rights than provisions made in either Britain or America.[135] However, with the onset of the global depression and the post-war reparations exacting a heavy toll on Germany, the disabled veterans would soon come to feel the pressures. If they were institutionalized, they would find the scene in hospitals bleak and unwelcoming. During and immediately after WWI, many German hospitals were unsafe and unsanitary, full of reported abuse and neglect cases. Burleigh estimates that up to 71,787 German patients died from a combination of hunger, disease, and neglect during World War I alone.[136] Yet the poor of Germany-- the chronically unemployed and widowed pensioners--would look enviously at the disabled veteran's benefits, however scant those benefits were. It was not long before complaints started to be voiced that the disabled were taking advantage of their situations and getting more than their fair share.

While several non-governmental, charitable, and benevolent agencies sought to provide relief and mitigate the more vicious aspects of the inter-war years, the newly formed Nazi party would lead the cause in honoring the disabled veteran. The National Socialists would honor the disabled soldiers as "the first citizens of the nation."[137] But such promises would prove to be short-lived. The Nazi rhetoric proved to be hollow and would not last long. The commitments to veterans by the Nazis would prove to be as thin as the promises made by the Weimar Republic. Disabled veterans would soon learn that the deep roots of prejudice affecting any political power structure, whether monarchical, democratic, or fascist, would quickly turn against them. The lessons of the western project ensconced in modernity would stress that the disabled were expendable, and they—the disabled—would find themselves the first sacrificed in times of crisis. In time, the killing machine of the Reich would turn on those same "first citizens" in its obsessive zeal to make Germany great again. The disabled veteran would face euthanasia programs as part of the cleansing of the Reich.

The plan to make a new Germany would not begin with the veterans but begin with disabled children. With the introduction of several euthanasia programs under the Reich, German children with disabilities would be the first in a wave of mass murders committed by the Nazis. The most infamous being the T4 program. While some disabled veterans, especially combat medal winners or those who had distinguished themselves with exemplary valor during WWI, would be given a reprieve, they would soon face the same horror. Klee reports that even those with records of distinguished service or recipients of medals might find themselves in hospital and removed to a euthanization center where they were killed.

Henry Friedlander cites the case of 58-year-old Karl Rueff, a lieutenant in the reserves awarded an Iron Cross First Class. He was institutionalized in south Germany due to a head wound he had suffered in the First World War. His disability pension paid for his institutional care, and he was relatively healthy, suffering only from an occasional epileptic seizure. Nevertheless, in 1940, he was transferred to Grafeneck—one of the first centers dedicated to euthanizing-- and gassed. On the site of a former medieval castle that served as a hunting lodge for the Dukes of Württemberg, near Marbach, in 1929, it was converted to a home for physically and mentally disabled persons. On 24 May 1939, Aktion T4 officials visited and inspected the former castle to see if it would be a suitable killing center.

Ernst Klee's well-documented "History of Euthanasia Program in the Third Reich" mentions others similarly treated and ultimately murdered by the Reich programs. He writes that we know of at least 36 former Wehrmacht soldiers who had been discharged from the Wehrmacht because of mental illnesses and were subsequently killed at the Hadamar facility in 1943. Thus, Hadamar would follow Grafneck in the initial phase of Nazi-era euthanasia programs. Hadamar personnel murdered 10,000 German patients by asphyxiating them with carbon monoxide in a gas chamber made to look like a shower room. Physicians ordered staff to kill these victims, including patients with disabilities, mentally disoriented elderly persons from bombed-out areas, "half Jewish" children from welfare institutions, psychologically and physically disabled forced laborers and their children, German soldiers and foreign Waffen-SS soldiers deemed psychologically incurable. The orders directed them to kill those patients by gassing, lethal drug overdose, or deliberate neglect.[138]

How were veterans with disabilities faring in the other nations? In the United States after the Civil War, every service member discharged would receive $60, a new suit, a train ticket home, and a discount to buy life insurance--every service veteran except the disabled. If you were disabled, your experience was going to be much different. At the end of the Civil War, the Federal Government enacted a set of laws to provide for the welfare of disabled soldiers. As we saw above, the regulations offered pensions, some subsidized housing, and a modest stipend for prosthetics. However, the resources would, as University of Penn historian of medicine Beth Linker reports, be significantly less:

"A veteran could receive a check three times a year, and he never had to return to work."[139]

But the check in the post-war economic decline proved not to be sufficient to cover medical or living costs, and by the onset of WWI, the Federal pension was proving too costly and was cut by Congress. In addition, Linker writes, "in the Progressive era, manliness was defined by a man's ability to labor." Lacking an outlet to express one's sense of worth, one can only imagine that the loss of self-esteem would have contributed to any number of mental health issues and drug and alcohol abuse. Things needed to change, and things were going to change and change they did, but not for the better as far as disabled veterans were concerned.

Any monies you received because of your disability would not be viewed as a pension but as compensation. This practice was not reversed until 1933, when payments to disabled veterans were reclassified as pensions. Congress tried to pass an act lobbied for by the American Legion, and other veterans groups called the World War Adjustment Compensation Act of 1924. It called for a dollar a day for time served and a quarter more for service overseas. However, there was a significant catch: if the total payment amounted to more than $50.00, it would be issued in a certificate form not redeemable for 20 years and not exceeding $1500.00. The legislation was opposed by Presidents Harding and Coolidge and failed to muster support and was defeated several times in both the house and senate before successful passage in 1924. In its final passage, it had to override two Presidential vetoes. Coolidge would snidely remark after his veto was defeated, "patriotism...bought and paid for is not patriotism."

The certificate could be used as collateral for loans. However, both disabled and non-disabled service members found that the post-war economic slump and depression would be too challenging to make a living. Recall that they could not collect on these certificates until 1945. It is important to note that the average age of a WWI service member at induction was 30 years old. If they were 30 years old between 1914-18, they would be in their mid-to late-50 and early 60's in 1945. According to the CDC, the average life expectancy of a person born in the last decade of the 19th century was somewhere between 40 and 50 years. Congress was trying to outsmart the veterans, and the veterans knew it. Most would have been dead before they could collect their benefit. Their frustration and anger over these attempts at subterfuge would lead to a series of marches on Washington protesting the lack of support for WWI veterans, especially protesting the so-called "Bonus Certificate."

The veteran's treatment prompted their peaceful march and gathering on Washington of the "Bonus Army." Some 40,000 WWI veterans, their families, friends, and allies gathered in Washington, D.C., in the summer of 1932. The Bonus army set up Hooverville's encampment on the Anacostia Flats, a marshy flatland near the Anacostia River just south of the 11th Street Bridge. They waited for President Hoover to act on their demands. Their wait proved to be fruitless, but it did evoke a reaction. On July 28th, Attorney General William Mitchell ordered the police to remove the soldiers. When they refused, a scuffle broke out, and in the ensuing melee, police shot and killed two veterans: William Hushka and Eric Carlson.[140]

Informed of the shootings, President Hoover ordered the U.S. Army to evict them under the command of General Douglas MacArthur. MacArthur's troops consisted of the 12th Infantry Regiment, out of Fort Howard, Maryland, and the 3rd Cavalry Regiment and six tanks under the command of Major George S. Patton. In confusion, the bonus marchers mistakenly believed that the arriving troops were coming to their defense, so they welcomed their brothers in arms with cheers until Macarthur ordered a charge on the unsuspecting and unarmed marchers. After the charge, he sent an infantry bayonet charge and deployed tear gas. Fearing a campaign and public relations nightmare, Hoover ordered the assault stopped, but MacArthur ignored the president's orders and ordered a second attack. The aftermath resulted in 55 veterans being injured and 135 arrested. In addition, a veteran's wife miscarried, and a 12-week-old baby, Bernard Myers, died from the tear gas attack. The official government report tried to squelch the deaths. Although none of the military commanders found that their cowardly actions compromised their careers, it proved politically disastrous for Hoover, who in the 1932 election would lose in a landslide to Franklin D. Roosevelt. As this and other incidences indicate, the United States was in this regard just like its former allies and enemies, not a welcoming place for veterans, disabled or not. With the coming economic downturn of the dust bowl and full-scale depression, things would only worsen for the disabled veteran.

The U.S. Federal Government's response to its veterans historically has always been, at best, tepid. At its worse, it was inhumane. Even if not on the viciousness and scale of what would subsequently happen in Germany, for such a wealthy, prosperous, and powerful nation with such strident patriotic overtures, its record of treating its veterans is surprising. Indeed, a decade earlier, as disabled veterans of the WWI American Expeditionary Forces started to return to home, the Federal Government relied on its largely ineffective and poorly funded Federal Bureau of Vocational Rehabilitation (FBVR). The FBVR began during the Reconstruction era to assist in rehabilitating and re-educating disabled Civil War soldiers for re-entry into the American workforce. It would prove to be a major failure. In the New York City area, a top FBVR official issued the infamous "Hard-boiled order" that instructed admitting officials not to heed the struggles of the veteran's stories but "be hard-boiled...put cotton in your ears and lock the door. If you're naturally sympathetic, work nights when nobody is there."[141]

The plight of the American disabled WWI veteran would be fraught with tragedy; however, the volume of the disabled on all sides of the conflict would change the nature of disability for the remainder of the 20th century as much as they would find themselves neglected and shunted to the margins. The disabled were no longer going to be relegated to the margins of society. Veterans with disabilities would lead the charge in the coming transformations. As Stiker notes, "earlier societies had failed to situate the disabled."[142] After both the U.S. Civil war and WWI, the presence of veterans with disabilities would slowly start appearing in mainstream institutions. The practical development of prosthetics and the growth of physical therapy meant that returning veterans with disabilities would have a set of possibilities earlier veterans did not enjoy. In their wake, modern physical therapy, or physiotherapy as it was known at the time, would grow. When the war broke out in 1914, there was no formal field as rehabilitation, although some European programs did exist. Prompted, in part, by experiences from the American Civil War, U. S. Army Major General William Crawford Gorgas--the U.S. Surgeon General of the Army--ordered a task force of Army medical officers to Europe to investigate the European rehabilitation programs. Gorgas established the Division of Special Hospitals and Physical Reconstruction as a direct result of the group's findings on Aug. 22, 1917.[143] The U.S Army's Office of Medical History defined physical therapy "as maximum mental and physical restoration of the individual achieved by the use of medicine and surgery, supplemented by physical therapy, occupational therapy or curative workshop activities, education, recreation, and vocational training."

At the time, physical therapy consisted of hydrotherapy, electrotherapy, and mechanotherapy, active exercise, indoor and outdoor games, and massage."[144] It was initially left up to Captain Granger to implement and develop this novel form of medical intervention. It was met with skepticism by the medical corps; the program met with obstacles at every step. A small indication of the resistance is evident when the first two "official" physical therapists were women; it was not considered a serious enough medical field for men. Nevertheless, women therapists would take advantage and become pioneers in physical therapy. Despite the scant resources and general skepticism, their singular efforts would positively affect the lives of thousands of disabled veterans. It is a story that still needs telling.

Two of the heroic women who met the challenge and helped forged the field of physical therapy, despite vigorous opposition was Marguerite Sanderson and Mary McMillan. The first Supervisor of Reconstruction Aides in the Surgeon General's Office was Marguerite Sanderson, the former president of the Boston School of Physical Education. She began her duty in January 1918 and was eventually transferred to the newly established Walter Reed General Hospital, primarily to organize units for deployment to overseas military hospitals. The first unit set sail for France in June 1918. Sanderson followed in September.

The second heroic woman was the first physical therapist with the Army, Mary McMillan. She began her work at Walter Reed in February of 1918 and almost immediately encountered obstacles. Not surprisingly, because of the new program's unfavorable reception, she was given no room for her clinic and was required to offer treatment in crowded hospital wards. In addition, she had to use an outdoor porch for space for any group exercise class that proved problematic in inclement weather.

As the number of wounded and disabled veterans started to trickle back home up to and following the armistice, it was necessary to enlarge the physical therapy program. However, as those numbers increased, pressures lead to the need to dedicate more resources to the veteran's care. To that end, and under considerable advocacy from McMillan and others, they would hire more staff, build buildings, and dedicate wings of existing buildings to rehabilitation. Again, the veterans benefited from the women's skilled therapy, and the Army brass noticed their dedicated work. Witness, for example, the following assessment from a member of the Army medical corps who worked closely with a physical therapy unit:

"I have never known of anything approaching the devotion of these girls to their work. They worked hard all day, attended lectures on technic after hours, held quizzes during the noon hour and in the evenings and could be found in the clinic until late hours trying out technics one upon the other. No corps ever displayed greater loyalty, more unselfishness, greater devotion."[145]

While the physical therapists were making a difference in the lives of the disabled veterans, they were unwittingly playing a central part in a larger drama that would affect the lives of persons with disabilities from then on. The establishment of the medical community's interest in rehabilitation would spawn an industry that would enrich and engulf the lives of persons with disabilities. Formerly persons with disabilities were largely ignored by the medical communities; they would now become extensive medical and scientific research subjects. This medicalization of disability is one of the critical relationships and developments of modernity. The lesson of the Enlightenment project of science and medicine here is that persons will be reduced to mere objects. The unsavory upshot would witness the development of the so-called "medical model" of disability whereby a person would become identified by their condition alone. Their complete, rich humanity would be reduced to a single physical condition, and their bodies would become controlled by medicine. They would lose the very autonomy of bodily ownership. As with most advancements in medicine and technology, this, too, was a double-edged sword with both positive and tragic results. To be sure, rehabilitation and the nascent medical technologies would alleviate much suffering and make many things possible for persons with disabilities that were before unheard of and perhaps once deemed impossible to conceive. And while these developments do bring many positive aspects, they would come at a sharp cost, a severe cost for the disabled themselves. As Snyder and Mitchell put it, "since the advent of the rehabilitation era, disabled people have resided within proximity to a scientific ethos that misidentifies objectivity with the debasement of its object of study."[146] One's full humanity is reduced to one's medical condition: one is a spinal cord injury even years after the accident; one is "confined to a wheelchair," "paralyzed," etc. This process described by Snyder and Mitchell is valid for other disabilities too--one is reduced to the condition of disability: one is blind, deaf, etc. Arguably this gave rise to the "medical model" of defining the word disability, where a person is reduced to a physical condition. But as Stiker suggests concerning the era of rehabilitation, there is something more concerning at play here too:

"The disabled were exceptions and stood for exceptionality, alterity; now that they have become ordinary, they have returned to ordinary life, to ordinary work."[147]

This is not your everyday ordinary. The disabled would no longer be the manufacturers of their own identities; instead, they become the raw material for others to practice their handiwork upon and are re-defined by their condition. This process of redefinition is also a reduction. "Consequently," as Snyder and Mitchell continue, "the phenomenon of disability has been routinely represented as the site of undesirability: one that only provides recourse to a battery of interventions involved in the alleviation, diminishment, normalization, oversight, and invasive management of disabled persons' lives."[148] What is of note here is that while there are demonstrable improvements for some of the disabled, especially compared to earlier historical epochs, the lives of the disabled will still be viewed as a great scourge to overcome, repair. But this time, not by returning them to god, ostracizing them, or scapegoating, but by the magic practices by the new gods in white lab coats.

"People with disabilities have seen themselves anchor a scientific research industry that continues to circle back to some variation on the age-old observation that disability is a misfortune because our research reveals that same point time and time again."[149]

To borrow a phrase from Marx and Engels, "whole populations will be conjured out of the ground." In this instance, the disability itself would result from the strange alchemy of science, medicine, rehabilitation, and the pressures of the constantly growing, rapidly industrializing culture of modernity. The disabled are made, not born.

25

Eugenics and the Disabled

By the late 19th century, Darwinian evolution had been transformed into and hijacked by social Darwinism. Social Darwinism, a non-empirically based world view, developed a virulent set of arguments against the poor, the "feeble-minded," and the disabled on the pretext of improving society and human evolution. Principally, social Darwinism comes from the reformist theories of social philosopher Herbert Spencer, the admixture of statistical analysis and poorly formed views in genetics, combined with the existing prejudices against the disabled to make a perfect storm of discrimination. The very concept of disability as impairment- the medical model of disability- owes its existence to the eugenic movement and social Darwinism. It augments the rise of the medical and therapeutic model of modernity with which we closed the last section. As Snyder and Mitchell write, "eugenics invented the category of 'disability' that grouped people with widely divergent physical and cognitive characteristics under a single heading of "defect."[150] This binary linguistic process would define the very nature of disability as a pure negative. It would take its lead from the millennia-long prejudices built up around the disabled and ground them in a specious, au courant theory covered in a veneer of a scientistic patina. The logic it assumes is strictly binary: on the one pole, you have ability, competence, and ethical, the good; while on the other, you have the defective, the impaired, and, by implication, the bad. Thus, terms such as impairment, disability, etc., are given a negative twist. The word "disability" appears first in the 1570s deriving from the Latin prefix "dis-" having a privative or negative sense and the stem "-abilitas," meaning to have the ability or aptitude. The word takes on its more common usage of a loss of ability in the late 19th century and will help pave the way for the social movement of eugenics and social Darwinism. It masks the ultimate Promethean hubris: what nature failed at, humankind can improve.

The term "eugenics" was coined by Francis Galton in 1883. Later, he defined the term in a 1904 issue of the American Journal of Sociology as "the science which deals with all influences that improve the inborn qualities of a race; also, with those that develop them to the utmost advantage." Galton believed that humans could direct their future by selectively breeding individuals who have certain "desired" traits. Thus, he famously coined the now-ubiquitous phrase, "nature versus nurture."

Breaking with Darwin's theory, Galton believed in a kind of deterministic heritable pattern with which we might intervene, direct, and produce desirable traits in humans the way farmers and breeders have been doing with plants and livestock for years. That the disabled take the place of plants or animals to be husbanded in this rhetoric is highly revealing. Darwin's assumption that only the fit survive is adopted wholesale and obsessively prized by Spencer and Galton precisely because it relegates the disabled to the ash pile of evolution.[151] The paternalistic attitudes that the aristocratic classes held toward the poor assisted in the development of this notion. The poor were to be controlled by the wealthy; they were viewed as incapable of self-improvement because they lacked the necessary desired traits. Their reasoning was a gross example of a common naturalistic fallacy where what is, is believed to be what ought to be. The poor were poor, the disabled, well disabled. Not, by the way, because of material lack, reactionary political choices, burdensome legislation, or inequities but because of something innate to their being, their nature. Combining Galton's theories with the British aristocracy's political and ethical upper-class snobbery, we can easily see why Galton and other's ideas of eugenics will take hold of upper-class intellectuals on both sides of the Atlantic. Stateside, Americans lacking a sense of identity were always imitating European, particularly British upper-class conventions and ideas. As a result, eugenics would thrive in America.

In the U.S. and elsewhere, these ideas form the foundation of a set of ideas that will lead to theories aimed at ridding society of the undesirable while simultaneously aggrandizing the upper class's values, beliefs, and skills. Many of Galton's ideas of the kinds of advantageous traits and who should live were based on Galton's earlier study of upper-class British society. These ideas would be accepted and advanced by the likes of Spencer, Huxley, and others. As a result, the work is imbued with British class-based, imperialistic, and racist prejudices. As an example, take the following racist and euro-centric sentiment from Galton in describing his work:

"The natural ability of which this book mainly treats is such as a modern European possesses in a much greater average share than the men of the lower races."[152]

Galton's position was widespread among the elites on both sides of the Atlantic. British academics, including Karl Pearson, head of the Department of Applied Statistics at University College, London, provided criteria for sterilization that included persons with tuberculosis, the insane, and those born "diseased" from birth.[153] At the department he headed, he would collect data used in future eugenic trials. Those chosen for eugenics would include hermaphrodites, hemophiliacs, the diabetic, the deaf, mute, those with harelips, and even those with different numbers and lengths of toes and fingers. Others, such as T.H. Huxley, who in describing the perceived differences between white Europeans and non-Europeans, specifically linked disability with race, further grounding 19th century notions of scientific racism and eugenics:

"No rational man, cognizant of the facts [could deny that the Negro is inherently inferior]. It is simply incredible that, when all his disabilities are removed, and our prognathous relative has a fair field and no favour, as well as no oppressor, he will be able to compete successfully with his bigger-brained and smaller-jawed rival, in a contest which is to be carried on by thoughts and not by bites."[154]

The link between disability, race, and social irrelevance was everywhere in the 19th century, and it becomes one of the most potent and unchecked assumptions of the 20th century. Herbert Spencer would become the heir to Galton and Huxley in advocating a social evolution based on these exclusionary categories. Differing radically from Darwin's conception of evolution as expressed in his "Origin of the Species," Spencer would later coin the phrase "survival of the fittest." A phrase wrongfully attributed to Darwin and somewhat surprising to people unacquainted with Darwin's writings is found nowhere in Darwin's published works. That is until Alfred Wallace wrote to Darwin advocating its use, and he adopted it after Spencer. To be clear, Darwin would use the term later but usually to refer to natural selection in the plant and animal kingdoms and not humans. For Spencer, the phrase embodied the eugenical ideal of the dominance of the fittest as it applied to humans. It will play the operative role in nearly all ideologies of discrimination, including those aimed at the disabled. He first approached and wrote about his thoughts on evolution in his 1857 essay, "Progress: Its Law and Cause," published in The Westminster Review. The essay would be the basis for later theories of pseudo-genetic prejudices. That it would be published in such an eminent journal is revelatory. The powerful influence of The Westminster Review would show in its list of editors and contributors. The philosophical radicals started the Review, including James Mill, Jeremy Bentham, and John Stuart Mill. The review became the organ for 19th-century liberalism and would see Mary Ann Evans (George Eliot) become an editor. Under her guidance, it published articles articulating the "law of progress" that would outline classist and racist theory adopted by later British and American intellectuals. The Review would feature the work of the scientific racist and population demagogue, Thomas Malthus. The Malthusian position blames the "upsurge" in lower-class populations for their uncontrollable innate desires leading to surges in population that would outpace the subsistence, leading to crime, disease, and famine. Malthus and others would then argue that it would be better to pre-emptively reduce these populations by cutting back on welfare, charity, and other social programs. Malthus' belief became the mantra of most conservative, libertarian, and right-wing ideologues in the 20th century.

Spencer would be a contributor to the Review. One of his essays from the review would form the basis of his book, the "First Principles of a New System of Philosophy," published in 1862, wherein he would articulate many of these ideas.

Contrary to Darwin's claims, he would hold that evolution had a goal or end. Teleological thinking is anathema to modern evolutionary theories following Darwin's aleatory open-ended evolution model, but Spencer would smuggle in his assumptions. Spencer's end-point model would, he argued, reach a final state of equilibrium. This equilibrium would likely see the triumph of his 19th-century social class. A position that Bertrand Russell criticized in a 1923 letter to Lady Beatrice Webb, writing,

"I don't know whether [Spencer] was ever made to realise the implications of the second law of thermodynamics; if so, he may well be upset. The law says that everything tends to uniformity and a dead level, diminishing (not increasing) heterogeneity."[155]

Spencer would then attempt to unite his interpretation of the theory of evolution with the current debates in biology, sociology, and ethics. Viewing society as a complex organism that had changed from a lower to a higher form became one of the essential and erroneous ideas embedded within social Darwinism. Thus, leading to the teleological ideal that Spencer argued we should work toward achieving. The desired endpoint requires us to do whatever is necessary to reach it, including, of course, improving those around us who may be hampering our ability to reach that pinnacle of social perfection. His indebtedness to his earlier studies and fascination with the French thinker Auguste de Comte is clear here. Comte had advanced the notion of an ever-evolving society that could and would reach, inevitably, a state of perfectibility. Comte's idea would influence a wide range of thinkers in the 19th century, including disparate thinkers from Spencer and Marx.[156] The idea of progress is, of course, one that lurks behind the unchecked presuppositions of eugenicists, too. Each of these thinkers, albeit in their way, believed in the perfectibility of humanity. For Spencer and the eugenicists, science becomes the vehicle of that perfection. In the end, Spencer provides the philosophical scaffolding that Galton, Huxley, and the eugenicists would need to construct the system of discrimination that eugenics provided. Armed with ableism, classism, and racialized science, social programs aim to remove the disabled from society, gain their teeth and start to cannibalize.

Herbert Spencer may have coined the phrase "survival of the fittest," but the upper echelons of British society would cleave wholeheartedly to such an idea and make it a creed. Prime Ministers A.J. Balfour, Neville Chamberlain, and Winston Churchill would all be social Darwinists and eugenicists.

Political affiliation seemed not to matter to many on the left, such as Sidney and Beatrice Webb and other Fabian Socialists, who would accept and promulgate eugenical ideas. They would join writers such as H.G. Wells, George Bernard Shaw, and economist John Maynard Keynes to name but a few. To this dubious tradition, American progressives would vigorously add the concept of 19th-century race and the attendant notion of "race suicide." First introduced by Edward A. Ross, a University of Wisconsin sociologist -who had been fired from Stanford University for his vitriolic opposition to Chinese and Japanese immigrants -the concept of race in science would become a popular notion with academics. To get a measure of the man, consider Ross's comments he made at an anti-Japanese rally,

"And should the worst come to the worst it would be better for us if we were to turn our guns upon every vessel bringing Japanese to our shores rather than to permit them to land."[157]

Fired from Stanford, he would hold appointments at the Universities of Nebraska, Wisconsin, and Chicago, become a best-selling author, and capture the ear of President Theodore Roosevelt, who became an ardent eugenicist. Ross would visit the Soviet Union and welcome the revolution, serve on the Dewey Commission that exonerated Leon Trotsky, and serve on the national committee of the ACLU. Yet, as this list demonstrates, the ideas we are exploring were widely accepted by vast sections of Americans. Many of the intelligentsia, left and right; academics; progressive and reactionary political leaders of the day, and ordinary people will subscribe to some version or other of this potent brew. A short-list of influential eugenicists includes Presidents Coolidge and Theodore Roosevelt; Senator Henry Cabot Lodge; Henry Ford; Alexander Graham Bell; Supreme Court Justice Oliver Wendell Holmes, Jr.; novelists Upton Sinclair and Sinclair Lewis, and activists Margaret Sanger, Helen Keller, and W.E.B. Dubois.[158] Even the anarchist Emma Goldman would espouse eugenics, arguing that states needed to decrease the birth rates of "paupers, syphilitics, epileptics, dipsomaniacs, cripples, criminals, degenerates, etc."[159] Political foes would find common cause in exterminating the poor and the disabled.

Eugenicists working in high and mighty institutions would wield power that would shape generations of Americans to come. Their collective influence was so widespread and came from their missionary-like zeal to protect the future. To achieve this goal, they would turn to new theories of social planning to begin their crusade. As mentioned earlier, Social Darwinists and eugenicists, following the leads of Huxley and Spencer, opposed most state aid, welfare, and support programs for and to the benefit of poor and disabled on the grounds of not wanting to provide them the means to procreate or reproduce. To allow them to reproduce would further burden society, so social engineers would focus on contraception, abortion, and forced sterilization as preemptive measures to control the population. The addition of economics to the mix of biological, ethical, and sociological theories completed the recipe for the new eugenicist philosophy. If the goal was to rid the system of the unfit, then depriving them of any material support from which they might gain advantage was a key, if inhumane, strategy. Oddly, none of these so-called evolutionary thinkers concluded that their fellow species members were cleverly adapting to the challenging conditions they found themselves born in and to; instead, they held a deterministic notion toward the entrepreneurial spirit of the poor, disabled and disenfranchised. Instead, the class-based, aristocratic nature of these thinkers' assumptions was immune to the diligent struggles and earnest efforts of many poor and disabled. The social engineers' self-imposed blinders allowed them to see only future perils for the nation and species if they failed to change the course of the ship of state. Unfortunately, the upper-class intelligentsia that adopted eugenics was all too quick to jump to the task of steering the ship of state. Their first act was to criticize the impoverished and disabled, a classic example of blaming the victim.

The upper classes rail at the poor that their own lifestyles and limitless demand for luxuries and thriving economies create; but offer little real relief or shared opportunity for actual improvement. To achieve their ends, they would take refuge in the popular pseudo-sciences of their day. The burden placed on the shoulders of the upper-class intelligentsia was enormous: they had to save their nation from impoverishment and rescue the species from these inferiors.

Because of these ideas and practices, persons with disabilities will suffer the most in modernity. Many will be forcibly institutionalized and shut away in single-sex institutions for life; or, where affordable, sterilized without providing consent. In addition, liberal reformers created separate schools and work-centers in their largesse, further segregating persons with less severe disabilities from mainstream society. The attempt to cleanse the unwanted poor and disabled from society would be the new banner for socially-minded progressives. But, unfortunately, it would lead to measures that are even more draconian by the middle of the century. Thus, a year after Galton's death in 1912, a eugenics conference was convened. As Dr. Howard Markel describes the meeting and the zeitgeist leading up to it:

"Sir Francis's social theories on who was eugenically worthy spread like wildfire among white intellectuals in almost every developed Western nation. For example, in July of 1912, one year after Galton's death, the threat of inferior races polluting the Western body politic was discussed at the first International Congress of Eugenics in Lon-

don. Sitting in the audience were Britain's Prime Minister Lord Balfour, Winston Churchill and Charles Darwin's son Leonard, along with
the ambassadors of Greece, France and (wait for it) Norway."[160]

As social Darwinist theories started to gain traction with the upper
classes, eugenicists would be further motivated to find themselves suddenly well-funded, leading to many tirelessly campaigning for and winning the battle for public opinion. They would convene conferences,
publish books, journals, articles, and change social policy. Finally, they
had the ears of the powerful, and they found themselves being heard.
The result was that they affected the sort of change they longed for and
long desired.

To start, they needed to identify and label with scientifically reason-
able terms and then apply the remedies. Unfortunately, the labels often
invoked included "idiots," "morons,"[161] or "imbeciles." All of this was
done, naturally, in the name of progress.

Its history can be traced to England in the 1890s. Mary Dendy would
advocate for segregating the "mentally subnormal" from the larger population: "to stem the great evil of feeble-mindedness in our country."
Such rhetoric was justified because it claims to prevent unspeakable
"evils" that would slow the advance of society if left unchecked. The
"evils" are coded words for perceived notions of criminality, disability,
poverty, and sexual promiscuity. The last item on the laundry list of
the "evils" prompts so many of this period to be obsessed with the sexual lives and reproductive nature of poor women and persons with disabilities. It would ultimately lead them to justify the practice of forced
sterilization. Falsified identifications of sexuality and prejudice would
be integral to other forms of discrimination; suffragists and persons of
color will be branded as sexual outlaws, perverts, predators, rapists, etc.
The two twin poles of these obsessions will be either a complete loss of
sexual ability or a super-human sexual prowess.

In England, Dendy's efforts would see the establishment of institutions and the passing of eugenics-inspired legislation used to in-
carcerate individuals deemed "feeble-minded." As we have seen,
feeble-mindedness became a lump term that would grow to include

anyone with any form of mental or social ineptitude or physical disability. In England, Dendy's efforts would establish a Royal Commission on Mental Deficiency that became a significant player advancing the new eugenics platform. This kind of thinking would eventually lead to the "Mental Disability Act of 1913" in England and Wales. The legislation would lead to economically powerless and vulnerable people--many with disabilities--being summarily deprived of their liberties in the U.K. This legislation would become the model for future laws abroad.

As Snyder and Mitchell indicate, the wedding of the eugenics movement with the mania for classifying and quantifying intelligence would become a potent brew for discriminatory attitudes and allow eugenics to become a widespread social phenomenon. The 19th-century popularity of anthropometric techniques and schemes inundated both professional and popular sciences of the day. Phrenology and other pseudo-scientific theories of measuring craniums would lead to measuring bits of intelligence, and a whole host of hierarchies would be produced showing males were more intelligent than females,[162] whites more intelligent than other, darker-skinned races[163]; and, of course, Europeans smarter than the rest of the world. Americans would-despite their protestations that they were not indebted to Europe-swallow these prejudices completely. When it came to matters of racism, Americans become proud Europeans. We would see that latter focus on the boon of administering I.Q. testing blossom in America. Snyder and Mitchell summarize this complex set of ideas manifesting in the new educational philosophies:

"While a theory of heredity gave scientific support for the formal exclusion of disabled people from mainstream social life, training schools were the setting for the formulation of a new diagnostic classification."[164]

The torchbearers of this new ideology of hate would take inspiration from leaders such as the American eugenicist Henry H. Goddard who spoke with an obsessive zeal about hunting down persons with disabilities,

"We need to study them very seriously and very thoroughly; we need to hunt them out in every possible place and take care of them."[165]

What would he mean? Solicitude? Compassion? No. We will see that "care" implies institutionalization, sterilization, and debasement. All disabled persons in modernity will soon feel like Flaubert's Hippolyte. The implied violence of this metaphor belies their aims at a progressive betterment of society. What is operative here is the fear of and hate of difference and disability that we have seen as part of the Western project. America, as we will soon see, would eventually become the fecund battleground for eugenics.

In the rhetoric of the late 19th-century empire builders and colonists, it became essential for them to feel a sense of superiority to other nations and races, even those indistinguishable from their own. The discourse of racism will dominate, but so, too, will ableist and sexist prejudices. For example, in 1881, the new nation of Italy convened the International Congress in Milan that would outlaw sign language. They feared that deaf people would outbreed hearing people and perhaps transduce a new language, shedding Italian.[166] But, beneath this fear is the fear of the other—in this sense, deaf Italians— and they will be caricatured as hypersexual, immoral, and anti-Italian and left unchecked would produce more of their kind (an essential assumption) than the good Italians. As we saw above, the Italian physician Cesare Lombroso had attempted to classify criminals by their physiology. He had earlier claimed to demonstrate that "criminals are apes in our midst, marked by the anatomical stigmata of atavism," which was a code for being outwardly disabled. The whole complex of hate-driven metaphors and unchecked assumptions is at play in Lombroso's warning.

Lombroso defined "epilepsy as a mark of criminality."[167] One can only wonder what prejudices and fears the hearing world thought the deaf were communicating via their cryptic sign language or the epileptic was trying to steal when they had a seizure. As with the oppression of all minority cultures, the dominating culture fears the language of the minority and quickly bans the use of that minority language. We saw this, for example, in the banning of indigenous languages in North America and elsewhere (e.g., the United States, Canada, and Australia). But it goes back as far as the Norman conquest of England when the French-speaking Normans would outlaw the Saxon.

An unprecedented level of international cooperation coalesced around eugenics and its advocates. Nation-states may not agree on trade tariffs, commerce, or boundaries, but they were unified in their fear of the disabled. For example, at the Second International Congress of Eugenics held in New York City at the American Museum of Natural History in 1921, virtually every industrialized nation had representatives present, including delegates from Belgium, Britain, Denmark, France, Italy, Norway, Sweden. Russia and Germany would like to have been present, but due to the recent national wounds of WWI, they were not allowed to attend in person, but their research and their voices were heeded, and their professionals kept within the fold.[168] The new century looked bleak for the disabled, and it was just the beginning.

26

Between the Wars:
Disability and Restriction

The period between the two world wars served as a period of readjustment of attitudes toward the concept of disability and the disabled themselves. As Snyder and Mitchell note discussing Fred Wiseman's interwar period documentaries on the disabled, "the period of U.S. History represented by these works is, concerning people with disabilities, the most dynamic and portentous period, which saw the development of an increasingly hostile and restrictive social context for all marginalized populations." We see this in eugenics, the treatment of the poor, the rise of antisemitism, the struggles of women for universal suffrage, colonial repression, and institutional and systemic racism.

The disabled suffer much in this period; indeed, as the long period between the U.S. Civil War and WWII witnesses, the general practice toward the disabled is less benevolent than in earlier periods. The larger medical community can be viewed as both partially at fault and as a potential remedy, but more importantly, as playing into the hegemonic attitudes pervasive in Western society toward the disabled. The medical community's cooperation is nothing but tragic. These attitudes are seen in the publication (1901) of a widely used medical textbook written by Gould and Pyle and called "Anomalies and Curiosities of Medicine" that contained detailed descriptions replete with grainy black and white photographs of "a veritable freak show of disabled bodies placed on display in medical photographs"[169] and which was a popular resource in medical colleges. While ostensibly being used to educate physicians, it seemed to build on and arouse attention by its blatantly voyeuristic tendencies too often found in the attraction of the other. Snyder and Mitchell conclude,

"From this perspective, research feeds the insatiable gristmill of science while fortifying our ideas of disability as a curiosity that invites the most prurient forms of speculation parading as empiricism."

The 20th century—the bloodiest and arguably most violent century for the disabled—would see eugenics emerge as the scientific justification for discrimination. The trans-Atlantic eugenics movement became a genuinely cooperative Euro-American movement beginning with the British and French biologists and moving to American psychologists and social planners and into the open arms of German social engineers and doctors. The widely popular yet pseudo-scientific notion that we can control our genetic future would become the rallying cry for a North Atlantic war against the disabled through human intervention.

The American movement in eugenics was funded by powerful, well-endowed American institutions such as Planned Parenthood, The National Geographic Society, the Carnegie Foundation, and many prestigious and influential American Universities. Eugenicists often came from the dominant white, Anglo-Saxon protestant liberal echelons. Much of their hate is aimed at the disabled, Catholics, Jews, persons of color, and others who do not belong to their privileged classes. To support these ideas, some U.S. leaders, private citizens, and corporations started channeling funds into eugenics studies at research institutes and universities with top scientists and politicians' full and uncritical support. The list of institutions and universities who profited or were deeply involved reads like a who's who of 20th century American wealth and power. Joining those mentioned above with guilty hands included the Rockefeller Foundation, the Harriman Foundation, the Kellogg Foundation, and elite universities such as Harvard, Princeton, Stanford, Bowdoin, and Vermont.

However, the Eugenics Records Office (ERO) was the leading American institution advocating eugenics. It was established in 1911 in Cold Springs Harbor, New York, by Charles Davenport. Davenport defined eugenics as the "science of the improvement of the human race by better breeding."[170] To give you a measure of the suspect nature of genetic knowledge at the time, Davenport believed that there was a single gene responsible for the "love of the sea," something he coined, "thalassophilia," and which could be used to explain why the sons of anglers and sailors became anglers and sailors. He argued that this genetic dispensation for the sea was why "naval careers ran in families."[171]

Davenport had persuaded the Carnegie Institute, John D. Rockefeller, Jr., and others to support the ERO. He then appointed Harry W. Laughlin as its first superintendent. Laughlin was the author of a flawed sociological study examining the "excessive mental defectiveness" of southern and eastern European immigrants. He authored a book on eugenics published in 1922 that examined American sterilization policy titled Eugenical Sterilization in the United States. It included an exhaustive list of those worthy of sterilization, including the feeble-minded, the insane, criminals, epileptics, alcoholics, blind persons, deaf persons, deformed persons, and indigent persons. Eighteen states passed laws based on Laughlin's flawed research.

Laughlin's suggestions were also quickly adopted in Nazi Germany. His model served as a basis for the infamous and stringently enforced Erbgesundhetsrecht and led the Reichstag to pass the Prevention of Hereditarily Diseased Offspring law in 1933. Laughlin's efforts would be rewarded. He received an honorary degree from the University of Heidelberg in 1936 for his work in the "science of racial cleansing."[172]

Laughlin and the rest of the ERO staff spent ample time and considerable resources surreptitiously tracking family histories. They assumed that the unfit always came from low-income families, recent immigrants, or were members of minorities. They also often lived with physical or mental disabilities. The ERO would track these people, and when states enacted sterilization laws, they would offer the names to the local boards over-seeing the process of sterilization. It led an entire generation of eugenic-inspired professionals -biologists, geneticists, engineers, psychologists, sociologists, social workers, statisticians- carrying out their policies. These professionals, as Friedlander writes, wanted to introduce rational social planning into human affairs and believed that biological manipulation would achieve their ends."[173] Their dominance in both the biological and social sciences reverberates to this day in American universities and governmental agencies. For example, these and similar researchers "demonstrated" that the undesirable traits in these families, such as poverty, were entirely due to genetics and not lack of resources or of existing inequities. If Davenport's flawed science explained the origins of sailors, it would work for the poor, too.

Prejudicially laden thinking led many social activists to adopt eugenics. One such figure was Margaret Sanger, who strenuously advocated against charitable organizations and argued for the institution of repressive social controls of minorities. Sanger would choose birth control, sterilization, and legalized abortion as the mechanisms to limit those she deemed unwanted and undesirable. How else can we explain the fact that Sanger willingly spoke to a KKK meeting in Silver Lake, New Jersey, in 1929?[174]

The Klan in 1926 was near its height in popularity, having gained many additional members in the early 20th century; its unchecked violence toward minorities was near an all-time high, too. Such violence was a tragic and common phenomenon in America. According to the University of Missouri-Kansas City Law Project,[175] 23 African Americans were lynched that year alone. The climate of hate is evident in the American sociologist Ross who would be a staunch and effective advocate for sterilization. Here are his thoughts on the subject:

"For my own part, I am entirely in favor of it. The objections to it are essentially sentimental, and will not bear inspection. Sterilization is not nearly so terrible as hanging a man, and the chances of sterilizing the fit are not nearly so great, as are the chances of hanging the innocent. In introducing the policy, the wedge should have a very thin end indeed. Sterilization should at first be applied only to extreme cases, where the commitments and the record pile up an overwhelming case. As the public becomes accustomed to it, and it is seen to be salutary and humane, it will be possible gradually to extend its scope until it fills its legitimate sphere of application."[176]

The chilling inhumanity of this passage will only be surpassed by the extent to which others would go to achieve the same goal. Ross was putting into words the dominant belief about those deemed undesirable, the disabled, the poor, and immigrants. One needs to place this quote into the historical context of systemic violence, such as the lynching of African Americans, reminding us of how starkly inhumane and commonplace these beliefs are rooted in American culture. Ross's comparison between lynching and sterilization becomes the two twin poles of hate leveled at those deemed undesirables- blacks and the disabled-that is so pervasive in American culture. The presence of so much hate and fear would inspire Abe Meerpool[177] to pen "Strange Fruit," which Time magazine named the American song of the century. Billie Holliday's haunting and soul-stirring rendition would make it famous in 1938, but even her soulful rendition could not stop the onslaught of violence.

Although coming from the same alchemy of intolerance, fear, and hate, much of the violence aimed at the disabled would be sublimated through bureaucracy and institutions and not through outright violent acts. State by state, committees, councils, and boards would be convened to offer solutions to the problem of the growing number of "undesirables" in the U.S. These undesirables were inevitably poor, disabled, and often members of minority groups. As members of these minority groups, barred from voicing their positions. In complete contrast and using the full power of his bully pulpit on the Supreme Court to advocate for eugenics, Justice Holmes would infamously opine that "three generations of imbeciles is enough" in the tragic Buck v Bell Supreme Court decision.[178]

"It is better for all the world if instead of waiting to execute degenerate offspring for crime or to let them starve for their imbecility, society can prevent those who are manifestly unfit from continuing their kind...Three generations of imbeciles are enough." (Buck v. Bell)

Holmes wrote the majority opinion for the Supreme Court's affirmative decision on the Buck v. Bell case. The case argued that a young woman, Vivian Buck, and her mother, Carrie, were deemed unfit and "not quite normal." It appears that such a determination was based entirely on their perceived sexual promiscuity of the Buck women. Carrie Buck had been raped at 17 and gave birth as an unwed mother. This seems to be the only basis for the Supreme Court decision about her proposed promiscuity. Oliver Wendell Holmes Jr. described her daughter, Vivian, as the "probable potential parent of socially inadequate offspring, likewise afflicted," stating that "her sterilization will promote her welfare and that of society." All the evidence gathered to mount a case against Vivian and Carrie was spurious and today would be quickly discredited. At the time, labeling anyone as "unfit" or "not normal" was tantamount to issuing a life sentence. Designations as "unfit" were applied to a host of people that did not fit the standards. The vilified would include the poor, illiterate, blind, deaf, deformed, disabled, diseased, gypsies, orphans, "ne'er-do-wells," homeless, tramps, paupers, and river rats.[179]

As the noted evolutionary biologist and science writer Stephen Jay Gould wrote,

"Restrictions upon immigration, with natural quotas set to discriminate against those deemed mentally unfit by early versions of IQ testing, marked the greatest triumph of the American eugenics movement—the flawed hereditarian doctrine, so popular earlier in our century and by no means extinct today, that attempted to "improve" our human stock by preventing the propagation of those deemed biologically unfit and encouraging procreation among the supposedly worthy. But the movement to enact and enforce laws for compulsory "eugenic" sterilization had an impact and success scarcely less pronounced. If we could debar the shiftless and the stupid from our shores, we might also prevent the propagation of those similarly affected but already here."[180]

As noted, a chief underlying set of assumptions fueling the eugenics movement were the fascination scientists developed with quantifying intelligence. Added to sociological and statistical analyses of family planning we noted earlier, eugenics would become a ruthless tool for the dominant class to wield against those deemed unfit. One of the early advocates of I.Q. testing in America, Lewis Terman, combined the concepts of family planning with intelligence measuring and genetics and worrying,

"The fecundity of the family stocks from which our most gifted children come appears to be definitely on the wane."[181]

Along with others, he would issue a call to limit the lower classes' birth rates, persons with disabilities, and immigrants based on I.Q. measurements decrying that if we did not take quick action, there would soon be fewer children from alumni of Harvard than Italians in America. From reasoning like this was born a new and powerful tool to segregate and label, the I.Q. test.

As New York Times columnist, David Brooks, points out in a 2007 article on I.Q., "over the past century, average I.Q. scores have risen at a rate about 3 to 6 points per decade." Brooks describes the well-known "Flynn Effect" coined by Charles Murray[182] and Richard Herrnstein in their 1994 book, "The Bell Curve," and named for the psychologist James R. Flynn. It is essential to mention here that Murray and Hernstein's research was built on and, in part, funded by the Pioneer Fund, an American not-for-profit started by Edsel Ford. In its 1937 incorporation, the Pioneer Fund modeled its goals on the Nazi Lebensborn breeding program. One of its first projects was to pay for the distribution of a Nazi propaganda film about eugenics. Harry Laughlin of the ERO served as the president of the Pioneer Fund from 1937 until 1941, opposing interracial marriage and providing funding to assist in enforcing Southern "race integrity laws." Laughlin also opposed Jewish refugees fleeing Nazi Germany entry into the United States. In 1949, one of the fund's leading proponents, Wickliff Preston Draper, met C. Nash Herndon of the Bowman Gray School of Medicine at Wake Forest to support Herndon's advocacy of compulsory sterilization programs in North Carolina. Today, the Southern Poverty Law Center lists the fund as a "racist and white supremacist" organization. The Sunday Telegraph described the Fund as a "neo-Nazi organization closely integrated with the far right in American politics." Indeed, following Jesse Helms's 1984 Senate re-election bid, The Washington Post journalists Thomas Edsall and David Vise reported how Helms was linked to the Pioneer Fund and its attempts to show whites were genetically superior to blacks.

The Flynn Effect is usually referred to as the effect of "secular rise in I.Q. scores." The noticeable trend has been explained, in part, by test familiarity, better nutrition, better living conditions, schools that are more effective at education, more intellectually stimulating environments, and a host of other plausible factors. All of which would be blissfully overlooked by I.Q. enthusiasts and eugenicists. Brooks notes that only about 48 % of human intelligence can be safely attributed to one's genes and that environment plays a more prominent role. The role of the environment must be taken into account--environmental and economic circumstances are precisely the conditions most eugenicists failed to consider. Brooks cites the work of H.M. Skeels, who studied developmentally disabled foster children and found that adopted children had a significant average increase in I.Q. than their unfortunate peers who remained in the orphanages. Brooks concludes, "it wasn't tutoring that produced the I.Q. spike; it was love."[183] The 20th century with its social engineering, urban planning, rapacious capitalism, strident nationalisms, hyper technology, and obsessive scientism would be the last place to look for love and compassion.

Analogously, we see the lack of compassion in U.S. immigration policy. Stricter immigration rules were enacted, including the passage of the draconian Immigration Restriction Act of 1924 that was explicit in its eugenic orientation. Laughlin had lobbied explicitly for its passage. Laughlin was called on to testify and called an "expert eugenical agent"[184] when his testimony was invoked. The law would be designed to limit southern and eastern Europeans who were viewed, at the time, as problematic to the dominant WASP culture. The immigration law sought to restrict the entry of those described as "swarthy," "unkempt," and "unassimilable."[185] In essence, eugenics and racism offered Americans in power an authoritative scientific language to substantiate their biases against those they feared.

The eugenicist's plan to sterilize "unfit" individuals to prevent them from passing on their negative traits became a widespread national project. During the early part of the 20th century, 33 states had sterilization programs in place. The U.S. was not alone in enacting sterilization laws against the disabled. Japan had a set of leprosy prevention laws mandating sterilization and forced abortions as early as 1907.

In the United States, Indiana was the first state to pass a forced euthanasia law. Their neighbor to the north and across Lake Michigan, Canada, would witness the passage of the Alberta Sexual Sterilization Act of 1927, which led to an estimated 3,000 forced sterilizations. While sterilization efforts initially targeted mentally ill people exclusively, later traits deemed severe enough to warrant sterilization would grow to include alcoholism, criminality, chronic poverty, blindness, deafness, drunkards, drug fiends, epileptics, feeble-mindedness, pauperism, and promiscuity (see Ludmerer, 1972). Establishing the criterion for many of these terms was suspect. As we have seen, measuring intelligence was challengingly opaque, and no two psychologists seem to agree on what it is nor how to measure it. Yet and perhaps because of its opacity, it is often used as a lightning rod to distinguish the desired traits.

During this period in America, it was not uncommon for African American and Native American women to be forcibly sterilized while other medical procedures were being performed, and, of course, without their prior consent or approval. Cases predominate where the individual sterilized did not know she had been.[186] Indeed, as we have seen, the eugenic prejudices against the disabled would be added to racism and class to concoct a potent mixture of discriminatory attitudes still operative well into the 21st century. Recall how, as recently as 1965, one-third of Puerto Rican women had undergone forced sterilization. Lest we get too complacent, forced sterilizations are still an all too frequent and grim reality for many persons living with disabilities across the globe today. In May of 2014, the World Health Organization published a joint, inter-agency statement addressing the need to eliminate forced, coercive, and otherwise involuntary sterilizations. The report's very existence speaks to the frequency of this barbaric practice. The report referenced the involuntary sterilization of several specific population groups, including the disabled; the other groups affected included many threatened groups, including cultural and racial minorities, indigenous persons, women, children, and transgender individuals. Persons with disabilities, predominantly intellectual and cognitive disabilities, are often still the targets of these violations. The report adds:

"Human rights bodies have recognized that sterilization of persons with disabilities without their consent constitutes discrimination, a form of violence and torture, or other cruel, inhuman or degrading treatment."

The report concludes that such practices are still in play today because persons with disabilities are "often treated as if they have no control, or should have no control, over their sexual and reproductive choices"[187] Part of the prejudices arrayed against persons of disabilities is the constant infantilizing of and reductive dehumanization of the disabled person's autonomy. It is a sobering reminder of how little we have progressed and how deeply set these prejudices have become.

Most people--then and now--subject to sterilizations had no choice. They did not give and were not asked for consent. Because the programs were run by the government or powerful non-governmental institutions backed by the government, they had little to no chance of escaping the procedure and certainly no recourse for appeal. Further, innovations in science and technology would valorize the new technology as a humane and cost-effective way of treating what formerly was never considered a problem. In this sense, science and technology will often manufacture a "problem" out of thin air merely to manufacture its value and increase its profitability for its backers and investors. Our deepest fears and political prejudices may manifest and control what and how science operates in this sense. Too often, science has been used as a tool of repression and division and an implement for social control by the upper classes. Science's veneer of objectivity is torn asunder to reveal its sordid underbelly looking to most suspiciously like a weapon for the rich. Indeed, as Stephen Jay Gould writes in his essay on Carrie Buck, the development of new medical technologies would further enhance the scope and reach of these modern Prometheans allowing their zeal to institute repressive programs:

"The movement for compulsory sterilization began in earnest during the 1890s, abetted by two major factors—the rise of eugenics as an influential political movement and the perfection of safe and simple operations (vasectomy for men and salpingectomy, the cutting, and tying of Fallopian tubes, for women) to replace castration and other socially unacceptable forms of mutilation."

The tragic upshot of these practices was that the all-reaching "benevolent" state and institutions of "care" could step in brandishing its new technology and have its self-appointed "experts" diagnose you as "unfit." If they do not already have a category to place you in, they will soon devise one for you and your condition. This significantly increased your chances that you could be sterilized, institutionalized, or, at least, be labeled. The zeal for classification and attendant process of pathologization would be in full swing in modern mid-century America. The Catholic priest and anarchist philosopher, Ivan Illich, is especially helpful in analyzing and diagnosing this tendency in modernity. In his insightful work, "Medical Nemesis," he introduces the concept of "specific diseconomy," which is the measure of social anomie occasioned when an institution gets out of hand. More technically, according to Illich, it refers to the institutionally counterproductive results created by a technological development gone amok. For example, one can use an illustration from medical practices where labels produce a specific illness to be treated by that medical practice. Alternatively, as this book shows, these practices define the very concept of disability as a pathology to be treated. In short, many conditions we understand as "disability" today were not pathologized before the development of the very technology advanced to identify, cure, treat, or end that exact condition. As such, we see examples ranging from medical technology fields that induce illness to educational institutions that create conceptions of ignorance, rankings, and endless comparisons, all creating self-fulfilling prophecies. Finally, the modern judicial and penal systems which perpetuate injustices in the very name of justice, the scientific and medical technologies used by the powers-that-be for and in their own narrow interests create a potent admixture of repression. When a specific diseconomy is increasing, the institution or industry responsible for that technology is increasingly counterproductive to its original intentions. The "Bell v Buck" decision is a textbook example when we see the decades of tragedy that would ensue from this decision and the medical technologies that made it all possible in the first place.

The rest of mainstream American culture will follow the lead of the upper class. Thus, the eugenical and ableist (as well as racist, homophobic and sexist) assumptions become pervasive and part of the normative assumptions of a society. In the U.S., the eugenics movement would attain its most significant height by the late 1930s, having begun in earnest in 1905. At state fairs and agricultural expositions in rural America, eugenicists capitalized on the rural nature of American and its agricultural basis by funding contests for "fitter families." One of the first contests was at the 1911 Iowa State Fair and was initially known as the "Fitter Families for Future Firesides" but became better known simply as "Fitter Families Contests." The contest was the brainchild of Mary Watts and Florence Brown Sherbon. Both Watts and Sherbon were two of the early pioneers of the Baby Health Examination movement, which sprang from a "Better Baby" contest that started at the 1911 Iowa State Fair and spread to 40 other states before WWI. Florence Sherbon[188] had studied nursing in Iowa and saw that part of her mission was to reduce the infant mortality rate by improving the health of the mother and child also by getting rid of midwives.

The contests grew in popularity with financial support provided by the American Eugenics Society's committee on popular education. Held at state and county fairs throughout the United States up to and through the 1920s, the contests became popular in rural America and the burgeoning middle classes. Prior to entering a competition, the families were required to view a puppet show on eugenics in what was called a "Mendel Theatre" --named after Gregor Mendel, the innovator of pea hybridization. Organizers would then demonstrate the principles of eugenics to the families, often using a black and white guinea pig, demonstrating dominant and recessive genetic traits.[189] The final hurdle was an interview by the organizers asking the families about their ancestry and race, and any known disabilities. If purity was determined, the chosen family was eligible to enter the contest. As the contests developed, families submitted a record of traits and underwent both physical and psychological examinations by teams of doctors paid for by the American Red Cross.[190] Next, doctors graded the families using a whole letter grade system, awarding a silver trophy to the "fittest." Awards were given in three categories for families of different sizes- small, medium, and large-- depending on the number of children in each family. The top prize for families earning a B+ or better would often bear the inscription:

"Yea, I have a goodly heritage."[191]

Quite predictably, such contests were open only to white families coming from western and northern European heritage. You did not bother entering if you or any member of your family had a psychiatric condition, lost a limb or digit from a farming accident, or did not meet any racial categories!

27

Immigration and Disability: Who Gets in and Who Doesn't: Telling Their Story

While we just learned that stricter immigration rules were one of the policies of the eugenics movements, earlier immigration policy exacted heavy burdens on disabled migrants trying to enter the United States. Immigration policy would become more restrictive and discriminatory through the 19th and 20th centuries. The land of liberty would start to look more like a 21st century gated community. The first Federal immigration law (1824) expressly prohibited the entry of any "lunatic" or "idiot." It would later be amended in 1891 to include anyone "unable to care of himself or herself," and most physical and mental disabilities would be added to the laundry list of conditions inspectors would look for and ban. That an inspector would "look" is a loose use of the term. They were given little to no training, so each inspector would fall back on and rely on their personal biases. In 1903, people with epilepsy were banned, and by 1917 the list of exclusions would include those with arthritis, asthma, bunions, deafness, deformities, flat feet, poor eyesight, spinal curvature, and varicose veins, to name but a few. Fiorello LaGuardia, later to be the 99th mayor of New York City, would report that while he worked as an interpreter on Ellis Island, "over fifty percent of the deportations for the alleged mental disease were unjustified."[192]

A declaration certifying a person unfit would lead to deportation, splitting families and dashing the dreams and hopes as well as the hard-earned money expended by the hopeful émigré. Not to mention the risks they encountered leaving their homeland only to face them once again after being deported.

The immigration services labeled any physical disability with the so-called LPC clause. The LPC clause meant a person was, in their eyes, "likely to become a public charge."[193] Even in cases where a citizen vouched for the person, had a job waiting for them, or a sponsor, a disability was enough to evoke a Kafkaesque tribunal set in motion. Nielsen reports of a Russian Jew, Moische Fischmann, who happened to be deaf and was deported despite having many guarantors of support. The LPC designation was not the only criterion available to the immigration officials. One medical officer explained that the actual ability to work was not the only factor: "even if he was able, employers of labor would not hire him"[194] This claim shows how the mere possibility of any future discriminatory act that the émigré may face was justification for denying entry. The sheer chance that the émigré may meet with discrimination once allowed to enter was used as justification for discriminating against them and barring them from entering in the first place. The Byzantine logic reveals the absurd levels institutions, policies, and people will stoop to discriminate against the disabled. Why would the state suddenly become so concerned about the well-being of the disabled?

The height of the absurdity is reached in the following strange case. It is the peculiar case of the Irish immigrant, Patrick Eagan. In his case, we witness the surreal nature of immigration in America. In 1909, Eagan was refused entry to the United States because officials thought the able-bodied laborer's penis was too small. Canady reports that immigration officials were looking for "effeminately developed" undesirables, and Eagan did not measure up. Evidently, able-bodied, future

Americans included a prescriptive normative ideal in genitalia, too. A small penis worried immigration officials because they thought it was either a sign of effeminacy or, in their thinking, a pervert.

"They then rejected Eagan on the basis that immigrants "effeminately developed" were "undesirable in any community."[195]

That one's genitals became a subject of state interest details how the discriminatory practices often use fears related to the sex lives of the disabled to create an invidious form of discrimination used to justify and promulgate their policies.

Immigration centers such as Ellis Island would become flashpoints of discrimination for the new nation. Not only were they protecting the shores against the disabled, but they were on the lookout for any confused gender expression to add to their religious and racial prejudices. As Dolmage would put it:

"At Ellis Island, the categories of defect and disability that adhere today were strongly grounded if not created, as was the diagnostic gaze that allowed for the nebulous application of the stigma of disability as we know it today. The space of Ellis Island circumscribed certain patterns of movement and practices of visualizing the body. The product was, often, the spectacle of Otherness. In addition, all who passed through Ellis Island also became subject to—and then possessor and executor of—a certain gaze and a certain bodily attitude. Ellis Island functioned as a heterotopic space. And not simply so—always in a tangle of definitions and as a repository of bad science and overlapping oppressions."[196]

It becomes clear that the logic of discrimination leveled first against the disabled immigrant would pave the way and become the model of notifying later ethnic, religious, and racial discrimination practices still operative today.

28

The Silent Villain: Television, Film and the Big Screen of Disability

The rise of cinema would prove a mixed blessing for persons with disabilities in the early 20th century. Despite its revolutionary possibilities in changing how we perceive our very selves, our bodies, and the world around us, cinema would be co-opted and used to reinforce society's deepest fears and prejudices. Stanford professor Paul Longmore has collated more than 3,000 examples of stories with disabled characters in early film and television, but these victories would be short-lived and largely pyrrhic. While many actors and directors would make a prosperous living out of portraying disabled characters negatively and stereotypically, the disabled themselves would receive little to no benefit. Lon Chaney Sr., for example, built his career playing disabled villains. The list he portrayed is long, including Quasimodo in adaptations of the Hunchback of Notre Dame and Erik in the Phantom of the Opera. Chaney starred in even more blatantly stereotypical roles, such as the amputee gangster in the 1920 production, The Penalty. In the 1927 film, The Unknown, Chaney played the armless carnival knife-thrower Alonzo the Armless. Chaney would work with Director Tod Browning in 10 films, often portraying mutilated characters. The ever-present link between evil and disability in myth, theatre, and literature was given visceral, visual support in the burgeoning film genre. Chaney viewed his career and his choice of characters as growing out of an exciting complex of motives and aspirations. Speaking about the roles he chose, Chaney wrote in a 1925 autobiographical piece for the trade publication, "Movie":

"I wanted to remind people that the lowest types of humanity may have within them the capacity for supreme self-sacrifice. The dwarfed, misshapen beggar of the streets may have the noblest ideals. Most of my roles since The Hunchback, such as The Phantom of the Opera, He Who Gets Slapped, The Unholy Three, etc., have carried the theme of self-sacrifice or renunciation. These are the stories which I wish to do."[197]

Chaney's quote reveals much about the treatment of persons with disabilities in the early 20th century. First, Chaney caricatures the roles of the disabled he was portraying as the "lowest types of humanity" and then he implies that it is through such debasement that somehow the disabled are being better represented.

Cinema would continue to use, advance, and exploit the idea of the disabled villain from its earliest form as silent movies up to today's multi-million-dollar blockbusters. One only needs a cursory look at any "bad guy" in a film, and you will find a continuation of this stereotype. In literature where the tragic character needs to possess an inner flaw—hamartia—there will always be an attendant outer disfigurement or condition. Cinema will do the same but reverses the order of presentation. The external flaw is obvious. Cinema's ability to visually depict the disabled body becomes even more effective in conveying stereotypes. It relies on the shorthand signs signifying the disabled to convey entire characters.

As Longmore writes:

"Look at current horror films and it's the same. The most popular ones all have disfigured villains -- Halloween, Nightmare on Elm Street, Friday the 13th, The Texas Chainsaw Massacre."

We can see this concept in action at the website called Tvtropes, where the bloggers list a section titled the "Evil Cripple." They define an "evil cripple" as a role where the character has a disabling condition that causes them to seek revenge on the able-bodied world. This trope re-introduces the long-held assumption of the "embittered gimp." The person with a disability, supposedly, seeks revenge on the world of the non-disabled because of perceived injustices that have rendered them disabled.[198] The use of disability as a symbol is as old as Greek theatre; what is new in this approach is the intention attributed to the character. We see cinema ratcheting up the intensity of the evil of the character with the disability:

"An Evil Cripple is a villain or generally morally perturbed character who also suffers a debilitating physical condition, often taking the form of paralysis requiring the use of a wheelchair. The Evil Cripple doubles as the Genius Cripple a lot, providing an intellectual threat to compensate for their physical frailty. Alternatively, the Evil Cripple can become a physical threat if they use futuristic enhancements to overcome their disability, such as replacing missing or defective limbs with superstrong Powered Armor or cybernetic parts."[199]

This trope is used to contrast the "hero," who is inevitably a strong, non-disabled male. His opposite, the anti-hero, is always disabled. The Tvtropes entry continues, "a disabled villain is usually compared to a morally upright and physically "perfect" hero." The obverse becomes true. The abled body hero is also a beautiful body too.

Longmore illustrates this trope in his 1985 essay, "Screening Stereotypes," where he reminds us of the popular western "Wild, Wild West" that ran on CBS from 1965 to 1974. In one episode, the arch-villain, a dwarf named Miguelito P. Loveless, says to the series' hero, James West: "I grow weary of you, Mr. West. I weary of the sight of your strong, straight body." The statement reveals the obsession the non-disabled world has about imputing motives on envy and jealousy to the disabled. As a result, the disabled are assumed to be living in envy of the able-bodied.

What is more, notice the implication from the name of the character. The idea of the character Loveless works as a condemnatory, double implication of social isolation. Not only is the disabled person physically disabled and envious of the abled, but the disabled character is incapable of being loved or of loving another. He is loveless. A sharper contrast with the hero could not be more apparent, as in all westerns: James West always gets the girl. He is as lucky in love as in life.

The trope exists, claim the website's authors, because it builds on a historic precedent created by the early 20th-century eugenics movement that demonized the disabled—viewing the trope as an example of the so-called "rule of symbolism" where a symbol is used to "stretch the willing suspension of belief" of the audience. The website lists other examples like this trope, including the depraved dwarf, the evil eunuch, and the evil albino. Tropes we can see in recent pop culture. An example of the depraved dwarf is the Tyrion Lannister character in the popular "Game of Thrones" mini-series. Tyrion is, in the words of New York Times writer Lev Grossman, "the brilliant, black-witted dwarf whose family has had the firmest grip on power for much of the series, though that is not saying much. Tyrion is another good example of what separates Tolkien and Martin. Tyrion is not a hearty, ax-wielding, gold-mining member of a noble dwarven race. He is not Gimli. Tyrion is an actual dwarf, achondroplastic and stubby-limbed, a joke to passers-by and an embarrassment to his family."[200]

Grossman mentions the first notion rooted in eugenics-based ideas linking disability or other physical deformities with a "natural" predisposition towards madness, criminality, vice, etc. The rule of symbolism is often at work here since a "crippled" body can be used to represent a "crippled" soul — and indeed, a disabled villain is usually put in contrast to a morally upright and physically "perfect" hero as we have seen. In the case of Tyrion, he has a doppelganger in his flawless brother, Jamie Lannister.[201]

29

The Forgotten Holocaust: The Disabled during WWII

"Forgetting the extermination is part of the extermination itself"

-Jean Baudrillard

A letter from a rural German community citizen reached Adolf Hitler dated July 1939. The Fuhrer received many letters, but this was no ordinary one. In this letter, Richard and Lina Kretschmar asked for permission to kill their five-month-old son, Gerhard. He had been born with only one leg and slight vision loss. They hated him; they called their son the "Monster." The Kretschmar's were convinced that his existence was contrary to the Aryan ideals of genetic purity and perfection being advanced by the Reich and which they firmly believed.

Hitler welcomed the letter and granted the permission in an unprecedented executive act, and the young child was murdered by Hitler's personal doctor Karl Brandt five days later. Gerhard would be buried in the local Lutheran churchyard, and the church records would say he died of a "weakness to the heart."[202] The only apparent weakness of heart was in the German culture itself.

Between 1939 and 1945, the Nazis murdered hundreds of thousands of people with disabilities.[203] The program, which is still little known, started with children with disabilities labeling them Ausschusskinderer or "garbage children." It paid German doctors, nurses, and administrators a fee to report infants up to three with any kind of disability. These children would be rounded up by special units and sent to "hunger houses" where they died slow, protracted deaths from starvation or were killed by lethal injections or gas. Children with any "defect" or "incurable" disease were subject to this program. Children with physical, neurological, cognitive, intellectual disabilities, or those with epilepsy, blindness, deafness, and cleft palates would be subject to extermination.

The extermination program would develop into an efficient killing machine under the guidance of Brandt and later Philip Bouhler and be known as "Aktion T4." The name was derived from the program's street address, Tiergarten Strasse No. 4 in Berlin. At its height between January 1940 and August 1941, it is estimated that at least 275,000 German children with disabilities were killed. This period would come to be known as the period of "wild euthanasia." After the war, no significant legal action, reparations, or apologies would be offered to the families of the murdered.

Today, historians consider Gerhard's tragic story a version of a "trial balloon" or an instance of "running it up of the flagpole" where a state or political party tests a tentative measure to gauge the response by the population. Will they reject or accept it? By all accounts, the case of Gerhard was received favorably. There were no protests or noticeable adverse reactions at all. It would take decades to track down and discover the name of the first disabled child—Gerhard-- killed by the Nazis. His existence will be forgotten and buried under the tragedy of history. In 2007, the German historian Ulf Schmidt revealed his identity in his biography of Hitler's doctor, who murdered Gerhard, Karl Brandt[204]. Brandt would later head the infamous T4 program and advocate for euthanizing and aborting disabled children and fetuses to strengthen the Reich. He traveled around Germany extensively, performing abortions primarily of non-Aryan fetuses. Such abortions were legal after the passage of the 1933 law to prevent hereditarily diseased offspring (Gesetz zur Verhütung erbkranken Nachwuchses). Judging that the reaction to Gerhard was favorable, the Nazis pursued their aim of ridding the Reich of inferior citizens, starting with their youngest and most vulnerable.

Hitler convened a committee to investigate implementing a more comprehensive policy of euthanasia of persons with disabilities and those of non-Aryan lineage in the Reich. He found avid support from academics in German universities researching malformations and congenital disabilities and members of the medical professions. Two early supporters were doctors Wolff and Hirt, both working in the field of teratology at the University of Strasbourg. Recall teratology was the study of abnormality. As chair of the anatomy department at Strasbourg, Brandt would receive thanks from Hitler for his service, shipping him a collection of Jewish skeletons[205]. Other Universities would profit from this period of euthanasia by receiving the organs of recently murdered inmates from the various "killing centers" around Germany and, later, their occupied lands. No consent was asked for, nor was any given by the victims or their families. By August of 1939, the official registering of future victims would begin in earnest, and the program would develop into a state-wide federal program. Thus, Germany became the 20th-century epicenter for the American ideas of exterminating the disabled.

The United States Holocaust Memorial Museum tells us that by "August 18, 1939, the Reich Ministry of the Interior circulated a decree compelling all physicians, nurses, and midwives to report newborn infants and children under the age of three who showed signs of severe mental or physical disability." To incentivize them, healthcare workers were given bonuses to report disabled children to the ministry. At first, only infants and toddlers under three were included, but soon, juveniles up to 17 were registered and slated to be killed. Estimating the number of physically and mentally disabled children murdered through starvation, gassing, or lethal medication overdose may be impossible. Why? The officials knew they were engaged in unethical practices and tried to cover their tracks by falsifying medical records and death certificates. We can briefly summarize the T4 program and Nazi policy with a quote from the United States Holocaust Memorial Museum online exhibition:

"The Nazi persecution of persons with disabilities in Germany was one component of radical public health policies aimed at excluding hereditarily "unfit" Germans from the national community. These strategies began with forced sterilization and escalated toward mass murder. The most extreme measure, the Euthanasia Program, was in itself a rehearsal for Nazi Germany's broader genocidal policies."

Yet even before the rise of the Reich in the 1930s, the precarious post-war German economic situation witnessed the rise of unsafe, unsanitary, and abusive situations in German hospitals, schools, and asylums. These conditions and the costs needed to change them would prompt officials to remove the burdens rather than caring for them as patients. When the Nazis rose to power, all the conditions were ripe. They just needed a case study. And Gerhard was offered by his parents.

Pleased with their success, the Nazi government would kill disabled adults in Poland and later in Germany. They called this euthanization program the "Charitable Foundation for Cure and Institutional Care" and housed it in the same nondescript building located on Tiergartenstraße 4 in Berlin. Thus, collectively they would come down through history as the T4 program.

The T4 program officially began in the fall of 1939 during the height of Nazism in Germany. Under the direction of Bouhler and Brandt, T4 was used as a euthanasia program to "mercy kill" those whose lives were viewed as "burdensome" and those viewed as unnecessary drains on the limited resources of post-WWI Germany. So-called "useless eaters" -- one of Brandt's favorite terms for the disabled--T4 would also function as a program to rid the Volkish of non-Aryans. It would tacitly emerge into a testing ground or school for future SS killers and concentration camp commandants. At the T4 program, the Nazis trained those they would later use to execute the mass murders in the death camps of the Holocaust. The meeting of the racist ideology, eugenics, and the cruel utilitarian policy of war-time economics brought together a policy of extermination and the killing of the least disadvantaged in German society.

The enforcing arm of the KdF, the Reich Department of the Interior (RMDI), would issue a decree in August of 1939 ordering all midwives, physicians, and nurses to report any infants born with deformities or having disabling conditions or those living with a disability or medical condition to the officials at T4. The KdF was the Kraft durch Freude (Strength through Joy),[206] a state-operated organization to develop healthy recreational and leisure activities to advance the Aryan fitness and health ideals. German popular culture would abound with images of Germans recreating in nature, alluding to the ancient Greek ideals of beauty, strength, and athleticism.

Ostensibly, all of this collecting was done under the guise of gathering scientifically objective data about severe medical conditions to achieve a healthy nation. In reality, the registry became the master list of the murdered. It specified the identification of feeble-mindedness, idiocy, mongolism, blindness, deafness, microcephaly, hydrocephaly, all deformities, missing limbs, dwarfism, and paralysis.[207] It is important to note that most of these children were by no measure terminally ill, sick, or dying. In many cases, they were active, loved members of their families.

How did it work? The officials would use the registry lists to gather the children and take them to any number of the newly established or recently converted "killing centers" in places such as Gorden near Brandenburg, Am Steinhoff in Vienna, Grafeneck, Hartheim, Sonnestein, Bernburg, Hadamar, and Eglfing-Haar near Munich.[208] At these centers, the children would be warehoused and either gassed, killed by injection, or deprived of food and water until they died.[209] There are accounts from staff under testimony recounting some of the patients crying out, "I don't want to die, I'm not sick."[210] Typically, a child would arrive, undergo a sham physical, be stripped naked, and be led to a room designed to poison them by gas. The gas they used was hydrogen chloride marketed as Zyklon-B, meaning "cyclone." It was long used as a fumigant on fruit trees in California. From 1929 on, the United States Public Health Service used it to fumigate freight trains and clothes of Mexican immigrants entering the United States. It would late be used to murder 1.1 million Jews in the Holocaust.[211]

After the child was killed, a process would start. The murdered child's family was eventually notified of their death, usually by listing a legitimate medical condition or complication due to a non-performed surgery or non-existent treatment. In short, the medical records were falsified.

The families would receive cremated remains claiming to be of their child. The ash in the urns they received had come from the mass cremeatoria. The falsified certificate of death accompanied the urns. Few people questioned the system. It seemed all very official. Where and when questions arose, the Reich would threaten the curious.

After killing the patients, the gruesome task of destroying the body began, and a group of so-called "stokers" and "decontaminators" would start the task of separating the bodies, remove any jewelry and knock out the deceased's teeth, scavenging any gold or silver fillings that they would send to the T4 office in Berlin. T4 Officials earned bonuses for the gold they could submit[212] to their overseers. Finally, the bodies were burned; the remains pulverized in grinders.

The role of the parents was confusing. Not all were as avid Nazis as the Kretschmars. The parents were indirectly responsible, for they would have to be required to relent to their child's "hospitalization" but would have been lied to and told that their children were going to medical treatment centers to receive advanced and experimental care. The program cynically played upon the hopes of the parents.

After the death of their child, the parents were lied to and told that their child had died from complications from the treatment or a botched surgery and given a falsified death certificate. While some parents may have welcomed the news of their child's death, many more did not and were powerless to find out what had transpired. The search for the truth would prove to be impossible. The Reich had hidden the program behind a nearly impenetrable wall of bureaucracy. If the stonewalling did not work, overly inquisitive parents could be directly threatened. Parents and family members would find themselves in a similar circumstance as the German philologist known only by his initials F.H. whom after learning of the death of his son, Hans, asked the doctor in charge:

"What have you done to our strong, physically well-developed son with your institutional treatment?"[213]

Of course, no explanation was provided other than the lie that Hans had died under treatment. Again, secrecy and conspiracy were the norms. In a final sickening and ironic twist, the Reich would then charge the parents for the costs of the child's euthanasia, claiming it was for the medical and cremation expenses.

After all the children were killed, the next to be euthanized were inmates at hospitals or asylums. After that, the killing machine turned to the orphaned and abandoned living as wards of the state. Finally, they targeted some with minor disabilities such as slight behavioral, cognitive, or learning disabilities.[214] Eventually, the lists would contain all but the most able-bodied Germans.

One's status in the world did not protect you either. There is the tragic case of Lia Graf nee Schwartz, a little person born in Germany and employed by Barnum. Used in a famous publicity stunt when she was placed on the lap of J.P. Morgan during a senate hearing, she was catapulted to an international celebrity. Despite the limelight, she would miss her homeland and return to Germany in 1935. Back home, she would fall into the category of a "useless person" and be transported to Auschwitz, where she was killed[215]. Despite the popularity of her AP image posing with the richest man in the world, her employment with the Barnum circus, and her popularity, she was still exterminated. Celebrity did not protect the Ovitch family either. The Ovitch's were a Romanian Jewish family that included seven dwarves. They had traveled all over Eastern Europe as a traveling troupe and achieved a degree of acclaim. Despite their status, they would end up in Auschwitz, where they were subjected to Josef Mengele's experiments as he attempted to investigate the genetic basis for dwarfism.

The erasure of persons with disabilities of the Western project was fulfilled in the actions of the thousand-year Reich. The admixture of prejudice, science, and social planning would combine into the deadly and efficient killing machine of the Nazis. Disabled people were removed, exterminated, and their very identities expunged. As Friedlander writes in the preface to his meticulously researched work, "The Origins of Nazi Genocide: From Euthanasia to the Final Solution:"

"I had always known that the use of the term "euthanasia" by the Nazi killers was a euphemism to camouflage their murder of human beings they had designated as "life unworthy of life"; their aim was not to shorten the lives of persons with painful terminal diseases but to kill human beings they considered inferior, who could have lived for many years...they were handicapped patients, persons who in the United States today are covered by the Act for Disabled Americas."[216]

Euthanasia itself has a long history, and it has not always been entwined with the lives of the disabled. Suetonius first conceived it as a noble way of dying in his biography of Augustus. Many years later, Francis Bacon, the English philosopher and one of the key figures in developing the scientific method, would introduce the word to English, borrowing it from Latin. Still, it would not carry the meaning of someone hastening or terminating life until the 19th century. Instead, a German doctor, Adolf Jost, would do the rest. Jost provided two aspects that would later fuel the euthanasia practices of the Nazis. The first was the concept called 'voluntary euthanasia, ' where an otherwise sane terminally ill person expresses a non-coerced wish to die to alleviate any probable future suffering. There is nothing in and of itself controversial about this aspect. Indeed, many, if not most contemporary ethicists, accept this as a fundamentally ethical act. The key will turn on how we come to understand the notion of voluntary consent.

Jost's second contribution is far more problematic. Jost introduced the notion that some lives burden the living; they ought to be killed. Jost believed those whose lives fit into this category did not even need a voluntary desire nor provide consent to die for the act to be ethically permissible.[217] This position—what is today called involuntary euthanasia—is morally repugnant and tantamount to murder. Let us consider Jost's position together with the influential paper on euthanasia co-authored by Binding and Hoche, "Allowing the Destruction of Life Unworthy of Life." We start to see a dangerous admixture of ideas that become lethal toward the most disadvantaged members of society when put into practice. The paper by Binding and Hoche argues for a moral imperative to end the life of anyone viewed as abnormal. Together Jost's, Binding, and Hoche's respective positions would be combined with the dominant theories of race, class, eugenics, and ableism, creating the perfect storm practiced by the Nazis in their T4 program.

In such a climate, T4 became the widespread forced institutionalization and extermination program of the disabled in Germany during the pre-and intra-war years of the 1920s and 1930s. Hitler had lauded eugenics and "selective breeding" as an essential tool for the "folkish" state in his 1923 semi-autobiographical "Mein Kampf." Under the rubric of eugenics, the Nazi-controlled practice would flourish, becoming a national policy that they would eventually import to all their conquered lands.

As a program to eliminate undesirables from the social order, the so-called mercy death program led to the direct death of an estimated 200,000 to 300,000[218] persons with physical or mental disabilities. The exact number is difficult to ascertain because the doctors falsified the death certificates and the direct cover-up immediately after the war.

The disabled are viewed as drains on both the future racial purity and the present economic situation. The radical eugenics as extermination movement spread under the Reich slogan, "Aufartung durch Ausmerzung," that Friedlander translates to "Regeneration through extermination."[219]

Who were these unfortunate undesirables? Many were, as Friedlander notes, retarded,[220] blind, deaf, or epileptic or had a physical deformity."[221] The killing of these people underscored the murderous impulse of the Nazi ideology, but it teaches us about the larger attitudes toward the disabled in the early 20th century. This did not happen in a vacuum. While it is well known that the Nazis sought to eradicate the

Jewish presence from the German racial stock completely, they did routinely kill their political opponents, too. Less known was how the disabled fared and were treated. By all accounts, the disabled were treated as inhumanely as the Jews, Sinti, and Roma. In many instances, one's ethnicity and disability or medical condition were added together to make one a target. Intersectionality has long existed in the world of the disabled. The twin evils of racism and ableism would be the fodder for the killing sprees of the Nazis. As Friedlander points out,

"The Nazis killed handicapped infants in hospital wards as well as elderly men and women in nursing homes."[222]

Friedlander concludes that the "regime systematically murdered only three groups of human beings: the handicapped, Jews and Gypsies." The three groups share a common history of being the groups most ostracized, projected, and feared as the other. The three groups would find themselves the object of the virulent hatred of this period, but the antecedents of the origins of hate directed toward each group arose from clear historic precedencies. As Evans points out in her exhaustive study "Forgotten Crimes: The Holocaust and People with Disabilities:"

"Since the 1980s, historians have dramatically increased our[223] understanding of Nazi Racism. Our information about Nazi persecution thus now includes a much greater awareness of the culpability of various German professionals, including doctors, scientists, professors, and psychiatrists, in the formation and implementation of Nazi racial policy."

In his "Racial Hygiene: Medicine under the Nazis," Proctor convincingly demonstrates the set of philosophical ideas and institutional practices that structured German thinking many years before the rise of the National Socialists came to power. The two dominating notions of racial inferiority and the labeling of different abilities as pathological began as we have seen in the enlightenment period but would lead directly to the complex of ideas taken as normative during this period. In the 19th century, the race to find a pure and dominant species and the long-standing search for an Ur-language foundational to culture fueled ethnocentric and exclusionary ideologies. The Western culture's obsession with race and racialism, nationalism and ableism, and the resulting stereotypes endorsed by influential thinkers such as Comte, Kant, Fichte, Schopenhauer, and Hegel would pave the way for these practices. The philosophers were often cited and used by others to advance racist or nationalist positions. Social Darwinists would provide the final scientific scaffolding to erect such systemic ideas of hate. From here, we see that the very nature of biological and natural sciences would add to the grist. The practical application of these ideas in medicine is where we then see the results.

Leading scientific figures such as the highly influential German naturalist and biologist Ernst Haeckel would add much to this debate. Haeckel introduced Darwinian evolutionary thinking to German-speaking audiences and offered a variation of Darwinian thought that would develop into scientific racism. Following the American biologist Morton and the Swiss naturalist Agassiz, Haeckel advanced a position known as polygenism. Polygenism is the idea that each "race" of present-day humans arose from separate historical species. As Haeckel put it,

"The Caucasian, or Mediterranean man (Homo Mediterraneus), has from time immemorial been placed at the head of all the races of men, as the most highly developed and perfect."[224]

He would call for the killing of the "weak" and "mentally defective" to store up what he perceived as the declining "Indo-Germanic race."[225] Noted American evolutionary theorist Stephen Jay Gould in his "Ontology and Phylogeny" succinctly characterizes Haeckel's position as preparing for the rise of the Nazis:

"[Haeckel's] evolutionary racism; his call to the German people for racial purity and unflinching devotion to a 'just' state; his belief that harsh, inexorable laws of evolution ruled human civilization and nature alike, conferring upon favored races the right to dominate others . . . all contributed to the rise of Nazism."

Haeckel's influence did not stop at the German borders. Historian Daniel Gasman details how Haeckel's influence spread through Europe and stimulated fascist ideology in France and Italy. Therefore, we see similar efforts to eradicate the disabled in all European nations, especially under Nazi control or influence. However, even those nations that resisted the Nazi hegemony were guilty of inhumane treatment toward the disabled. For example, refugees fleeing the Nazis and seeking refuge in Switzerland would be subject to a new restriction. Fully 15-20% of Jewish refugees with disabilities were refused entry. The historically neutral county was far from neutral in this tragedy. As early as 1925, the Swiss passed laws restricting entry if one could not marry, was of "unsound mind," or was assessed as "unfit." These classifications were cast in the broadest of determinations and without medical evidence or support.[226] In this, Switzerland was a trendsetter. By 1928, the Swiss had passed the world's first forced sterilization law of the disabled. The 1928 law called for compulsory sterilization of the disabled and was admired and imitated by Hitler.

Odd as it may sound, but for the disabled, extermination was not the only assault that they faced. If the person with a disability could productively work, then the utilitarian thinking of the Nazis kicked into gear, and the person may find themselves spared and put to work. The risk to the German racial stock was still too significant to allow them to reproduce, so the Nazis followed the Swiss and later American models of forced sterilization and forced institutionalization. As a result, an additional 300 to 400,000 Germans were forcibly sterilized. In 1933 after the Nazis came to power, they passed a law for the Prevention of Progeny with Hereditary Diseases aimed exclusively at stopping the "decline" of the German racial stock. The law established "Health Courts" (Erbgesundheitsgerichte) to make decisions based on the evidence compiled by healthcare workers. The lists determined who was unfit for possible reproduction, and the healthcare workers were given financial incentives to list as many as possible. These lists contained virtually all the disabled citizens of Germany. As we saw, the healthcare staff were mandated by law to report all persons included under the mandatory sterilization law, but they were incentivized through rewards. The law also scrapped any notion of consent. If you found yourself on such a list, then you were forced into a program of sterilization. You had no recourse.

In the first year of operation, over 60,000 persons would be forcibly sterilized. Two years later, in 1935, the Nuremberg Laws provided for the forced sterilization of all the unfit.[227] Given the power of both legal and medical authority, the program could cast its net broader and include anyone deemed risky to the purity and health of the German people. Therefore, a person identified as racially, genetically, intellectually, or physically inferior may be sterilized by a medical procedure without recourse. Chemicals, surgery, or even X-ray devices surreptitiously hidden under countertops were commonly used to sterilize unsuspecting citizens. Evans's work includes several first-hand accounts of the brutality and side effects of these procedures. Data from this time describes hundreds of German citizens dying from botched procedures and thousands more living with chronic pain.

The background justification for the program was twofold: First, it sought to remove undesirables from the German gene population—the protoplasm-- ensuring a superior racial identity; and second, it sought to stimulate the post-depression economy by eliminating and reducing what it claimed were the costly burdens of caring for the disabled. Indeed, to help catalyze the German population's reception of the burdensome costs of the disabled, German textbooks turned to simple math instruction and tasked schoolchildren to solve real-world math problems such as:

"The Construction of a lunatic asylum costs 6 million RM (Reich marks). How many houses at 15,000 RM each could have been built for that amount?"[228]

The ideas would settle in and become unassailable by exposing and inuring Germany's children to this propaganda early enough. Both goals and their related practices were based on granting the disabled a "mercy death" (German: Gnadentod) and a release from "life unworthy of life." The architects of these ideas would go so far as to argue that disabled people had a duty to die for the nation. At heart, the deciding factor of who decides who lives, who dies, is at the root of this policy. But, of course, the decision of whose life was worth living was always made by someone else—usually cloaked in the authority of science or medicine-- and never the person whose life was in question. The same was true for sterilization procedures, although there was an appellate procedure, in theory. However, the propaganda worked. After this steady diet of propaganda, the view that the disabled were a burden on society became normative within the German population and is still operative throughout much of Europe. Generally, viewed as a humane choice and used by the Nazi policymakers as a test or precursor to the mass exterminations practiced in the concentration camps against Jews and others. Thus, the disabled were the test cases for the Holocaust and extermination of the Jews, Sinti, Romas, and others. Indeed, as we saw, many killing technologies, such as the types of poisonous gases later used in the death camps, were initially tested and developed in the T4 program.

Lost in the fog of war would be the infamous camp-based euthanasia program to exterminate those deemed unfit or labeled "dead weight prisoners." Those not immediately euthanized by T4 may have found themselves deported to a work camp where they would be exterminated after working them to near death as "dead weight." In the camps, they worked to death or faced another policy of euthanasia. The camp-based program was called the "Sonderbehandlung (special treatment) 14f13" and was known simply by the code Aktion 14f13. It ran from 1941 to 1944 under Philip Bouhler, the SS official responsible for the T4 program that killed adults and children with disabilities. He took his skills into the camps as the co-initiator of Aktion 14f13 and was directly responsible for killing 15,000–20,000 concentration camp prisoners. Those categorized and exterminated were persons with disabilities, mental illness, and laborers from Eastern Europe, Soviet prisoners of war, and, of course, Jews and Romas. They were classified as unfit because they could no longer work due to illness or disability.

One may be transferred to a camp if one fell into one of the following categories that enabled local police to initiate the process culminating in being sent to the gas chambers. Those individuals included and taken into what was called Schutzhaft ("protective custody") were "gypsies, vagrants, tramps, the "work-shy," idlers, beggars, prostitutes, troublemakers, career criminals, rowdies, traffic violators, psychopaths and the mentally ill." Lombroso's criminal profiling was adopted in the Reich and widespread practice in vogue throughout Europe. There was no escape from the long arm of the Nazi disability hunters.

What we do know is who perpetrated these atrocities. At first, government officials were in charge of running these programs. Some had medical backgrounds, and some did not. The SS would use the T4 program to assess the resolve of future concentration camp staff. If they passed, as in the cases of officers Franz Stangl and Gustav Wagner, they would receive favorable appointments to work in and command concentration camps. Stangl and Wagner would see their careers advanced because of their success and willingness to kill disabled persons at T4. In 1940, Stangl was transferred from a euthanasia center to the SS-Sonderkommando Sobibór extermination camp, where he served as camp commander implementing the Wannsee Conference's "Final Solution." His performance as commander was executed so well there that in 1942 he was transferred to Treblinka. Stangl was the longest-serving commandant at Treblinka. Nicknamed "white death" from his occasional wearing of an all-white uniform complete with a white whip, he tried to give the camp an atmosphere of medical and scientific gloss by having guards greet the newly arrived prisoners wearing lab coats. During his commandant, he would guide the camp through the deadliest period of the camp's history under Operation Reinhard. It is estimated that between 700,000 and 900,000 Jews and about 2,000 Romani were killed under his command. More Jews were killed in Treblinka than at any other camp apart from Auschwitz. The training at T4 had been a successful proving ground.

Another T4 graduate was Major Christian Wirth, a former detective and member of the elite SS corps. He was transferred from his duties at a T4 euthanasia center in Wertheim to become a supervisor at Chelmno. Chelmno was the first of six extermination camps in Poland. His expertise in mass euthanizing seems to have been the primary consideration of his appointment. Stengl had described Wirth as a "gross and florid man" who claimed he would "puke" at the sight of disabled people. Wirth would later go on to serve at Belzec-the first camp set up to institute Operation Reinhard.

The consequence of all this seemed to be that if they could kill the disabled inmates and patients without concern, the authorities reasoned, then they would likely be able to kill others deemed unworthy of living, too. Having trained these emotionless killers and brainwashed them into believing they were engaged in a humane task, the perfect killing machine was fine-tuned.[229] Others would soon join the disabled as targets for extermination, including Jews, Roma, communists, Jehovah's Witnesses, homosexuals, and later anyone who openly resisted Nazi policies. However, lest we forget, the roots of this practice of exterminating the disabled did not begin with the Nazis but two millennia ago in the ancient Greek myths and the Spartan practice of exposure. It is a small step from Oedipus to Treblinka.

The reach of the T4 program would extend far beyond the unassuming building on the Strasse from which it took its name. The Nazis would establish multiple centers for euthanizing the disabled across central Europe or convert existing hospitals or wards by building gas chambers and crematoria all over Germany and then into the lands they occupied. These new centers were established throughout Germany and the occupied lands to develop the efficiency of killing the disabled. As Hans-Heinrich Wilhelm's research details, the locations were many, and the numbers were staggering:

"The first large-scale euthanasia action seems to have taken place in Pomerania and eastern Prussia shortly after the Polish campaign. During 1940, four euthanasia institutions went into operation: Grafeneck, Brandenburg, Hartheim, and Sonnenstein. In the first half of the year alone, 8,765 persons were gassed in these institutions. The staff eagerly jumped into the task at hand-- three-quarters of the deaths occurred by June. By the end of 1940, 26,459 patients had been killed. In the following year, 1941, an additional 35,049 were "disinfected." These were the figures given by the accounting section of T4's head office. ("The

Euthanasia Program," in "The Encyclopaedia of the Holocaust," Vol II, pp.452-454)[230]

Until the end of the war and the horrors of the Holocaust became well known and clear, doctors throughout Europe and America lauded this policy. Several of the doctors would remain convinced that they were doing the right things. Despite the lack of international protest, the Nazis tried to keep this systematic extermination secret, and only the Catholic Church protested the war. Some clergy would question local authorities, but a threat from the SS typically put an end to such protests.

Who gets to decide what kind of life is worth living? The answer, in short, is medical authorities. They are not experts in living or the philosophies of living, nor do they possess first-hand experiences of differing abilities, cultures, or peoples. The training of medical professionals often advances the status quo by its very nature. How this practice came to be in Germany did not occur in a vacuum. It is essential to grasp that the Nazi doctors were not some aberrations from European or Western culture; indeed, as we have seen, the horrors of this period are the predictable outcomes from the prejudices and beliefs percolating against the disabled from time immemorial. The same texts, practices, and methods used to train doctors in Germany were the same ones used throughout the world's medical schools.

In Nazi Germany, what, if anything, is different is the scale and efficiency due to technological innovations and social planning development. The extermination of the disabled and the attempted exterminations of Jews and Gypsies fit solidly into the prejudices of leading scientists, medical authorities, and most Europeans and, for that matter, Americans of the early 20th century. As Friedlander describes it, paraphrasing Müller-Hill's "Tödliche Wissenschaft," the German bureaucratic, professional, and scientific elite provided the legitimacy the regime needed to implement this policy smoothly. The hierarchy of value, binary thinking, and the quasi-scientific theories abounding would conspire to strive for a future universe populated by only the elite. At the same time, the disabled, the under trodden, the unfit, would be destroyed and forgotten.

Anthropological, biological, ethnographical, and sociological sciences and many scientists working within these fields in the 19th and early 20th centuries adopted the prejudices of their times without a shred of confirmable evidence or compassion. Reflecting the biases and prejudices of their times, these scientists wrongly concluded that all human differences were based on hereditary (Galton's "nature") and so could be controlled at will. Others, such as the influential Italian criminologist Cesare Lombroso would extend these pseudo-scientific theories and conclusions into other research areas. A tenet in his "positive school of criminology" accepted the notion that some criminals were irrefutably "born for evil" and that one could identify this because he would be born with some identifying congenital or physical disabilities. Beliefs like this harken back to the quasi-science of phrenology. Despite being refuted, it remains lurking in our ideas. A variation of phrenology -where a particular phenotype determines a behavior -remains in use with the definition of the medical model of disability. We reduce a person to a single aspect or aspect of their physical condition. The veneer of the "scientific" and "medical" authority here enabled politicians and others vying for power and seeking to capitalize and gain political advantages to frame these ideologies of hate, exclusion, and extermination into policies. It happened long enough to achieve a kind of epistemological verity.

There exists convincing evidence that the euthanasia policy of disabled children pre-existed the rise of the Reich and the onset of WWII.[231] In his meticulous study on euthanasia in Germany, Friedlander argues that the "attack on handicapped patients in state hospitals and nursing homes began in 1933. He reports that in 1935 three years before the onset of hostilities, Hitler told the Reich's top doctor Gerhard Wagner that he would initiate a euthanasia program once the war started. When Germany invaded Poland on 1 September 1939, he proved good on his word. Hitler believed that the "fog of war" would disguise the brutalization of an entire population. He was right.

As culpably criminal as the Nazis are, the history of these ideas precedes the formation of the "Thousand Year Reich" and Hitler's ascendancy. In the economic crises of the 1920s and because of both burdensome costs of post-WWI reparations and the declining global economy, Germany would see shortages manifest in scarcity in the medical communities. In times of economic scarcity, many start to look for a scapegoat. In 1920, Karl Bonhoeffer, the chairman of the German Psychiatric Association, would describe how the scarcity caused "a change in the concept of humanity." Medical staff became accustomed to "watching...patients die of malnutrition in vast numbers, almost approving of this, in the knowledge that perhaps the healthy could be kept alive through these sacrifices."[232] The next step is easy: medical professionals claim they were humane in peremptorily euthanizing those deemed unworthy.

We see this in the climate of the 1920s. The intellectual foundation for the T4 extermination program and the widespread practice of euthanizing the disabled would be given a solid foundation in a well-received paper written in and published in 1920 by the German legal scholar and jurist Karl Binding and psychiatrist Alfred Hoche titled, "Permitting the Destruction of Life Unworthy of Living." In their book, they called for accepting the "lesser of two evils" in permitting for the killing of "living human beings whose death would be a deliverance both for themselves and society and especially for the state."[233] Written before the rise of the National Socialists, they had initially intended the paper to advance the argument for the deliberate killing of the "incurably sick." However, it would soon include those labeled mentally ill or disabled, children with cognitive deficits, and those deemed "genetically" dangerous to Aryan ideals. During times of scarcity, those economically irksome to German society would be blamed for Germany's problems. In the widely read and circulated paper, one of the more disturbing qualities is how they write as if they were such perfect utilitarians arguing from a deep social conscience for the good of all. Killing the disabled is a burden required for the betterment of society. They even go so far as to appeal to the selflessness of the person to be sacrificed. All in the name of the common good! Recall Homais' advice to Hippolyte in "Madame Bovary."

The enacting of the euthanasia program would essentially replace sterilization as a policy to achieve their eugenic goals. Killing the patient seemed to prove more cost-effective and efficient than sterilization. Nevertheless, as Friedlander tells us, there were still an estimated 75,000 sterilizations after the onset of hostilities. The occupied people of Poland, the Sudetenland, and other regions now not only needed to fear the Luftwaffe, SS, and Panzer divisions but sterilization and euthanasia as the Nazis would import these practices to their occupied territories. In total, Friedlander's research suggests that a conservative estimate of forced sterilization would amount to about 0.5 percent of the entire German population or roughly 375,000 persons. This was a new face of war: riding in on the brutal wave of the Blitzkrieg was an army of ruthless castrators.

The bubble did not burst. Hitler and his cronies took the success of the T4 program and ran with it. In 1939, building on the unparalleled successes of murdering disabled children, Hitler called for and initiated a program to "eliminate those people," referring to institutionalized disabled adults—including WWI veterans-in German hospitals. The same WWI veterans Hitler and other top-ranking Nazis had once extolled as heroes were now targeted for extermination. They would finally turn to a population Hitler had sworn to protect: disabled WWI and WWII veterans. They would be the following targets. The once honored "first citizens of the nation" that Hitler had formerly lauded would find themselves being placed on the registers of the unworthy. As the war intensified, the killing machine became rapacious. Few records were reliable, and while there is little available evidence, we know of at least 36 disabled veterans euthanized through these state-sponsored euthanasia programs. Recalling what Hitler had said, "Wartime is the best time for the elimination of the disabled," he knew that as the nation's focus was drawn to other matters, he could work his will. He was right. Until the end of the war in 1945, the killing of persons with disabilities continued totaling around 70,000 innocents, added to the hundreds of thousands of children and countless numbers of the death camps. We may never know the final numbers with any degree of certainty. After the war, the American-led Nuremberg trials would conclude, "this program involved the systematic and secret execution of the aged, insane, incurably ill, or deformed children and other persons by gas, lethal injections, and diverse other means in nursing homes, hospitals, and asylums."[234]

To prepare the citizens for the task and the broader implementation of these policies, the Nazis skillfully used the emergent powers of cinema. But they were equally skillful in winning the hearts and minds of Germans through anti-Semitic and ableist ideology. As a result, Germans who grew up under the Nazi regime are much more anti-Semitic than those born before or after that period.[235] School-based propaganda worked, but another medium was available: cinema. It is well known and well-documented how Leni Riefenstahl effectively filmed propagandistic films for the Reich's ideology; what is less well known is how other directors would use the same emergent media technologies and social forces to produce and distribute a series of propaganda films designed to show how Germans with disabilities were 'useless eaters' (unnütze Esser), and unnecessary burdens (Ballanstexistenzen). Movies, such as the enormously popular "Das Erbe" (Inheritance), helped build public support for the government policies of euthanizing the disabled by stigmatizing them and drawing attention to the extravagant and inflated economic costs of their care. However, the 1941 film "Ich Klage An" (I Accuse) would reach into the subconsciousness of the German citizenry and strike a chord. "Ich Klage An," directed by Wolfgang Liebeneiner,[236] was commissioned by Joseph Goebbels and won a prize at the Venice Biennale. This film would seek to "convince" people of the reasonableness of killing the disabled. The film was based on the novel "Sendung und Gewissen" written by Hellmuth Unger, an ophthalmologist who traveled internationally, advancing eugenic ideas. He was a prominent member of the top-secret Nazi euthanasia planning committee that spoke directly to Hitler; The committee was named the Kanzlei des Führeres and known by the acronym, KdF (Chancellery of the Führer). Although Unger was one of the program's chief architects for killing children, he escaped the war unscathed and was subsequently released by Allied investigators after brief captivity. He died in 1953.

Similar to the effects Riefenstahl's films wielded on the public imagination, these films played an essential role in justifying Nazi policy to the public. "Ich Klage An" played a significant role in advancing the concept of the 'mercy killing' of the disabled. It is the first of a long line of disability "snuff" films still being produced in Hollywood. Decades later, movies such as Clint Eastwood's 2004 Academy Award-winning, "Million Dollar Baby," and in 2016, "Me Before You," would continue the idea that disabled lives were not worth living. The former film is an adaptation of F.J O'Toole's short story about the real-life tragedy of a woman boxer who was disabled by a boxing mishap. In O'Toole's story, she continues living as an artist. Eastwood rewrote the account, having the film's character want to die after being disabled in the match. The film comes to the crescendo with the boxer becoming a quadriplegic who wants to die—her life is, as she views it, is not worth living. Finally, her trainer relents and "mercifully" kills her.

In the 2016 film, "Me Before You," a wealthy young quadriplegic decides his life is not worth living and heads to Switzerland to take advantage of that nation's liberal death with dignity laws.

The presence of these films tells us a remarkably similar story, especially when we consider the context of the dedicated push in the last few decades for so-called "death with dignity" laws. With this history in one's mind, one cannot help seeing the parallels and fear for disabled people in the 21st century.[237]

Let us look more closely at the film, "Ich Klage An." The storyline of "Ich Klage An" concerns itself with the story of a young, aspiring doctor whose wife develops multiple sclerosis, falls into depression, and desires only to die. Unfortunately, her husband abides by her wishes and kills her. As a result, he is put on trial for murder. The film's ending revolves around the doctor's defense, where he acquits himself by turning the tables on his accusers, declaring that they are the cruel ones for not allowing her to die when her life was not worth living. This echoed arguments by Binding, Hoche, and others when they reached the position that the disabled had a duty to die. However, existing pre-Nazi laws made euthanasia illegal, and Hitler and Goebbels realized that they needed to overturn that legislation to develop the practices they wanted to enact. They appealed to the Volk and were wise enough to understand that they first needed the Volk to be on their side to cause any radical social change. Recognizing the power of cinema, the Nazi authorities knew cinema could shape public opinion, be a catalyst for change and work as an inexpensive form of education or propaganda. So, a film with a subtle message such as "Ich Klage An" fits their message.

As mentioned, films such as "Ich Klage An" were not their only tool. During this period, as we have seen, Nazi-edited public-school math textbooks posed math problems in an attempt to normalize this kind of thinking.

In the dire inter-war economic crisis, these questions reverberated with many poor Germans. It caused them to see the disabled and others as easy targets of hate and recrimination. Capitalizing on this scapegoating, Hitler and his staff knew that if they changed the culture, they could achieve their goals of extirpating the disabled from the German soil.

In "Ich Klage An," the doctor becomes a populist hero--successfully arguing against the elite lawyers of the state and the faceless and uncaring legislatures and acquits himself, winning a moral victory. His winning position argues that what is truly cruel is a society that will not euthanize the disabled. Incidentally, this would be the justification of many of those later implicated with these policies: They all thought that they were doing the right thing to do. It is estimated that at the time, the film was seen by 13.5 million Germans.[238] While it was criticized by a few Germans, including Catholic and Protestant churches members, it was warmly received by the German medical community and highly effective in swaying public opinion. Hitler and Goebbels had won. Disabled Germans would pay with their lives. And disabled people around the globe are still paying.

It is easy to point at the Nazi atrocities and reduce all arguments to blaming them alone. However, to do so puts us at risk of ignoring other similarly inhumane policies, many of which predate WWII and the rise of German fascism. The first forced sterilization laws were passed in the United States and later followed by those in Switzerland. In 1929, Denmark passed a law legalizing forced sterilization of the disabled and followed five years later by Norway. The movement to sterilize the unwanted spread to adopted laws in Cuba, Czechoslovakia, Estonia, Finland, Hungary, Iceland, Latvia, Turkey, and the USSR. The whole globe was turning against the disabled.

In 1941, the French surgeon and Nobel laureate Alexis Carrel had called for the extermination of the mentally disabled as a cost-effective and humane form of treatment, echoing Binding and Hoche's position. Carrel was co-inventor along with Charles Lindbergh of a heat pump, and like Lindberg, he too would come to welcome the Nazis. Before the T4 program had even begun, Carrell advocated for the use of poisonous gas to rid humanity of so-called "defectives." In his popular, scientific works, he would argue for eugenics and the need to strengthen humanity against defectives. In the German edition of a 1936 publication, he fawned over the Nazi policies.

"The German government has taken energetic measures against the propagation of the defective, the mentally diseased, and the criminal. The ideal solution would be the suppression of each of these individuals as soon as he has proven himself to be dangerous."

Interestingly, he omitted that passage from non-German editions. *The Journal of American Psychiatric Association* repeated his call to euthanize "retarded children," labeling them "nature's mistakes." With the widespread belief in and practices of eugenics, it is hardly surprising that during the Nuremberg War Crimes Trials, the Nazi doctors deflected any wrongdoing by pointing to their American and European colleagues. Pointing to the actions of the Allied medical and scientific communities, they claimed they were no guiltier than their counterparts. In this, they were not far from the truth. This may explain why only three of the architects of the T4 program would receive any punishment. The countless doctors, nurses, orderlies, and associated professionals would walk away carrying their guilt with them.

We see then that the Nazis' path of ridding the world of the disabled was well paved and preceded by the rise and widespread success of the eugenics movement that capitalized on the notion of exploiting the disabled. In 1930, Julian Huxley, secretary of the London Zoological Society and chair of the Eugenics Society, wrote:

"What are we going to do? Every defective man, woman, and child is a burden. Every defective is an extra body for the nation to feed and clothe, but produces little or nothing in return."

This rhetoric sounds like it could come directly from Nazi propaganda. However, it was before the Nazis came to power. This kind of hate-filled and inflammatory rhetoric would prepare for and set up the horror of the eugenics movement, which would ultimately lead to the T4 program and, as we have seen, the Holocaust. The architects of the Holocaust would defend their actions at the Nuremberg trials by referencing American eugenics laws and policies. They were not dissembling. Many of the horrors of the Holocaust seen in a broader outline reveal similar programs in the United States. Federal Government actions and policies, including the genocidal treatment of native peoples, the American Indian reservation system and their forced relocations, the internment of Japanese Americans in WWII, racial quotas and biased immigration laws, as well as the acceptance of the scientific racism of the likes of Carrell, Galton, Haeckel, Laughlin, Spencer, and others, reveal the depths to which American culture is implicated. The eugenics movement abetted by discriminatory policies and practices before WWII and found in many nations would make the Nazi extermination machine a reality. The Nazis, of course, took these to brutal extremes, but the antecedents were present and widespread.

Finally, it must be doubly emphasized that the Americans and Nazis were not alone in this inhumane practice of forced sterilization and the mercy killing of the disabled. We find many other countries, including Denmark, Norway, Sweden, Switzerland, and the Soviet Union, which developed and formed forced sterilization programs and eugenics laws aimed at the disabled.[239] The long legacy of removing the disabled remains today, as any disabled traveler to any of these countries may tell you regarding the lack of access, the absence of persons with disabilities, and the generally negative attitudes toward the disabled nearly a century later. It is clear that the dehumanization of the disabled did not begin, nor did it end with the Nazis. It is placing the disabled into a category and deeming them worthless that sets up an inevitable dynamic. The person is labeled as inferior and, based on that label, is then denied access to justice, healthcare, education, economic possibility, and the opportunity to live. The result is a self-fulfilling prophecy.

In today's zeitgeist, the disabled are viewed as sad objects of scorn or an aspirational so-called "super-gimp." Lurking beneath much of today's attitudes is still the vestiges of the religiously inspired idea of divine agency, bad luck, or blood. These beliefs still permeate the complex set of attitudes towards the disabled in many modern democracies. Because of this belief in agency and merit, the successful often heap scorn upon you without worrying about any consequences. For example, in the 2016 campaign for the U.S. Presidency, Republican candidate Donald Trump could make fun of a reporter's disability and see very little rebuttal or reprisal from either mainstream or alternative press. When Donald Trump ridiculed the New York Times reporter Serge Kovaleski who happens to live with a disability, because Kovaleski was critical of Trump, it underscored the acceptability of scapegoating or attacking the disabled in contemporary American society.

Moreover, one can and will get away with it. Trump is doing what Hitler and his cronies did. Oddly, for Trump, it was not the first time he had stooped to this form of hate. Trump had earlier ridiculed conservative columnist Charles Krauthammer[240] who happened to be a quadriplegic as "someone who just sits there" and a "man who can't buy his own pants." (Huffington Post). Just as disturbingly, Trump's real estate empire is on record for being one of the most egregious violators of the ADA. In addition, in 1991, he led a campaign to banish disabled veterans permitted to vend on 5th Avenue. Disabled veterans were granted an exception to market on the streets of New York City after the U.S.

Civil War. In a 1991 letter to the NYC Assembly, Trump wrote, "While disabled veterans should be given every opportunity to earn a living, is it fair to do so to the detriment of the city as a whole or its tax-paying citizens and business." According to The Daily News, the veterans were granted licenses to peddle dating back to the 1890s as an effort to assist disabled U.S. Civil War veterans. In 2004, he wrote to then NYC Mayor Michael Bloomberg,

"Whether they are veterans or not, they should not be allowed to sell on this most important and prestigious shopping street," he wrote. "The image of New York City will suffer... I hope you can stop this very deplorable situation before it is too late."

Yet despite his attacks on persons with disabilities and especially disabled veterans,[241] his popularity and poll numbers lauded as revealing what Americans felt but dare not say. What do we make of this form of discrimination?

An unanticipated upshot of these discriminatory beliefs of trying to ban or eradicate disability is the administration of PAPP-A tests to screen for the potential for Downs syndrome. As a result, there has been a 90% drop in babies born with Downs over the past decade. This decrease is due to pressures placed on expectant moms to abort by medical professionals. Those professionals argue that the parents will face emotional burdens and financial expenses because of their child's disability. This practice is akin to the Nazi eugenics of killing the disabled as unworthy of living and is essentially saying that a person with Downs is not living a life worth living. The respective societies sought to hide or remove the disabled from the community, some using liberal notions of concern, others brutal disregard, and still others programs of mass killings.

With an eye to the future, Suzanne Evans concludes in her book, "Forgotten Crimes: The Holocaust and People with Disabilities," a book that I have relied on for much of my material:

"In short, these policies implemented by the Nazis to victimize and exploit people with disabilities were part of a pervasive and lasting legacy of discrimination toward people with disabilities. The rise to power in some European countries in recent years of ultra-right and nationalistic parties (which tend to view anyone 'different' with 'hostility') adds to concern for the future. The Holocaust for people with disabilities must be viewed in a larger context that links memory, present realities, and future solutions."

30

America Meeting Americans: Of Freaks and Geeks in the Sideshow of Life

"When you're born, you get a ticket to the freak show.
When you're born in America, you get a front row seat."
-George Carlin

In the mid-20th century, a proliferation of stories about grotesques and freaks would later appear so often in the stories of Flannery O'Connor, the photography of Diane Arbus, and other places. It would be a good and popular source of entertainment for unscrupulous entrepreneurs. A century earlier, exploiting persons with disabilities and those with rare conditions would already be a profitable enterprise at sideshows, circuses, and amusement parks. Rooted in practice going back as early as the 17th and 18th centuries with their fascination with medical anomalies or oddities, scientists, artists, and others would collect specimens of medical oddities in museums—the "cabinets of curiosity," or wunderkammern, allowing the public to view them for the price of admission.

One example we might cite is the peculiar case of the Irish giant Charles Byrne who stood eight-foot-four. Although he profited by his height by touring county fairs across the UK, the English doctor, John Hunter, approached the teenage boy and asked to buy his corpse when he died. Horrified, Byrne refused. A few years later, at age 22, Byrn died, and Hunter stole his body. Hunter then dissected, boiled the flesh off the skeleton, and displayed it for cash. Sadly, Byrne's skeleton remains on display at the Museum of the Royal College of Surgeons in London, where it has been attracting gawkers for nearly two centuries.[242]

In many other instances, as in the Mutter Museum[243] in Philadelphia today, many specimens are from disabled individuals. In the dawn of science and medicine, curious researchers sought to explain if not make a profit on some oddities that would, in most circles, be known as "monsters." The history of the notion of a freak of nature can be traced back to antiquity. Aristotle, for example, had defined an aberration of natural form as a lusus naturae in Latin. In his hierarchy of being--the Scala Naturae—the lusus naturae was a freak, an anomaly. With a twist, the Roman naturalist Pliny the Elder held that anomalies in nature were a joke of nature. He argued that fossils, for example, were nature carving into stone as a joke. Later and by the 18th century, in his taxonomy of being, botanist Carl Linnaeus would distinguish three kinds of humans: Homo sapiens (rational man), homo ferus (wild mind), and homo monstrosus (the man-monster).

The Enlightenment mania for categorizing and classifying reached a peak in his work. Following in this tradition, Charles Darwin, in his On the Origin of Species, postulated a homo monstrosus as a hybrid from a cross-species reproduction giving his theory a subtle racist overtone given all the fears of miscegenation in the air at that time. At root with this fascination is not only the inclination to inquire into nature's workings but the all-too-human sense of curiosity. According to the OED, the English word "curious" comes from Middle English and Old French "curios," ultimately deriving from the Latin, "curiosus" suggesting the idea of 'careful." As Yunte Huang covers in his recent and insightful study of the con-joined twins Chen and Eng in his 2018 "Inseparable: The Original Siamese Twins and their Rendezvous' with American History," the concept of curiosity is both a gift and a burden. Thus, the two-fold notion of interest and care is folded into its meaning. In the first sense, the word as Thomas Hobbes understood it as the foundation of language, science, and religious institutions.[244] His fellow philosopher, David Hume, viewed it similarly as that essential quality of "that love of truth, which [is] the first source of all our inquiries." However, Huang reminds us of the second sense too, which may carry a more sinister connotation. In Ecclesiastes 3:23, we are told that curiosity is "the cause of mankind's errors." In either of the two senses, to be the object of another's curiosity can be discomfiting. The upshot becomes whether a monster, a freak of nature, a bad joke, or the unfortunate by-product of a strange coupling, a person with a disability looked at with curiosity was going to find themselves the object of fear, ridicule, or a subject to be examined, probed and studied. The only option left was for them to be exploited for other's entertainment. Enter the freak show.

By the 19th century, people with medical anomalies and rare conditions would find themselves at the center of attention and potential exploitation due to traveling circuses and sideshows. By the late 19th and early 20th century, the sideshow attraction of "freaks" was a mainstay and popular pull for audiences. It was as if science's curiosity had jettisoned the oddities of nature and left them to the unscrupulous showmen to exploit as freaks.

It would prove profitable, at least for the impresarios. P.T. Barnum began exploiting people's disabilities when he purchased an elderly blind and partially paralyzed slave named Joice Heth. He billed her as "the 161-year-old nurse of George Washington." For over a year, Barnum put Heth on display six days a week for as long as 12 hours a day. Then, to capitalize on her popularity, when Heth died on February 19, 1836, Barnum charged a fee--50 cents--allowing spectators to watch a public autopsy.[245] Indeed, even the dead bodies of disabled people were not off-limits. Nothing was sacrosanct to these petite-capitalists who were hell-bent on exploiting the disabled even if dead.

A South African woman renamed Saartje Baartman, a member of the Khoikhoi who was orphaned and taken captive by the Dutch was brought to Europe to display. Why? Due to her large buttocks--she would be exhibited under the title of the "Hottentot Venus." Hottentot is a racially abusive term used to describe the Khoikhoi people, a nomadic, non-Bantu people of southwestern Africa. She was displayed from Africa to England, Scotland to France, arousing spectators' prurient curiosity wherever she was forced to go. Her death did not relieve her of these struggles. Even after she died in Paris on 29 December 1815, her exhibitions continued. Science blogger Brian Switek tells us that the scientific community was not dismayed by her death but sought opportunities to exploit her corpse:

"As reported in The Literary Panorama and National Register the naturalists waiting to examine her body were glad to see that "her size and enormous protuberances are not diminished." After they were through, a wax cast was made of her body, her brain was removed, and her skeleton was stripped of flesh."[246]

Twenty years after her death, she was still in the public limelight. In 1843, "The Family Magazine," an English periodical, compared her profile with a "Grecian ideal" to make an argument for beauty and explain why she was not eligible. The idea was that by comparing different races' facial profiles illustrating the beauty of the Grecian (read European or white), you could see how far Saartje's face was from the purported ideal.

Saartje's brain, skeleton, and sexual organs remained on display in a Paris museum until 1974. Her remains were not returned to South Africa until after President Nelson Mandela lobbied for them; she was finally laid to rest in 2002.

The "freaks" were inevitably individuals with various disabilities or rare and often undiagnosed medical conditions and deformations. One was Myrtle Corbin, billed as "the 4-legged girl from Texas," She was a popular attraction for Barnum and later with the Ringling Brothers at

Coney Island. One of the most popular sideshow freaks, she was known to earn as much as 450 dollars a week. However, she had a condition known as dipygus, a congenital condition that may lead to the twining of a pelvis, or as in Myrtle's case, an extra set of non-functioning legs. In addition, she was born with a clubfoot, making mobility challenges.

Nonetheless, Barnum would place her on display at age thirteen. After performing for six years, she left the side-show-biz, married, and raised a family. She would bear eight children, four of whom died in infancy. Due to economic hardship, she later returned to performing in sideshows performing at Coney Island aged 41. She would die at 59, and her family had to bury her in a sealed concrete casket to prevent grave robbers from stealing her corpse. The family had been the recipients of several offers to purchase her body. They wanted to save her from the fates of Byrne and Saartje.

Throughout much of the early 20th century, the traveling sideshow became popular leisure and entertainment for the burgeoning middle classes, particularly during the Great Depression. Several artists, including Reginald Marsh, Eudora Welty, and Ben Shahn, wrote about or photographed many sideshow performers.[247] The dehumanizing spectacle that was the sideshow nevertheless did allow some of those with these conditions to eke out a living. It could not, however, be either a very pleasant or a highly profitable life. Many of the performers were forced as children into the business, where they could expect a life of abuse and neglect. Indeed, Barnum started displaying Tom Thumb at age 10. He would be one of the first successful acts after Barnum's success with Heth.

Charles Sherwood Stratton, better known by his stage name, General Tom Thumb, was a little person Barnum advertised as Napoleon and other historical characters. Barnum built on the long and storied English folk tales of Tom Thumb and profited from Tom's diminutive stature. Although Stratton started working at 10, he would eventually eclipse his former impresario living in the most fashionable neighborhoods. Later, when Barnum's circus hit financial ruin, he bailed out the failing empire of his former boss.

Stratton had a variation of a condition known as dwarfism caused by a deficiency in a growth hormone. At the time, there was no medical diagnosis known for his condition. He traveled with P.T. Barnum's Circus for 40 years, amassing a fortune (it has been estimated to be over a million dollars in today's dollars) and would be feted by celebrities, royalty, and U.S. Presidents. He was invited to the Lincoln White House and performed for Queen Victoria at Buckingham Palace. He died of a stroke aged 45.

While Tom Thumb and Myrtle Corbin's lives were successful by any standard, they would be notable exceptions; indeed, most sideshow performers would live short and economically dispirited lives, dying in poverty and fading into obscurity. Criss-crossing America were countless traveling circuses, many with their sideshows and freakshows displaying people with disabilities at the mercy of unscrupulous circus owners and charlatans.

Barnum's success with Joice Heth and General Tom Thumb and the public's seemingly insatiable "curiosity" led Barnum to continue seeking and hiring other people with disabilities. During the ensuing half-century of the 19th century, Barnum would later hire and exploit the conjoined twins, Chang and Eng Bunker,[248] a family of albinos, and many others.

Phineas T. Barnum began exploiting the American public's credulity early in his life using lotteries and odd "biological" specimens. He would usually manufacture the latter from the parts of dead and preserved animals. In 1842, his first significant success along this line was the "Feejee Mermaid." It was a torso of a monkey sewn to the body of a fish that a ship's captain had sold to a Boston Circus owner who had, in turn, sold it to Barnum. The discourse of a half-mammal, half-animal exotic creature would play on the racist, colonialist and ableist rhetoric of the 19th century. The "mermaid" would also allude to the controversial debates raging around evolution. However, despite critics and skeptics of such hoaxes, Barnum and others would profit from their suspect enterprises. Barnum's successes allowed him to purchase the American Museum on Broadway and gather an ensemble of disabled Americans, creating a "rotating roster of freaks: albinos, midgets, giants, exotic animals."[249] Barnum capitalized on the prejudicial attitudes of Americans, turning the freak show into a highly profitable business for himself while degrading its performers and piquing the curiosity of the American populace.

Never one to lose an opportunity to exploit, we see Barnum taking advantage of the rhetoric of prejudice of the 19th century; he jumped on the controversy surrounding the 1859 publication of Charles Darwin's "The Origins of the Species" by hiring William Henry Johnson. Johnson was the child of former slaves now living in New Jersey and had been born with a mild case of microcephaly. It left him with a cranial deformity which Barnum exploited, transforming Johnson into "Zip the Pinhead" and billed as the "missing link." Barnum billed Johnson as the definitive proof for Darwin's evolutionary theory between humans and apes. In his billing, Barnum advertised Johnson as a "different race of human found during a gorilla trekking expedition near the Gambia River in western Africa." Johnson's head was kept shaven except for a topknot, dressed in fur, placed in a cage, and ordered to grunt to further Barnum's ruse. In addition, he was paid a dollar a day not to talk.

It is well known that Charles Dickens and the Prince of Wales took a perverse interest in Johnson, and both visited the show while on tour in America. After a life of such oppression, Johnson, who lived well into his eighties, tried to market himself in 1925 during the "Scopes Trial" as living proof of evolution.[250] He reportedly died wealthy and was reputed to say on his deathbed to his sister: "we fooled 'em for a long time, didn't we?"

Barnum was not the first to capitalize and exploit persons with disabilities, but he did become one of the most influential producers of museums, sideshows, and circuses. He brought into the American mainstream a new business built on the exploitation of persons with disabilities.

P.T. Barnum was born Phineas Taylor Barnum in Bethel, Connecticut, to a merchant family. Barnum would try his hand at several economic enterprises designed to trick gullible consumers into parting with their money. His visit to a freak show in Philadelphia that featured Joice Heath was the catalyst for his entry into the sideshow business. He saw her at a sideshow and purchased her from her owner for $1,000. He would display the blind, toothless, and partly paralyzed 80-year-old woman up and down the east coast--Albany, Boston, New York, and beyond. As we saw, Barnum would try and capitalize on her death by marketing her autopsy, eerily foreshadowing by a century how the medical and pharmaceutical industries would capitalize on the death of Henrietta Lack's cervical cells.[251] Undeterred, Barnum would open the American Museum in New York in 1842, developing into a profitable and popular attraction featuring primarily persons with disabilities on display for the curious. At its height of popularity, the museum saw up to 15,000 visitors a day.[252] It has been estimated that 38 million customers attended the museum.

What were they paying to see? For the price of their admission--25 cents--they would be exposed to any number of displays, artifacts, and exhibitions that ranged from wildlife to entertainment, but many came to see the oddities, the freaks. Featuring 13 different acts or human curiosities, the museum's Freakshow would at different periods have included General Tom Thumb, Cheng and Eng Bunker, a family of albinos, the Living Aztecs, three dwarfs, a black mother with her two albino children, the Swiss Bearded Lady, the Highland Fat Boys, Henry Johnson, the giantess Anna Swan and Commodore Nutt--the eventual replacement for Tom Thumb. Barnum knew how to advertise and take advantage of the lesser angels of the American appetite for entertainment.

Most of the participants of freak shows, circuses, and other entertainments lived precariously on the margins of society, barely eking out a meager living, often fuelled with alcohol and other problems. For example, Saartje Baartman would die young her health compromised from alcohol and tobacco addictions. The weekly or daily routine of being gawked at, laughed at, ridiculed, and derided would erode the self-esteem of anyone. Most of these participants came from dysfunctional backgrounds, were economically impoverished, and were forced or sold into the business when children. Coming as so many of them did from such underprivileged backgrounds, few had any formal education. Considering Baartman, Cheng and Eng, they were brought to countries where they had no knowledge of the language or customs and would need to rely on their handlers, however unscrupulous those handlers were.

Many of the sideshow participants were like "Maggie, the Last of the Aztec Children." Charlatans cruelly exploited them. Maggie, a male, was the stage name of Schlitze Surtees, possibly born as Simon Metz. Schlitze, as he was known, was born with microcephaly and was estimated to have the cognitive capacity of a three-year-old. He would be displayed in an androgynous outfit sometimes as "Maggie" and at other times as "The Monkey Girl," "Pinhead," or "the Missing Link." Due to his disability, Schlitze was incontinent, needing to wear diapers while on display, and would often sit for hours in his soiled costume. His career was controlled by unscrupulous handlers who took advantage of him and bounced him around, selling him from circus to circus, sideshow to sideshow. Over his career, Schlitze performed with various circuses, including the Ringling Bros. and Barnum & Bailey Circus, the Clyde Beatty Circus, and the Tom Mix Circus. In 1928, Schlitze was in the film "The Sideshow," a drama set in a circus. Four years later, in 1932, Schlitze was used in Tod Browning's 1932 exploitative horror film "Freaks."

The circus sideshows, freakshows, and museums along American boardwalks became a mainstay of entertainment for Americans through the latter 20th century. Some lasted until the 1950s and early '60s but would see their fortunes slowly eclipsed by the rise of television as the dominant and beloved form of entertainment for middle-class Americans. Television would bring a shift in American's consumption of entertainment, but larger forces were at play as well. The burgeoning civil and disability rights movements during the latter part of the 20th century played a minor role in ending such exploitative enterprises. The actual demise of the circus and its attendant side- and freakshows, however, was due to the changing pastimes of middle-class Americas. Television and the movie industry would sound the death knell to the American circus.

At the same time, some persons with disabilities were able to profit from the entertainment. The denigrating and exploitative aspect of the shows built on and advanced the longer cultural and historical nature of discrimination against persons with disabilities. As such, these shows make this an especially nefarious aspect of 20th-century American popular culture. Today performers in "Freak Shows" are not forced into performing and are seldom abandoned to a life of squalor. More importantly, they are consenting adults and usually working within the context of art, performance theatre, or retro-vaudevillian acts. Today's performers likely come from comfortable, middle-class backgrounds, are often college graduates trained in art, theatre, or performance, and see it as a viable, provocative way of making a living by performing in a quasi-vaudevillian aspect of show biz.

There is still the problematic nature of exploiting disability and difference. In this sense, "the look" or "gaze" of "the other" has become a useful political tool available to artists and even performers in the art world. Many contemporary performers see their performances as subverting dominant practices of oppression. As Rachel Adams puts it in her work, "Disability and the Circus:"

"The thrill of the freak show is in its promise of a close and unmediated encounter with otherness. Live performance also gives the freak the possibility of agency. However, much she is objectified, the freak maintains her capacity to look back, challenging the audience to recognize her humanity and to be mindful of the impulse behind the urge to stare."

In this reading, the performer becomes a real, living, and embodied "Olympia," returning an unsettling gaze to the consumer of her flesh, her body, and, in the process, causes the viewer to re-examine their culpability in framing and sustaining notions of ability/disability. Modern Freaks have attempted to turn an exploitative and dark chapter in American entertainment into politically engaged performative art.

However, a serious and pragmatic objection arises here. As much as the audience understands the origins of their curiosity and is informed critically of the historic background assumptions of the discriminatory and prejudicial beliefs toward persons with disabilities, they may view such performances critically and appreciate the political statement being offered. The critically informed consumer is not, however, the average one. Rather, it is more likely that some element of titillation and curiosity is still at play in modern iterations of freak shows. Suppose the viewer leaves the performance without any awareness of the history of discriminatory treatment of the disabled. In that case, they will likely adopt those prejudices through their passive and unthinking consumption. I doubt that the person drawn to a freak show is a well-read cultural or philosophical thinker steeped in the history of disability studies trying to plumb the depths of social discrimination. Instead, they, too, are drawn as earlier consumers were drawn to freak shows—curiosity. They, too, are thoughtlessly imbibing the cultural and historically induced sets of prejudices about disability, the novelty of the other, the freak.

Of course, something more practical and financial was at play with these performances for Barnum and others. As Dalton Brown wrote focusing on Barnum,

"Barnum was a leader in the business of stealing humanity from people, creating "human curiosities" to entertain curious humans. It seems the idea of "human curiosity" defines how freakshows captured a nation's attention for so long. Showmen like P.T. Barnum took advantage of human nature's natural disposition to gawk at what it finds unusual, piquing people's curiosity for decades. Unfortunately, showmen had a societal impact in exploiting this disposition, exacerbating the notion that disability was something to be gawked at and shamed by the masses. Instead of appreciating differences, freak shows mock, disrespect, and exploit these differences for financial gain."[253]

Historically, these freak shows and sideshow performances were not universally accepted. They were often lumped together as the kind of lower-class forms of entertainment that well-educated and up-standing citizens did not deign to attend. Apart, of course, from Queens, Presidents, and famous writers. Some earlier 19th century critics of these inhumane practices and performances offered serious objections to the popularity of the sideshows and the effects on the performers. In 1861, the British historian, reformer, and co-founder of the satirical magazine, "Punch," Henry Mayhew, wrote:

"Instead of being a means for illustrating a moral precept, [freak shows] turned into a platform to teach the cruelest debauchery...The men who preside over these infamous places know too well the failings of their audience."

Mayhew viewed sideshows as lacking any edifying moral purpose and as exploitative to both the performer and the audience. Degradation is a double-edged sword scarring both the performer with a disability and the paying customer. The only one who can indeed be said to gain from the situation is the circus owner.

As late as 1950, a 16-year-old girl from North Carolina, Carol Grant, who was disabled from birth and had visited a sideshow, was so shocked by the degradation she witnessed that she wrote an impassioned letter to the North Carolina Agricultural Commissioner:

"Handicapped people are seeking more in life than being stared at in a sideshow."

And perhaps our final word on this topic should come from a former performer himself, Frank Lentini, a three-legged known as the "King of the Freaks," who wrote,

"My limb does not bother me," he wrote, "as much as the curious, critical gaze."

Sadly, for some, they are still set exploiting the disabilities of others. For example, nearly 30 years after Lentini's death, the rock band "Alice in Chains" used a photograph of Lentini on their album to generate sales. The use of minority bodies to stimulate profit is a problematic area of pop culture and fine arts in the 21st century. That a rock band uses an image of a disabled person is, in itself, not the problem. The problem arises when the image is used to attract the consumer based on the consumer's prurient interest or curiosity, based on the consumer holding invidious stereotypes. As such, it is used as a marketing ploy to drive sales. We see this same treatment within the use of other minority communities. For example, take the controversy around Dana Schutz's painting of the murdered black teenager, Emmet Till. Her painting "Open Casket" has drawn the ire of artists such as Hannah Black, who writes:

"It is not acceptable for a white person to transmute Black suffering into profit and fun, though the practice has been normalized for a long time."

Because the dominant classes often use black and minority bodies for profit within the context of racism, we see the obvious negative consequences of such an act. Disabled bodies in freak shows, television, and art are treated similarly and exploited for profit. This sort of commodification fuels discrimination and exploitation of persons with disabilities and is alive and thriving in America and beyond.

Today the phenomenon of reality television has brought the freak show into your living room. This phenomenon gained resurgence in the popularity of television shows that emerged in the first decade of the 21st century. Major television stations that once prided themselves on providing educational programmings such as The Learning Channel, BBC, and the Discovery Channel, found that they could gather more viewers and make more money by exploiting persons with disabilities. To that end, the first decade of the 21st century saw a flood of "reality-television" programs whose fundamental precept is to display people who are disabled. Programs such as "My 600 Pound Life," "Little People, Big World," "Born This Way, "The Undateables," and "Autism in Love" may bring some financial reward to the participants who are paid handsomely by the producers but are dependent on the larger context of discrimination of the disabled. Indeed, it is estimated by GLADD[254] that less than 1.4% of television roles and characters of some 813 overall regular characters on broadcast primetime depict actual people with real disabilities. Instead, the only depictions viewers will see are those portrayed on reality television. The only place you will see a character or portrayal of a person with a disability relegated to reality television speaks volumes about the current state of prejudice aimed at the disabled. Frances Ryan analyzes British reality television programs that depict the lives of persons with disabilities:

"When depicting disability, mainstream broadcasters give us the good, but they give us the bad and the ugly – and in the case of Bodyshock or Extraordinary People, do so while calling them exactly that. The modern-day freak show, these ratings hits mix deformity, disability and obesity into a one-size-fits-all hatchet job of ignorance."

31

Ugly Laws in America: The Cult of Beauty

"It is the reflection of my face. Often in these lost days I study it: I can understand nothing of this face. The faces of others have some sense, some direction. Not mine. I cannot even decide whether it is handsome or ugly. I think it is ugly because I have been told so. But it doesn't strike me. At heart, I am even shocked that anyone can attribute qualities of this kind to it, as if you called a clod of earth or a block of stone beautiful or ugly."

-Sartre, "Nausea"

In 2003 while being interviewed by a British Film director, Nobel laureate, and co-founder of the DNA molecule, James Watson, argued for using genetic techniques to prevent the births of "ugly girls." He added, "people say it would be terrible if we made all girls pretty," he explained, "I think it would be great." There seems something profoundly flawed and offensive about this claim coming from anyone, but coming from the mouth of a Nobel laureate, it is especially worrisome. One is inclined to dismiss Watson's comments as the socially inappropriate comments of a nerdy scientist. But that simply will not be acceptable. Too often, those in power say outrageously offensive things showing their ignorance and claiming to be misunderstood non-conforming geniuses. He may have been a capable chemist, but his grasp of history, ethics, and social phenomena is deeply and profoundly flawed.

History suggests something more nefarious is at play in our understanding of disability and beauty. As we will see, the aesthetics of beauty and sense of decency in our public spaces are decidedly ableist as well as fraught with profound consequences for the disabled, then and now. Across America, neighborhoods, condominiums, and villages enact Homeowners Associations' Regulations and Bylaws pointedly burdensome or discriminatory for the disabled. Architects reject as a limit on their artistic creativity the humane need to integrate accessible designs. The person with a disability may be and was banned from pools, schools, or any number of public facilities. The oft-used notion of public "decency" or "safety" may be invoked, but the upshot was always to keep the disabled either out of view or from accessing the corridors of public space. So it follows, too, from the corridors of political power, where they can become a potent political agent for change. As we will see, Watson's comments and the laws that limit public access for people with disabilities are, well, as American as apple pie. But when municipalities started to pass legislation and ordinances banning disabled people from public places, the real threat became apparent. Ugly laws will function as that threat.

The disability rights scholar and Dean of Arts and Humanities, Susan Schweik, in her article, "Kicked to the Curb: Ugly Law Then and Now," recounts the story of "Mother Hastings":

"Sometime during the second decade of the twentieth century, a woman commonly known as "Mother Hastings" was told by authorities in Portland, Oregon that she was "too terrible a sight for the children to see": "They meant my crippled hands, I guess," she told a reporter, "[t]hey gave me money to get out of town." "Mother Hastings" complied, moving to Los Angeles just as that city's leaders were discussing enacting a version of the city ordinance that had targeted her in Portland."

Such legislative acts would sweep across the land of freedom, curtailing the liberties of the disabled and those deemed ugly in America.

As surprising as this may seem to some, some of these so-called "ugly laws" were still on the books well into the 21st century. In the movie about the life of the disability rights advocate and disabled Vietnam War veteran Richard Pimentel, called "The Music Within," there is a poignant scene in a restaurant where he and his friend, Art Honneyman, were celebrating Honneyman's birthday with a pancake breakfast. The waitress commented on Honneyman's cerebral palsy, saying he was "the ugliest, most disgusting thing" she had seen, and threatened to call the police and have them arrested under the "Ugly Law" if they did not leave her restaurant. They refused and were subsequently arrested and charged under the San Francisco "Ugly Law." That was in the early 1970s!

Ugly laws started to appear in the United States and Europe from the late nineteenth century and would continue until the 1970s. Many municipalities had enacted and promulgated ugly laws to curb beggars and panhandlers, but their execution proved far more sinister. Ugly laws made it illegal and punishable for persons who were viewed as "ugly," "unsightly," or "unseemly" to appear in public. Euphemistically, the laws were known as "unsightly beggar ordinances," but were the laws aimed at curing indigents? The laws were ostensibly directed at removing persons viewed as "unsightly" or "unseemly" who otherwise upset the community's aesthetics. However, in practice, they soon engendered a very fluid criterion of what was considered "unsightly" or "unseemly." Into that criterion would fall the disabled, deformed, and poor. Too often, the laws would be directed at those with disabilities, as in the case of Honneyman. The 19th-century link between physical appearance, suspected criminality, and deviance would form the ground for these ordinances. Watson does not need genetic manipulation when you could have laws to achieve his end.

The first ugly law was passed in San Francisco in 1867 — Order No. 783.[255] The law describes whom it is intended to affect, including "any person who is diseased, maimed, mutilated, or in any way deformed to be an unsightly or disgusting object or an improper person." The ordinance further includes that any person "without means of support, and physically unable to earn a livelihood" shall be subject to imprisonment and a fine of $25.[256] Thus, the combination of poverty and disability becomes a double whammy. Soon cities, municipalities, and towns-large and small-around the country would follow suit and enact "Ugly Laws" directed at the disabled poor. These laws were reminiscent of Queen Elizabeth's laws against the "helpless poor," which we saw passed in the 1600s. Ostensibly those laws were enacted to curb a social problem, too. However, they were ultimately directed at the disabled just as the later laws would be directed in major American cities such as Chicago, Columbus (OH), Denver, Omaha, New Orleans, and Portland. They all followed San Francisco's lead enacting their own set of ordinances.

Let us look at the wording of one municipality. Chicago would pass its legislation in 1881, and it may be found in the Chicago Municipal Code, sec. 36034. Here it clearly expresses whom the law is aimed at:

"No person who is diseased, maimed, mutilated or in any way deformed so as to be an unsightly, disgusting or improper is to be allowed in or on the public ways or other public places in this city, or shall therein or thereon expose himself to public view, under penalty of not less than one dollar nor more than fifty dollars for each offense."[257]

Diseased. Maimed. Mutilated, Deformed. We are talking here about persons with disabilities. Not the poor and not panhandlers. In this statute, we hear the voice of a virulent form of discrimination borne from the deep and irrational fear of difference and aimed directly at those with disabilities. It is particularly loathsome because these laws were motivated, framed, and passed into the ordinance by people far more privileged, powerful, and, in every practical sense, better off than those the laws were aimed at it. It also presupposes a highly debatable idea of beauty.

Moreover, the use of the terms such as "maimed," "unsightly," "disgusting," and "improper" are without any universal or objective assent. Precisely what do they mean? Or reference? The terms as written are entirely subjective and open to vast and relativistic interpretations making these laws even more unpredictable and biased. The apparent aim of these laws was to limit the begging and pan-handling from business and shopping districts. In practice and enforcement, however, they were written as ways to limit the public access of persons with disabilities that the mainstream found distasteful, unpleasant, or aesthetically unsettling. In essence, these laws and others similar to them take a political mandate and convert them to an anesthetization[258] of the public space that is detrimental to the disabled. To appear in public now carries a cost, a severe cost. The ugly laws have their intended effect of keeping people with disabilities out of the public purview by imposing apartheid of ability that often and over time will become a learned behavior internalized by most, including many of the disabled themselves. Call a person ugly long enough...

The justifications for enacting ugly laws stemmed from a protective impulse by members of the councils who believed themselves offering a veneer of protection from the riff-raff of society. The same people making the laws and those it is protecting would also be flocking to gawk at the disabled being displayed in freaks shows and cabinets of curiosities across America. As syndicated columnist Cecil Adams wrote, "while the revelation of a disfigured limb may have offended the sensibilities of some, it no doubt offered a voyeuristic pleasure to others."[259] However, this impulse does little to affirm the humanity of a person with a disability caught as you would be between the positions of being the object derision or fear or the object of a paternalistic sense of care. Either treatment would bridle even the most tolerant of persons. Placing these laws within their historical context- the rise of eugenics, sterilizations, and the forced institutionalization of many disabled -these laws take on a nefarious meaning.

The larger zeitgeist of the late 19th and early 20th centuries can be viewed as a time when the construction of urban and municipal public space was being framed by the wealthier classes and working toward understanding what constitutes the aesthetics of public health. As such, they brought their exclusionary values to bear in the manufacturing of built space. These values were profoundly mistrustful of differences of any degree and type. They were based on misunderstanding, lack of awareness, fear, and reactionary political reasoning. Rooted in fear, especially fear of the other and disability, they would be super-added to existing fears of race, sexual deviance, class, immigrants, and women's liberation to create a perfect storm of intolerance.[260] The public sphere was fast becoming overly sanitized, hyper-policed, and forcefully homogenized in the name of public safety or public health. The arena of public space would be where Orwellian tactics would first and most successfully be placed into action. Schweik suggests both "anti-freak" and ugly laws had the same effect of outlawing the disabled body from the public purview. They treated the anomalous body as something outside the social norm. An upshot of these laws will be that judges were more likely to sentence the disabled or "unsightly" more harshly.[261] Violence against the disabled would become a recurrent and all-too-common historical fact. These laws will also spawn the institutionalization of violence created by enacting statutes that further sanctioned systemic violence. Law has the effect of normalizing a behavior and abetting others to act accordingly or similarly. It forms the foundation of socially acceptable behaviors. We do what we are allowed to do.

Historically we have known that violence toward the disabled has always been widespread. As early as 1948, German criminologist Hans von Hentig identified disability as a significant factor in people being selected and subjected to violence.[262] Current research sees that violence continuing throughout the 20th century.[263]

Taking the larger view and placing these laws within the various period's emergent pseudo-sciences of eugenics and the variety of medical practices that would denigrate the disabled such as craniometrics, phrenology, we see how the latter 20th century will be framed. The powerful forces arrayed against the disabled will contribute to an oppressive social order. We can see how high the deck was stacked against the disabled in the 20th century, especially in America.[264]

All these practices become normalized. As Snyder and Mitchell write, "this enfeebling discourse ultimately becomes the basis for legalized segregation."[265] In concert with the near-total absence of persons with disabilities from the public space, the bans on immigrants with disabilities, you were unlikely to hear any countervailing voices or see any evidence to the contrary. The few exceptions were noted precisely for overcoming their disability (e.g., Helen Keller, FDR, et al.). Decades of forced institutionalization, extermination, and isolation had worked.

The erasure of the disabled that began in antiquity was nearly complete in the middle of the 20th century. By the advent of the 21st, it would be almost complete. As disability policy analyst Bobby Silverstein summarizes:[266]

"Disability issues are civil rights issues. Historically, we've tried to fix people with disabilities. If we could not fix them, we supported exclusion and segregation. Sometimes we banned people with disabilities from being seen in public. Sometimes we forced people with disabilities into institutions and sterilized them. People with disabilities were perceived as vulnerable and dependent, and somebody had to take care of them."

As we have seen in several other contexts in our study of disability, these prejudices endure for a very long time. Moreover, they can manifest in many subtle and some less subtle ways long after corrective actions have been made to redress the original wrongs. Micro-aggressive actions emerge as sublimated behaviors of people expressing their biases and fears against the disabled. For example, Chicago repealed their "ugly laws" in 1971 but over a decade and a half later, some Americans were still expressing their sense of distaste at disabled persons appearing in public. For example, in a September 22, 1986 opinion and advice column, Ann Landers responded to critics of an earlier letter posted by a reader. The reader found it offensive that a disabled person was dining at a restaurant. In the original letter, the woman said the sight of the disabled person made her feel "like throwing up." In many of the response letters to Ann Landers' rebuttal, the writers upbraided Landers and complained about persons with disabilities "flaunting" themselves and their disabilities in public. One letter suggested that if persons with disabilities are allowed access to public spaces, then "restaurants should have a special section for handicapped people—partially hidden by palms or other greenery so that other guests do not see them."[267] Judith Heumann writes how in the 1960s, the New York Board of Education banned her from teaching because her presence with a disability, polio, itself was viewed as harmful to her potential students.

This deep-seated and irrational fear of disability exemplified here often manifests in abusive micro-aggressions but can be seen as producing greater violence toward persons with disabilities once it has been institutionalized. These institutionalized and systemic forms of violence against people with disabilities abets personal acts of great violence. We see that latter aspect in Japan with the 2016 case of mass murderer Satoshi Uematsu. A 26-year-old Japanese man fantasized about killing people with disabilities. He wrote letters to the local Japanese authorities about his "dream of euthanizing disabled people." In the letter, Uematsu wrote of his willingness to kill persons with disabilities. In the letter, Uematsu argued that the Japanese government should permit euthanasia for disabled people, noting that he would be willing to carry out such killings. He even provided gruesome details on how he would do it. "I envision a world where a person with multiple disabilities can be euthanized," Uematsu wrote and added he could "wipe out a total of 470 disabled individuals" by attacking two residential facilities for disabled people during the night, "when staffing is low."[268] The authorities never investigated him.

He would go on to act on his plan. At 2 AM on Tuesday, July 26th, Uematsu broke into the Tsukui Yamayuri En (Tsukui Lily Garden) facility, where he had formerly worked and proceeded to murder 19 people. By the end of the carnage, nine men and ten women, aged 19-70, were dead, and 25 others were seriously injured. He then drove to the nearby police station and turned himself in, calmly telling the police, "I did it." Then, allegedly adding, "It is better that disabled people disappear."[269]

We cannot easily dismiss Uematsu as an isolated case, either. In the United States, there is a similar case of a healthcare worker Donald Harvey. Harvey became known as the "Angel of Death" for committing up to 87 murders over 17 years while working in hospitals, including several V.A. hospitals. He claimed to be motivated by empathy. Most of his patients were disabled or elderly--killing many of them by injecting them with poisons or sera tainted with HIV or Hepatitis. He killed two patients by stuffing oversized catheters into their bladders until they broke through the men's bladder walls. The men would die from internal bleeding or sepsis.

It should be noted that both Uematsu and Harvey viewed their actions as borne out of good intentions and empathy. It is of note that in Gilbert's case, he had joined a neo-Nazi party. The degree to which he shared the Nazi belief of euthanizing the disabled is unclear.[270] However, the strong link between the fear of disability leading to prejudice and violence against persons with disabilities is undeniable. Recent research shows the preponderance of such violence. In 2015, the United States Department of Justice reported that disabled people were almost three times more likely than non-disabled peers to experience violence.

Moreover, the data shows that the nature of the crimes tends to be severe and violent. For example, crimes perpetrated against the disabled such as sexual assaults, aggravated assaults, and robberies, are far more disproportionate than any other population.[271] I will end with the haunting words allegedly confessed by Uematsu: "It is better that disabled people disappear."[272]

Footnotes

1.   ^ Davis, L.J. "Enforcing Normalcy: Disability, Deafness and the Body," p. 7. Verson

2.   ^ Albrecht, G., "Encyclopaedia of Disability," p.253

3.   ^ http://www.nytimes.com/2012/12/18/science/ancient-bones-that-tell-a-story-of-compassion.

4.   ^ Retrieved from, https://arstechnica.com/science/2018/09/mummy-of-paraplegic-child-shows-how-perus-nasca-culture-treated-disability/

5.   ^ http://www.nytimes.com/2012/12/18/science/ancient-bones-that-tell-a-story-of-compassion.

6.   ^ vis-à-vis: Explorations in Anthropology, vol11, no 1 (2011)

7.   ^ Wright, Cassady and Yoder, "Recent Progress in Bioarchaeology: Approaches to the Osteological Paradox," Journal of Archaeological Research, Vol. 11, No. 1, March 2003

8.   ^ Stiker, p. 42

9.   ^ Audlin, J. *Circle of Life: Traditional Teachings of Native American Elders.* Santa Fe, N.M.: Clear Light Publishers, 2006.

10.   ^ Pattanaik, D. *Lakshmi: The Goddess of Wealth and Fortune-An Introduction.* Vakils Feffer & Simons Ltd, 2003

11.   ^ An interesting contrast exists in the semiotics between Alakshmi and Athena (later Minerva) both of whom use the owl as their symbol. For Athena, the owl is wisdom, whereas, for Alakshmi, the owl represents arrogance and stupidity.

12.   ^ Mogk, M. (ed.), "Different Bodies: Essays on Disability in Film and Television," McFarland, p. 123

13.   ^ Retrieved from http://infidels.org/library/modern/michael_moore/disabled.html

14.   ^ Dunlap and Vorpanya, "Buddhist Ideology Towards Children with Disabilities in Thailand" p. 234

15.   ^ Moore

16.   ^ https://www.theguardian.com/world/iran-blog/2015/dec/10/iranian-americans-scapegoats-for-terrorist-acts-by-us-congress-hr158

17.   ^ http://www.jewishencyclopedia.com/articles/2203-azazel

18.   ^ Stiker, H. "A History of Disability" University of Michigan Press, Ann Arbor.

19. ^ Stiker, H. "A History of Disability" University of Michigan Press, Ann Arbor.

20. ^ Maimonides, The Guide for the Perplexed, p. 357

21. ^ Metzler, "Disability in Medieval Europe: Thinking about Physical Impairment in the middle Ages, circa 1100-1400," Routledge. PP 83-4.

22. ^ Moore

23. ^ http://www.fountainmagazine.com/Issue/detail/People-with-Disabilities-from-an-Islamic-Perspective, June 2008, Issue 63.

24. ^ Stiker, p. 25

25. ^ Al-Aloufi, H., Islam and the cultural conceptualisation of disability, International Journal of Adolescence and Youth, Vol. 17, 2012 - Issue 4

26. ^ Schumm and Stoltzfus (ed.) "Disability in Judaism, Christianity, and Islam: Sacred Texts, Historical Traditions, and Social Analysis," Palgrave Macmillan, 2011: xii-xxiii.

27. ^ See Davis, Enforcing Normalcy, pp-126 passim

28. ^ The Routledge History of Disability. pp-10 passim

29. ^ Aristotle, The Politics, (439-44).

30. ^ Baker, P.S. "Training Warriors in Ancient Sparta."

31. ^ Stiker, "A History of Disability"

32. ^ The ancient Medes allied to the Persians were people coming from present day Iran, Iraq and Syria and
formed one of the first major refugee migrations into what would become the people of Western Europe.

33. ^ Thayer's Greek-English Lexicon

34. ^ Mayor, "The Amazons: Lives and Legends of Warrior Women across the Ancient World" p. 156

35. ^ Isidore of Seville (560-636), the Spanish cleric, is thought to have begun this etymological derivation from a-mazonia rather than ama-zoonia. The latter might be a formation that would underscore living without and in this case, men.

36. ^ https://languages.oup.com/google-dictionary-en/

37. ^ https://vocabbett.com/podcast-37/ retrieved 13 August 2021

38. ^ Retrieved at https://philosophynow.org/issues/75/Oedipus_A_Thinker_At_The_Crossroads

39. ^ In the 2019-2021 COVID crisis we witnessed the "hard" decisions of denying medical treatment to the disabled to "save" it for more deserving cases. In the early 20th century, Nazi's would classify the disabled as worthless eaters saving resources for those deemed more deserving of those scarce resources.

40. ^ American immigration policy often bans disabled refugees from even applying for immigration. See Nielsen's "*A Disability History if the United States.*"

41. ^ Dolon was the other

42. ˆ *Iliad* 2. 217-219

43. ˆ Many in the disability rights and activists' communities remind able-bodied persons that they will likely encounter some form of disability in their lives and have offered the acronym T.A.B. as a reminder. It stands for temporary abled bodied and reverses the process of labelling the other. We are not the disabled; you are the temporarily abled bodied.

44. ˆ For an instructive memoir on the déclassé nature of disability see Robert Murphy's "The Body Silent"

45. ˆ This may account for the reason why U.S. President Donald Trump would ridicule the decorated American veteran, Senator John McCain.

46. ˆ Martha Edwards, "Philoctetes in Historical Context," from Gerber, Disabled Veterans in History, p, 63

47. ˆ Edmund Wilson, The Wound and the Bow, Oxford, 1965, p.233

48. ˆ Freeman, K., Ancilla to the Pre-Socratic Philosophers, p. 18, Harvard University Press

49. ˆ http://www.newstatesman.com/blogs/crips-column/2008/04/disabled-slaves-child-roman.

50. ˆ Jackson, R., Doctors, *Death and Diseases in the Roman Empire*, University of Oklahoma Press: Norman and London, pp 177-178.

51. ˆ Stainton, Reason, Value and Persons, Routledge History of Disability, p. 14

52. ˆ Retrieved from https://www.theguardian.com/education/2006/dec/01/highereducation.uk

53. ˆ C Brunhölzl, "Thoughts on the illness of Hermann von Reichenau (1019–1054)", Sudhoffs Arch. 83 (2) (1999), 239-243.

54. ˆ Retrieved from https://historicengland.org.uk.

55. ˆ Prior to the papal condemnation of torture by Pope Nicholas V in 866 punishments for legal transgressions were practiced widely throughout Europe. The methods of punishment and legal torture such as the thumbscrew, the boot as well as amputations would result in permanent disability inflicted on the malefactor.

56. ˆ Stiker, A History of Disability, p. 66

57. ˆ Metzler, I. "Reflections on Disability in Medieval Legal Texts: Exclusion-Protection-Compensation," in "Disability and Medieval Law: History, Literature."

58. ˆ Bans on disabled people teaching would last well into the 1970s. See Heumann's memoir, *"Being Heumann"* that follows her struggles to teach in NY.

59. ˆ Eyler, "Disability in the Medieval Ages: Reconsiderations and Reverberations."

60.   ^ Eyler, "Disability in the Middle Ages: Reconsiderations and Reverbera-
       tions," p. 90
61.   ^ Seedorf, Knud. *Osteogenesis imperfecta: A study of clinical features and hered-
       ity based on 55 Danish families*, 1949.
62.   ^ Kelly, F, *A Guide to Early Irish Law*, 1988, Early Irish Law Series 3. Dublin
63.   ^ Risse, G.B. *"Mending bodies, saving souls: a history of hospitals,"* Oxford Uni-
       versity Press, 1990. p. 56
64.   ^ Stiker, p.78
65.   ^ Stiker, p. 94 passim
66.   ^ Ariès, P, "Centuries of Childhood"
67.   ^ Stiker, p. 218
68.   ^Miles, "Martin Luther and Childhood Disability in 16th Century Ger-
       many: What did he write? What did he say?" Retrieved from http://www.in-
       dependentliving.org/docs7/miles2005b.html
69.   ^ Retrieved from https://attitudes2disability.wordpress.com/category/un-
       categorized/historical-outline/
70.   ^ http://arthistoryteachingresources.org/lessons/disability-in-art-history/
71.   ^ Hobgood, A. "Caesar Hath the Falling Sickness: The Legibility of Early
       Modern Disability in Shakespearean Drama" Disability Studies Quarterly, Vol
       29, No 4 (2009)
72.   ^ Ibid Hobgood
73.   ^ Ibid Hobgood
74.   ^ Incidentally, this may be the origin of the erroneous etymology of the
       word handicapped. It was popularly held and often still mistakenly claimed
       that the word's origin stemmed from this time when disabled beggars were
       given a cap to beg with and voila, hand-in-cap became "handicapped". One
       usually finds such simple linguistic explanations are, sadly, wrong.
75.   ^ Allderidge, P. "Management and Mismanagement at Bedlam, 1547–1633."
       In: Webster, Charles. Health, Medicine and Mortality in the Sixteenth Cen-
       tury. Cambridge University Press; 1979 p. 141–164.
76.   ^ Retrieved from http://linguafranca.mirror.theinfo.org/9802/ip.html
77.   ^ Bowman and Jaeger, (ed), Understanding Disability: Inclusion, Access,
       Diversity, and Civil Rights
78.   ^ Fiedler, Freaks, p. 246
79.   ^ This explains how anti-Clinton forces concocted conspiracies of a child-
       sex ring in a pizza parlor that would rivet many Americans fears. The pizza
       gate conspiracy was used by Trump supporters to smear Hilary Clinton's bid
       for the U.S. presidency
80.   ^ Snyder and Mitchell, p. 214
81.   ^ Nocks, L., "Frankenstein in a Better Light"
82.   ^ Retrieved from http://www.iga.stir.ac.uk/showblog.php?id=202

83.   ^ Wren, K. (1993). *Introduction Victor Hugo: The Hunchback of Notre-Dame.* London: Wordsworth Classics.

84.   ^ Pop and Widrich, *Ugliness: The Non-beautiful in Art and Theory*; p. 17

85.   ^ Pop and Widrich, *Ugliness: The Non-beautiful in Art and Theory*

86.   ^ Pop and Widrich, Ugliness: The Non-beautiful in Art and Theory

87.   ^ Pop and Widrich, Ugliness: The Non-beautiful in Art and Theory

88.   ^ Pop and Widrich, Ugliness: The Non-beautiful in Art and Theory

89.   ^ Lenotre, G. "Romances of the French revolution," p. 175, Vol., 1 1909, Heinemann, London.

90.   ^ Schama, Citizens: A Chronicle of the French Revolution, p. 383 1989 Random House.

91.   ^ Benton, J.H. Warning Out in New England, W. B. Clarke Company, 1911

92.   ^ Snyder and Mitchell, p. 37

93.   ^ Retrieved from The Writer's Almanac 8/17

94.   ^ Foner, E. Free Soil, Free Labour, Free Men: The Ideology of the Republican Party before the Civil War, Oxford University Press. P.xii

95.   ^ Retrieved from http://www.amandahughesauthor.com/disabilities-in-colonial-america.html#.V68MPZgrJhE

96.   ^ Retrieved from https://attitudes2disability.wordpress.com/2007/02/03/the-19th-century/

97.   ^ Retrieved from "Healing Spas and Ugly Clubs: How Victorians Taught Us to Treat People With Disabilities."

98.   ^ Retrieved from https://shoddyexhibition.wordpress.com/2016/03/06/disabled-mill-workers-shoddy-fever-harsh-times-positive-contributions/

99.   ^ ibid

100.   ^ Dodd, W., "A Narrative of the Experience and Sufferings of William Dodd: A Factory Cripple," p.13

101.   ^ Retrieved from https://streetsofsalem.com/2017/03/26/a-scalping-in-salem/

102.   ^ Taylor, A. J. P. "John Bright and the Crimean War," *From Napoleon to the Second International: Essays on Nineteenth-Century Europe.* P.228.

103.   ^ Davis, L.J. (ed.) "The Disability Studies Reader," p. 20

104.   ^ Ibid p. 20

105.   ^ ibid

106.   ^ Jarvis, E, "Report on insanity and Idiocy in Massachusetts, 1855." P.62

107.   ^ Retrieved from https://www.britannica.com/topic/phrenology

108.   ^ Retrieved from https://www.smithsonianmag.com/history/facing-a-bumpy-history-144497373/

109.   ^ Huang, *Inseparable: The Original Siamese Twins and Their Rendezvous with American History*, p.173

110. ^ Walsh, Anthony A., "George Combe: A portrait of a heretofore generally unknown behaviorist". *Journal of the History of the Behavioural Sciences.*7 (3): 269–278.

111. ^ Retrieved from https://garfieldnps.wordpress.com/2012/08/31/phrenology-in-victorian-america/

112. ^ See the recent spate of pseudo-medical clinics and rehab facilities claiming that through rigorous and sometimes controversial therapies the paralyzed can walk again

113. ^ While it was during the Crimean war when soldiers' first witnessed the first widespread use of rifled infantry weapons, the heavy toll was clear in the Civil War.

114. ^ Manring, M. M.; Hawk, Alan; Calhoun, Jason H.; Andersen, Romney C. "Treatment of War Wounds: A Historical Review."

115. ^ Retrieved at www.nlm.nih.gov/exhibition/lifeandlimb/honor-ablescars.html

116. ^ Stiker,p.100

117. ^ http://www.vermontcivilwar.org/units/vrc/

118. ^ http://www.civilwarzone.com/TheInvalidCorps.html

119. ^ https://penncurrent.upenn.edu/2011-12-15/research/rehabilitating-soldiers-after-war.

120. ^ Retrieved at www.nlm.nih.gov/exhibition/lifeandlimb/honor-ablescars.html

121. ^ Kean, *The Icepick Surgeon: Murder, Fraud, Sabotage, Piracy, and Other Dastardly Deeds Perpetrated in the Name of Science,"* p.23.

122. ^ Retrieved at http://www.bbc.co.uk/history/worldwars/wwone/shellshock_01.shtml.

123. ^ Jones, E, Fear, N and Wessely, S. "Shell Shock and Mild Traumatic Brain Injury: A Historical Review". *Am J Psychiatry* 2007; 164:1641–1645.

124. ^ Winter, J.M. "The Great War and the British People". Hampshire: Palgrave Macmillan; 2003.

125. ^ Du Feu, J., "Factors Influencing Rehabilitation of British Soldiers After World War I." Retrieved from http:// http://www.medicinae.org/e10

126. ^

127. ^ Soc Hist Med. 2011 Dec; 24(3): 666–685.
Published online 2011 Feb 27. doi: 10.1093/shm/hkq095

128. ^ BBC Four series Blood and Guts: A History of Surgery

129. ^ http://www.smithsonianmag.com/arts-culture/faces-of-war-145799854/

130. ^ http://etd.lsu.edu/docs/available/etd-07072016-124553/unrestricted/Pritchard_thesis.pdf

131. ^ Chttps://www.theatlantic.com/health/archive/2014/08/the-first-face-transplants-were-masks/375527/ohen, D. "The War Come Home: Disabled Veterans in Britain and Germany, 1914-1939." P. 59

132. ^ Cohen, p.102

133. ^ Cohen, p.102

134. ^ Cohen, p.89

135. ^ Cohen p.154

136. ^ Burleigh, M. "Ethics and extermination: Reflections on Nazi genocide," p. 114

137. ^ Cohen, p. 97

138. ^ https://encyclopedia.ushmm.org/content/en/Hadamar/oduction-to-the-holocaust. Accessed on August 6, 2021.

139. ^ Linker, B. *"War's Waste: Rehabilitation in World War I America,"* University of Chicago Press.

140. ^ In a small but late action to redeem themselves, the U.S. Defense department allowed the burial of both soldiers at Arlington National Cemetery.

141. ^ Gelber, S. (2005). "A 'Hard-Boiled Order': The Re-education of Disabled WWI Veterans in New York City." *Journal of Social History, 39*(1), 161-180. Retrieved from http://www.jstor.org/stable/3790534

142. ^ Stiker, p. 128

143. ^ http://history.amedd.army.mil/corps/medical_spec/chapterIII.html

144. ^ http://history.amedd.army.mil/corps/medical_spec/chapterIII.html

145. ^ Sampson, C. M.: Physiotherapy Technic. St. Louis: C. V. Mosby Co., 1923, pp. 9, 412-413.

146. ^ Snyder and Mitchell, Cultural Locations of Disability, University of Chicago Press, p.21

147. ^ Ibid 128

148. ^ Snyder and Mitchell, Cultural Locations of Disability, university of Chicago Press, p. 21

149. ^ Snyder and Mitchell, p. 21

150. ^ Ibid p.113

151. ^ See Davis, L., *Enforcing Normalcy*

152. ^ F. Galton, *Hereditary Genius* (London: Macmillan, 1869)

153. ^ David, L., *Enforcing Normalcy*, p.35

154. ^ S. Rose, Scientific Racism and Ideology: The IQ Racket from Galton to Jensen; *The Political Economy of Science,* pp 112-141.

155. ^ quoted in Egan, Kieran *(2002).* Getting it wrong from the beginning.

156. ^ Marx's attitude toward disability is complex. He views the horrors of capitalist production as being partly responsible for the bodily damage so often and predictably found in the proletariat. Coincidentally, although on the op-

posite ends of the political spectrum, both Marx and Spencer would come to share a common burial ground: Highgate Cemetery in North London.

157. ^ Stanford University, The Independent, Volume 66, Issues 3148-3160. P. 679

158. ^ Retrieved from https://www.pbs.org/newshour/nation/column-the-false-racist-theory-of-eugenics-once-ruled-science-lets-never-let-that-happen-again

159. ^ Kelves, Daniel, J., *In the Name of Eugenics: Genetics and the Uses of Human Hereditary*, Knopf

160. ^Retrieved from https://www.pbs.org/newshour/nation/column-the-false-racist-theory-of-eugenics-once-ruled-science-lets-never-let-that-happen-again

161. ^ The term "moron" would be coined in this time derived from the Greek for stupid.

162. ^ The founder of social psychology Gustave Le Bon once wrote that many Parisian women's brains were similar in size to gorillas.

163. ^ The German anatomist Vogt was particularly offensive here

164. ^ Snyder and Mitchell, p, 117

165. ^ Ibid p.117

166. ^ Retrieved from https://attitudes2disability.wordpress.com/2007/02/03/the-19th-century/

167. ^ Friedlander, "The Origins of Nazi Genocide: From Euthanasia to the Final Solution," p. 3

168. ^ Snyder and Mitchell p/120

169. ^ Snyder and Mitchell, p. 27

170. ^ Friedlander, H. "The Origins of Nazi Genocide: From Euthanasia to the Final Solution." P. 4

171. ^ Friedlander, H. "The Origins of Nazi Genocide: From Euthanasia to the Final Solution." P. 4

172. ^ Bruinius, Harry (2007). *"Better for All the World: The Secret History of Forced Sterilization and America's Quest for Racial Purity"*.

173. ^ Ibid, p.5

174. ^ You can read about Sanger's account of her speech in her 1938 autobiography.

175. ^ Retrieved from http://law2.umkc.edu/faculty/projects/ftrials/shipp/lynchingyear.html

176. ^ "Sterilization: A Progressive Measure?". The Wisconsin Magazine of History. 43: 190–202

177. ^ Retrieved from http://www.npr.org/2012/09/05/158933012/the-strange-story-of-the-man-behind-strange-fruit

178.　＾ Stephen Jay Gould, "Carrie Buck's Daughter" *Natural History* 93 (July): 14-18

179.　＾　http://www.huffingtonpost.com/entry/eugenics-sterilization-anti-choice_b_1227929

180.　＾ Stephen Jay Gould, "Carrie Buck's Daughter" *Natural History* 93 (July): 14-18

181.　＾ Hubbard, R., "Abortion and Disability: Who Should and Should Not Inhabit the World?" in "The Disability Studies Reader" p. 76

182.　＾ Murray confessed to burning a cross on a yard when growing up in Iowa. Burning crosses was a common form of violence used by the KKK and other hate groups to intimidate Jewish and Black families.

183.　＾ All quotes from Brooks column retrieved fromhttp://www.nytimes.com/2007/09/14/opinion/14brooks.html?_r=0

184.　＾ Hubbard, p.77

185.　＾ Retrieved from https://www.pbs.org/newshour/nation/column-the-false-racist-theory-of-eugenics-once-ruled-science-lets-never-let-that-happen-again

186.　＾ Retrieved at https://www.ourbodiesourselves.org/book-excerpts/health-article/forced-sterilization/, 8/9/2021

187.　＾ All material concerning contemporary forced sterilizations are from the W.H.O. document retrieved from http://apps.who.int/iris/bitstream/10665/112848/1/9789241507325_eng.pdf?ua=1

188.　＾ Lovett, L. "Fitter Families for Future Firesides: Florence Sherbon and Popular Eugenics,
The Public Historian."

189.　＾ Retrieved from http://prattpsychology.blogspot.com/2013/04/my-family-is-fitter-than-yours-fitter.html

190.　＾ Retrieved from http://rarehistoricalphotos.com/fittest-family-eugenics-1925/

191.　＾ Retrieved from https://www.dnalc.org/view/15804-Fitter-Family-Contest-medal.html. As etymology points out "goodly" may derive from "godly".

192.　＾ Longmore and Umansky, p. 46

193.　＾ Nielsen, p. 108

194.　＾ Longmore and Umansky, p.50

195.　＾Nielsen, K. *A Disability History of the United States.*

196.　＾ Dolmage, J., "Disabled Upon Arrival The Rhetorical Construction if Disability and Race at Elis Island, " Cultural Critique 77, Winter 2011

197.　＾ Retrieved from Wikipedia

198.　＾ Again, many people with disabilities find this assumption of bitterness surprising. Recall Hippolyte and for a recent insight see Judith Huemann's memoir *"Being Heumann: An Unrepentant Memoir of a Disability Rights Activist."*

199. ^ Retrieved from http://tvtropes.org/pmwiki/pmwiki.php/Main/Evil-Cripple

200. ^ Grossman, Lev (July 7, 2011). "George R.R. Martin's Dance with Dragons: A Masterpiece Worthy of Tolkien".

201. ^ Mention here should point out that Jamie joined the ranks of the disabled when he loses a hand. It is not a radical departure because he too has a flaw namely an incestuous obsession with his sister, Cersei.

202. ^ Schmidt, *"Karl Brandt: The Nazi Doctor,"* p. 122

203. ^ Evans, S., Forgotten crimes, p. 15

204. ^ Annas, George, The Nazi Doctors and the Nuremberg Code. Unapologetic to the end, Brandt would be tried and found guilty on two counts at Nuremburg infamously remarking at his hanging, "It is no shame to stand upon the scaffold. This is nothing but political revenge. I have served my Fatherland as others before me. Yet oddly he had earlier been arrested by the Gestapo for trying to flee Germany toward the war's end and used to brag that he was the one German no one would hang!

205. ^ Fiedler, Freaks, p, 242

206. ^ One of the outcomes of the KdF was the people's car or Volkswagen. Many years later the *Star Wars* movies would use the KdF motto as the motto of Princess Leia.

207. ^ Friedlander, p. 45

208. ^ Evans, p.48

209. ^ For an account of the inside of one of these clinics consult Friedlander's research regarding the testimony of a German POW in Britain who recounted a tour he was on at Eglfing-Haar where he was shown babies dying of starvation when the doctor leading the tour "pulled a child from a crib. Displaying it like a dead rabbit, he said: "With this one, for example, it will still take two to three days." I can still clearly visualize the spectacle of this fat and smirking man with the whimpering skeleton in his fleshy hand, surrounded by other starving children" p. 50

210. ^ Friedlander, p. 186.

211. ^ Christianson, S., *The Last Gasp: The Rise and Fall of the American Gas Chamber*, Berkeley: University of California Press. p.92.

212. ^ Evans. p/ 58

213. ^ Friedlander, p. 180

214. ^ Ibid p. 61

215. ^ Fiedler, L., *Freaks: Myths and Images of the Secret Self*, Anchor p. 85.

216. ^ Friedlander, H., "The Origins of Nazi Genocide: From Euthanasia to the Final Solution," p. XI

217. ^ Burleigh, M., "Death and deliverance: "Euthanasia in Germany: 1900-1945" Cambridge University Press, p. 12

218.	^ Since the Nazi medical officials falsified death certificates it is impossible to know exactly how many were killed.
219.	^ Schulze, R., The Holocaust in History and Memory, Vol., 5 (2012) p. 18
220.	^ We are aware of and practice the avoidance of such terms as "retarded" because of their negative effects it may have on others; however, in and when it is used by an author merely as an historical descriptor, we will let it stand.
221.	^ Friedlander, H., "The Origins of Nazi Genocide: From Euthanasia to the Final Solution," p.xiii
222.	^ Friedlander, H., "The Origins of Nazi Genocide: From Euthanasia to the Final Solution," p.xiii
223.	^ Evans, S., *Forgotten Crimes: The Holocaust and People with Disabilities*. Chicago: Ivan R. Dee, 2004.p. 96
224.	^ Haeckel, *The History of Creation*, 6th edition (1914), volume 2, page 429.
225.	^ Evans, p.98
226.	^ Evans, p. 140
227.	^ Retrieved from http://www.jewishvirtuallibrary.org/jsource/Holocaust/t4.html
228.	^ Schulze, R., The Holocaust in History and Memory, Vol., 5 (2012) p.20
229.	^ It is a little-known fact of Nazi ideology that anyone black or mulatto would be subject to forced sterilization as well. The so-called Commission #3 would ferret out any mixed-race child and forcibly sterilize them. It is estimated that at least 400 to 500 such children were sterilized mostly of mixed German and African ancestry-the children of French colonial troops stationed in the Rhineland in the early 1920s. (source: Jewish Virtual Library)
230.	^ Retrieved from http://www.jewishvirtuallibrary.org/jsource/Holocaust/t4.html
231.	^ Friedlander, p. 39
232.	^ Burleigh, M., "Death and Deliverance. 'Euthanasia' in Germany 1900-1945" Cambridge University Press, p. 11
233.	^ Retrieved from http://germanhistorydocs.ghi-dc.org/sub_document.cfm?document_id=4496
234.	^ Friedlander, p.62
235.	^Voigtländerand Voth, *Nazi indoctrination and anti-Semitic Beliefs"*, Proceedings of the National Academy of Sciences, Jun 2015, 112 (26) 7931-7936
236.	^ Liebeneiner would escape any post-war punishment and in fact go on to have a successful post-war career including filming and directing "The Trapp Family" the origins of the Broadway musical, "The Sound of Music."
237.	^ Despite opposition from the AMA, many hospitals and courageous advocacy groups such as "Not Dead Yet", the latter being a consortium of senior citizens and disabled activists, legislators have passed several laws allowing for active euthanasia or physician assisted suicide. While ethically justifiable in

certain instances, the room for abuse and lack of any careful oversight well may mean more disabled people being euthanized.

238.   ^ Retrieved at https://attitudes2disability.wordpress.com/category/uncategorized/historical-outline/

239.   ^ Luty, J., Psychiatry and the dark side: eugenics, Nazi and Soviet psychiatry, "Advances in Psychiatric Treatment," Jan 2014, 20 (1) 52-60.

240.   ^ During the writing of this book, Krauthammer died, and we all lost a principled and thoughtful voice.

241.   ^ Politico magazine did a revealing article about this topic, and it sensitively portrays the veterans using the permitting process. It may be retrieved online at http://www.politico.com/magazine/gallery/2016/05/trumps-war-on-disabled-veteran-vendors-000637?slide=0

242.   ^ To be fair and perhaps as a welcome sign of a change in medicine, there has been a robust debate to provide Byrne with the funeral he had desired. See Devlin, H. (22 June 2018). *"'Irish giant' may finally get respectful burial after 200 years on display". The Guardian.*

243.   ^ The liver from the famous Siamese twins, Chang and Eng Bunker is on display at the Mutter

244.   ^ Huang, *"Inseparable: The Original Siamese Twins and their Rendezvous' with American History,"* p.40

245.   ^ Retrieved from http://docsouth.unc.edu/neh/heth/summary.html

246.   ^ http://scienceblogs.com/laelaps/2009/02/27/the-tragedy-of-the-hottentot-v/

247.   ^ http://arthistoryteachingresources.org/lessons/disability-in-art-history/

248.   ^ For a brilliant and insightful account of Cheng and Eng consult Huang's "Inseparable"

249.   ^ Quoted in Crockett, Z. from http://priceonomics.com/the-rise-and-fall-of-circus-freakshows/

250.   ^ Quoted in Crockett, Z. from http://priceonomics.com/the-rise-and-fall-of-circus-freakshows/

251.   ^ For a treatment into Henrietta Lacks see Skloot's, *"The Immortal Life of Henrietta Lacks."*

252.   ^ Kelley, T. "A Museum to Visit from an Armchair". *The New York Times.*

253.   ^ Retrieved from http://www.rootedinrights.org/freak-shows-a-dehumanizing-display/

254.   ^ http://www.glaad.org/ GLADD is an organization that monitors media for the treatment of LGBQT issues but also does other important tracking.

255.   ^ Schweik, S. "The Ugly Laws: Disability in Public" p. 291

256.   ^ The American practice of laying prohibitively exacting fines and fees on the poor is beyond understanding.

257.   ˆ Retrieved from http://www.stuffmomnevertoldyou.com/blog/when-americas-ugly-laws-hid-the-disabled-poor-from-the-public-eye/

258.   ˆ This is no dissimilar to the attempt aestheticize the political and public space in Germany practiced so effectively by the Nazis.

259.   ˆ Schweik, S, "The Ugly Laws: Disability in Public," p. 102

260.   ˆ Snyder and Mitchell's chapter of the subnormal in their "Cultural Locations of Disability" carefully scrutinizes these fears and the forces that were put in play to ally them in early 20th century public health practices.

261.   ˆ Schweik, p. 107

262.   ˆ Von Hentig, The Criminal and his Victim (1948)

263.   ˆ Hollomotz," Disability, Oppression and Violence: Towards a Sociological Explanation"; Sociology, 2012; p. 1-17.

264.   ˆ I take it this is also the reason why you see an outpouring of aspirational memoirs of persons with disabilities in the 20th and 21st centuries. Their accounts become meaningful to the degree that they face nearly insurmountable odds. For every memoirist we can assume there are 100's or 100's of the disabled left voiceless.

265.   ˆ Snyder and Mitchell, "Cultural Locations of Disability" p.98

266.   ˆ http://www.cpdusu.org/featuredstories/093013/

267.   ˆ Retrieved from https://news.google.com

268.   ˆ Retrieved from https://www.theguardian.com/world/2016/jul/26/japan-care-home-attack-satoshi-uematsu-horrifying-vision-disabled-people

269.   ˆ Retrieved from https://www.theguardian.com/world/2016/jul/26/japan-care-home-attack-satoshi-uematsu-horrifying-vision-disabled-people

270.   ˆ Retrieved from http://maamodt.asp.radford.edu/Psyc%20405/serial%20killers/Harvey,%20Donald%20-%20fall,%202005.pdf

271.   ˆ United States. Department of Justice. Office of Justice Programs. Bureau of Justice Statistics. (2017). Crimes against Persons with Disabilities, 2009-2015 by E. Harrell. Retrieved from https://www.bjs.gov/content/pub/pdf/capd0915st.pdf

272.   ˆ Retrieved from https://www.theguardian.com/world/2016/jul/26/japan-care-home-attack-satoshi-uematsu-horrifying-vision-disabled-people

Select Bibliography

Binding, K., & Hoche, A., Allowing the Destruction of Life Unworthy of Life, Suzeteo Enterprises.

Bourrier, Karen, The Measures of Manliness: Disability and Masculinity in the Mid-Victorian Novel, University of Michigan Press.

Bruinius, Harry, Better for All the World: The Secret History of Forced Sterilization and America's Quest for Racial Purity.

Burleigh, M., "Ethics and Extermination: Reflections on Nazi Genocide," Cambridge University Press.

Burleigh, M., "Death and Deliverance: 'Euthanasia' in Germany 1900-1945, Cambridge University Press.

Clark, Peter, British Clubs and Societies: 1580-1800: The Origins of An Associational World. Oxford: Oxford University Press.

Cohen, Deborah, The War Come Home: Disabled Veterans in Britain and Germany, 1914-1939, University of California Press.

Dans, P., Review of The Cinema of Isolation: A History of Physical Disability in the Movies, Bulletin of the History of Medicine, Johns Hopkins University Press, Vol. 70, No. 2, Summer 1996, pp. 346-347.

Davis, L. (ed.), The Disability Studies Reader, 4th edition, Routledge.

Davis, L., "Enforcing Normalcy: Disability, Deafness, and the Body," Verso, London 1995.

Dunai, Eleanor C. Surviving in Silence: A Deaf Boy in the Holocaust: The Harry I. Dunai Story. Washington, DC: Gallaudet University Press, 2002.

Evans, Suzanne E. Forgotten Crimes: The Holocaust and People with Disabilities. Chicago, Ivan R. Dee, 2004.

Eyler, J. "Disability in the Medieval Ages: Reconsiderations and Reverberations." Ashgate Publications.

Fiedler, L., "Freaks: Myths and Images of the Secret Self," Anchor Books, 1978.

Flaubert, G., Madame Bovary.

Friedlander, H, "The Origins of Nazi Genocide: From Euthanasia to the Final Solution," University of North Carolina Press, Chapel Hill.

Friedlander, Henry. "Registering the Handicapped in Nazi Germany: A Case Study." Jewish History 11, no. 2 (1997): 89-98.

Gallagher, Hugh Gregory. "Holocaust: Disabled Peoples." In Century of Genocide: Critical Essays and Eyewitness Accounts, edited by Samuel Totten, William S. Parsons, and Israel Charny, 205-230. New York: Routledge, 2004.

Henderson, Gretchen E. "The Ugly Face Club: A Case Study in the Tangled Politics and Aesthetics of Deformity." Ugliness: The Non-Beautiful in Art and Theory. Eds. Andrei Pop and Mechtild Widrich. London: I.B. Tauris, 2014.

Huang, "Inseparable: The Original Siamese Twins and their Rendezvous' with American History, Liverright Publishing, 2018.

Ilich, Ivan, Deschooling Society. 1971.

Illich, I., Tools for Conviviality. 1973.

Illich, I., Energy and Equity. 1974.

Illich, I., Medical Nemesis. London.

Kelves, Daniel, J., In the Name of Eugenics: Genetics and the Uses of Human Hereditary, Knopf, 1985.

Metzler, I. "Reflections on Disability in Medieval Legal Texts: Exclusion-Protection-Compensation," in "Disability and Medieval Law: History, Literature."

Mayor, A. "The Amazons: Lives and Legends of Warrior Women across the Ancient World" Princeton University Press

Munyi, C.W., "Past and Present Perceptions Towards Disability: A Historical Perspective," Disability Studies Quarterly.

Norden, M., The Cinema of Isolation: A History of Physical Disability in the Movies, Rutgers University Press.

Oe, K, "A Personal Matter."

O'Neill, Sandy. "First They Killed the 'Crazies' and 'Cripples': The Ableist Persecution and Murders of People with Disabilities by Nazi Germany 1933-45: An Anthropological Perspective." Ph.D. dissertation, California Institute of Integral Studies, 2000.

Pop and Widrich, Ugliness: The Non-beautiful in Art and Theory, I.B. Tauris, 2013.

Schmidt, U., Karl Brandt: The Nazi Doctor. Medicine and Power in the Third Reich, London: Continuum. 2007.

Schweik, S., "The Ugly Laws: Disability in Public," NYU Press 2010.

Schulze, R. (ed.), "The Holocaust in History and Memory," vol., 5 (2012).

Schumm and Stoltzfus (ed.) "Disability in Judaism, Christianity, and Islam: Sacred Texts, Historical Traditions, and Social Analysis," Palgrave Macmillan

Snyder and Mitchell, "Cultural Locations of Disability," The University of Chicago Press.

Sontag, S., "Illness as Metaphor," Farrar, Strauss, and Giroux, 1978.

Stiker, Henri-Jacques, "A History of Disability," (trnsl., W. Sayers) The University of Michigan Press, 2000.

Thomson, Rosemarie Garland, "Extraordinary Bodies: Figuring Physical Disability in American Culture and Literature," Columbia University Press, 1997.

Tomlinson, "The Paintings and the Journal of Joseph Whiting Stock," Wesleyan University Press.

Acknowledgements

A book I have come to realize is not the work of a single author; rather, a book is a collaboration of many minds. Many people contributed to this book, some in obvious ways, others in less obvious ways. All the teachers who gave their time selflessly, activists who stood in solidarity, and good friends in earnest conversation are the ones who helped in the obvious ways. In that first group, particular praise goes to Chris Rose for her skillful eye proofreading the early editions. Early readers Beth Fastiggi, Brad Stephenson, Kathy, and Eric Stengel, must also be mentioned. If there are any errors, omissions, or mistakes, they are mine.

I need to mention the debt I owe to my teachers and professors, who provided a model for living the life of the mind, shared their passion for research, and offered advice on writing. Patrick Hutton, Will Miller, Charles Guignon, Richard Kearney, Robert Nash, and Teodros Kiros stand out.

I also owe my colleagues to Saint Michael's College, especially the Alliot lunchtime group Nat Lew, Declan McCabe, George Dameron, Adam Weaver, Paul Constantino, Jeff Trumbower, Lou Dimasi, and Mark Tarnaki. My colleagues at UVM, especially Susan Kasser and Nancy Gell, deserve mention, as do my colleagues in the SMC philosophy department.

Finally, mention needs to be made to my fellow PWD's who, over the years, shared experiences, thoughts, and insights that would guide, stimulate and offer perspectives I was unaware of existing: Diana Viets, Trey Trefethen, Eric Rose, Nate Besio, Ed Paquin, Cleary Buckley, Jordan Carrell, Heather Berg, among many others merit mention.

About the Author

Patrick Standen lectures in philosophy at Saint Michael's College and medical ethics at the University of Vermont. He lives in Burlington, Vermont.